IN ROME WE TRUST

IN ROME
WE TRUST

THE RISE OF CATHOLICS
IN AMERICAN POLITICAL LIFE

Manlio Graziano

Stanford University Press
Stanford, California

Stanford University Press
Stanford, California

In Rome We Trust: The Rise of Catholics in American Political Life was
originally published in Italian in 2016 under the title *In Rome We Trust:
L'ascesa dei cattolici e politica nella vita politica degli Stati Uniti* ©2016,
Il Mulino. Translated into English by Marina Korobko.

Printed in the United States of America on acid-free, archival-quality paper

Library of Congress Cataloging-in-Publication Data

Names: Graziano, Manlio, 1958– author.
Title: In Rome we trust : the rise of Catholics in American political life /
Manlio Graziano.
Other titles: In Rome we trust. English
Description: Stanford, California : Stanford University Press, 2017. |
"A version of this book appeared in Italian in 2016 as In Rome We Trust." |
Includes bibliographical references and index.
Identifiers: LCCN 2016035777 | ISBN 9781503600355 (cloth : alk. paper) |
ISBN 9781503601819 (pbk. : alk. paper) | ISBN 9781503601833 (ebook)
Subjects: LCSH: Catholics—Political activity—United States—History. |
Christianity and politics—United States—History. | Catholic
Church—United States—History. | United States—Politics and government.
Classification: LCC BX1407.P63 G7313 2017 | DDC 320.088/28273—dc23
LC record available at https://lccn.loc.gov/2016035777

Typeset by Bruce Lundquist in 10/15 Sabon

To the memory of Tullio Pastura (1926–2015)
Writer, then partisan, then uncle

Contents

Acknowledgments

I HAVE HAD MANY GOOD MASTERS, and I regret that I cannot thank them all here. I am grateful to them for teaching me how to see more clearly in a world that every day seems more obscure and for teaching me, above all, how not to confuse reality with dreams and that dreams can come true only if one knows and deals with reality, however unpleasant it may be. These mentors deserve my unconditional gratitude.

I owe a personal thank you to two of the most lucid Italian analysts of international affairs, Sergio Romano and Lucio Caracciolo, who have always proven extremely helpful and generous to me. This book would never have seen the light of day without the special consideration of Professor Vera Negri Zamagni of the University of Bologna. This English version was realized thanks to the kind involvement of Professors Stanislao Pugliese of Hofstra University and Timothy A. Byrnes of Colgate University and to the indispensable help of Paola Pecchioli of Il Mulino, my Italian publisher, who put me in touch with Emily-Jane Cohen at Stanford University Press.

Emily-Jane, wholeheartedly supporting the idea of publishing this book in the United States, has followed up systematically and thoroughly in all phases of its production, accomplishing an immense job beyond even her specific professional duties as editor. I deeply appreciate her steadfastness, her patience, and her private lessons about the (for me mysterious) American world of publishing houses. Thanks also to Micah Siegel of Stanford University Press, whose attentive care helped me greatly in the final phases of production.

I also owe a special mention to my wonderful and very patient friend and translator, Marina Korobko, and to my friend Constance Cooper, whose excellent English and deep interest in my work made her an ideal first reader of this book.

IN ROME WE TRUST

Introduction

FOR SEVERAL DECADES there has been a quantitative and qualitative growth in the role Catholics play in American political life and, not coincidentally, in the role American prelates play in the life of the Catholic Church. My purpose here is to explore how and why this has come to pass.

This book is born of the merging of two themes on which my research has focused in recent years: the geopolitics of the Catholic Church and the geopolitics of the global shift of power—in other words, of a new international context that is less and less American and more and more multipolar.

Geopolitical analysis of the Catholic Church reveals that the particular dynamism of the world's oldest institution allows it, at least potentially, to take the lead in a general process of desecularization. In other words, the Catholic Church's vitality allows it to offer guidance and specific objectives for the return of religions to the public sphere after three centuries of secularization in the political realm.[1]

Among abundant evidence of the regained strength of the Catholic Church is a series of indisputable facts: the number of seminarians (which is to say, candidates for priesthood) in the world nearly doubled between 1978 (the year John Paul II was elected) and 2013, growing from 63,882 to 118,251. Consequently, the number of priests has risen as well, from 403,173 in 1990 to 415,348 by the end of 2013. And the number of permanent deacons has also soared, increasing from 7,654 in 1980 to more than 43,000 in 2013. Despite an equally indisputable decline in the number of nuns, the "forces of the apostolate" (bishops, priests, permanent deacons, monks, nuns, members of secular institutions, secular missionaries, and catechists) grew worldwide by almost 300,000 between just 2005 and 2013, for a total of 4,762,458 people. In this same period the number of Catholics in the world grew by 12 percent, a growth rate faster than that of the population in Asia and Africa, corresponding in pace to demographic growth in the Americas and declining growth in Europe.[2]

Along with its quantitative achievements, the Church has regained, to some extent, the authority and credibility that it had gradually lost beginning in 1648, when the Peace of Westphalia inaugurated the process of secularization in international politics. This is certainly true for the nearly two hundred countries that today have diplomatic relations with the Holy See and for most leaders of great and small powers that sooner or later find an opportunity to bow before the pope and secure his benevolent attention. Even for the most prominent personalities and the authorities of the other great world religions, the head of the Catholic Church is today a point of reference, and the Church itself is a channel of communication and collaboration.

To these proofs of dynamism we must add another specific and far from anodyne piece of evidence: personnel of Catholic origin occupy an increasingly important place in the political life of the United States. Particularly striking are not just the dimensions of this phenomenon but the fact that very few have noticed it or tried to account for it.

This is in itself a sufficient invitation to try to fill the existing gap. It is necessary, however, to add two significant motivations for my study here. The first has to do with the geopolitics of the Catholic Church. It is impossible not to notice the increasing presence of US personnel at the top of the Vatican's hierarchical structure, in particular within the College of Cardinals, where prelates from the United States form the second largest national group after Italians. But, most important, it is impossible not to notice a progressive influence of the American Catholic experience on the universal Roman Catholic Church as a whole, beginning with the encyclical *Rerum novarum* (1891) and leading to the acceptance of the principle of religious freedom at the Second Vatican Council, as well as, of course, to the election of a "Pan-American" pope who was strongly backed by the US cardinals and who is the expounder of a pastoral teaching in which *life, liberty, and the pursuit of happiness* seem to have become new mantras. This aspect has been generally overlooked as well, or treated in teleological terms, as a sort of parallel "Manifest Destiny" that might gradually dissipate harsh but futile mutual misunderstandings of the past and finally lead the Church and the United States to walk the same path toward the same objectives.

The second motivation, from the viewpoint of the geopolitics of shifting power, is that the influence of the Catholic Church—direct and indirect— is growing in many non-Catholic countries as well, including India, South Korea, and the United Kingdom. But in no other non-Catholic country is its influence growing the way it is in the United States. And this applies not only to the number of politicians, military, and judiciary personnel at the top levels but also to the growth of social services offered to the population. This is all the more remarkable given that the United States is today the main "loser," in relative terms, in the global shift of power, doomed to see the vanishing of its hegemony, undisputed in the twentieth century, in international politics.

The hypothesis of a correlation between the relative decline of the United States and the increase of the Catholic presence in the ruling class of the country is therefore worth testing. It is also worthwhile to test the hypothesis of a correlation between increased American influence (and presence) within the universal Roman Catholic Church and its renewed dynamism.

THE MASSIVE LITERATURE on the Catholic Church in the United States and on the history of American Catholics, as well as the scarce texts on the relationship between the United States and the universal Roman Catholic Church, have until now been almost exclusively written by Catholic scholars, almost all of whom have been American. This peculiarity has allowed for abundant firsthand information and for studies that come from as many different angles as there are sensitivities within Catholicism, particularly in the United States. Anyone who engages in the study of the Catholic Church must pay tribute to the deep, erudite, and well-documented work conducted from within, without which critical analysis would be virtually impossible.

What is lacking, then, is not material, nor is it specific knowledge of events, but rather a fresh approach. What is missing is an external point of view, one not directly affected by the discussions, at times refined and at times turbulent, between the various currents of American and non-American Catholicism. And what is particularly missing is a geopolitical approach.

This book attempts just that. It provides an explanation of the increased role of Catholics in American life and the role of Americans in the life of the Church through a geopolitical analysis of the relations between the United States and Catholicism. It is a geopolitical book both in subject and method. In subject it aims to provide tools for analyzing the impact that these relations have on American domestic policy, on the internal policy of the Church, and on the entire system of international relations. In method it proposes to look, albeit briefly, into the totality of circumstances that have led to the current state of affairs.

Geopolitics is a dynamic discipline. As Nicholas Spykman put it in 1938, its task consists in finding "in the enormous mass of historical material, correlations between conditioning factors and types of foreign policy."[3] Put another way, the aim of geopolitics is to study constraints that restrict, condition, and steer the will of political actors through history. Both measurable (geography, economics, demography, military power, alliances, institutions, and leadership) and nonmeasurable constraints (traditions, habits, ideologies, prejudices, and, of course, religions) deposit sediment throughout history and leave their marks across the centuries. At the same time, they evolve and change. Long-term phenomena (whether a river basin, economic supremacy, or cultural influence) are the grammar of international relations; their modifications are its syntax.

This is why a geopolitical approach to the relationship between the United States and Catholicism cannot overlook the Church's historical development—not in order to repeat what can be found in dozens of other books but to review this history from a different perspective, a long-term perspective. Such a perspective proves, among other things, that geopolitics is not, as many believe, a flatly deterministic discipline in which certain premises necessarily give rise to certain conclusions. Throughout the history of American Catholicism, from the time of the thirteen colonies and beyond, there are almost no preconditions that would lead one to anticipate the decisive role of American prelates in the selection of a pope; no preconditions that would forecast a pope who speaks before Congress, received with the warm and abundant applause of American congressmen and congresswomen. Nor are there preconditions for more than a third of these congressmen and congresswomen being Catholic, or for the vice president, the speaker of the House, one-third of the cabinet, nineteen governors, all the military and defense leadership, and, in particular, two-thirds of the Supreme Court members also being practitioners of "Roman papolatry," followers of the "whore of Babylon," as Catholicism and the Catholic Church were long characterized in the United States.

The crises that broke the deterministic thread in the history of relations between the United States and Catholicism have mostly been "external," that is, not directly determined by the relation itself. They include, with regard to the Church, its defeat—albeit temporary—on the secularization front, its loss of contact with urbanized and proletarianized peasant masses, the carnage among European Catholic powers during 1914 to 1918, and, last but not least, decolonization. For the United States the biggest crisis has been the awareness that "the age of America's nearly total dominance of the world stage was drawing to a close."[4] Henry Kissinger dates this awareness to the end of the 1960s, while other specialists place it in the second half of the 1980s, concomitant with Japan's spectacular economic growth.

Faced with the prospect of decline, the United States and the Catholic Church adopted countermeasures, trying, if not to reverse the pace, at least to slow it down. Two men in particular have successfully embodied this attempt: Ronald Reagan and Karol Wojtyła. Whatever their personal roles may have actually been, it is certain that Reagan and Wojtyła managed, with different means and objectives, to restore confidence and stability in the institutions they were responsible to. In the process, both adopted with resolute firmness a missionary attitude and an apocalyptic bent that corresponds to the very nature of both the United States and the Catholic Church.

For eight years Reagan and Wojtyła served in parallel as heads of their respective institutions at a time when the crisis of the Soviet Union gave them a weakened common enemy whom they could use to rescue their faltering identities. Thanks to the existence of this enemy, and to the spontaneous empathy between the two men, both of exceptional caliber, was born the legend of a "holy alliance" between the United States and the Vatican whose aim was to liquidate the "evil empire." The myth arose along converging paths, leading in the same direction, to fight the same evil and assert the same purposes.

It could be said that this myth results from an excess of empiricism. But the mere accumulation of facts does not produce a theory. And sometimes it leads to a dead end. The United States needed to give spiritual depth to its recovered strength, and the will of the Roman Catholic Church required historical depth for its recent conversion to the principles of freedom of religion and conscience. Yet this myth does not stand up to historical, let alone geopolitical, analysis.

The Catholic Church and the United States, in fact, have different priorities, different goals, and, of course, different methods. Their current mutual cordiality is explained by the fact that, like all other geopolitical actors, they need allies in the pursuit of their goals; and since, generally speaking, the more powerful the ally, the broader the scope (at least potentially), it is understandable that they appreciate a rapprochement when one comes to pass.

But the two-centuries-long relationship between the United States and the Catholic Church has been essentially characterized by suspicion, sometimes by open hostility, and, since the end of World War I, by harsh competition on the field of universal values, that is to say, on the field of the moral leadership of the world. Both the Catholic Church and the United States are persuaded that God has blessed them with a manifest destiny; but it is hardly the same God, and it is certainly a different destiny.

The United States was born as a Protestant country or, more precisely, a puritanical one, and as such was anti-Catholic. Since the very beginning, however, there has been an overriding concern not to import the religious wars and persecutions of the Old World, from which the *Mayflower*'s passengers had fled, into the New. The most durable legacy of that concern is the First Amendment of the US Constitution, ratified in 1791, which prohibits the establishment of any religion. Yet long before the founding of the United States, the colonies were imbued with an implacable anti-Catholic sentiment. The first law banning Catholics was passed in Virginia in 1642, and other colonies followed suit. The hostility has known its violent moments, including the rise, in the nineteenth century, of tumultuous anti-Catholic movements. Such hostility was long present in the Protestant heart of the American nation, to the point that even during the Second World War, and again during the presidential campaign of 1960, pamphlets and caricatures circulated in which Catholics were depicted as the potential fifth column of a pope intent on "ruling America."

For its part the Church was no less hostile to the United States, whose territorial growth came at the expense of Catholic powers—France, Spain, and Mexico—with a failed attempt to conquer also the mainly Catholic Quebec. Moreover, the values carved in the US Constitution, beginning with freedom of conscience, were irreconcilably opposed to those defended and propagated by the Roman Catholic Church for centuries. At the end of the nineteenth century Pope Leo XIII officially condemned the assimilationist tendency of many American bishops, that is, their tendency to absorb some American values, such as religious pluralism and even the principle of the separation of church and state.

The universal Catholic Church came into conflict very often with American foreign and domestic policies: on the issue of slavery, on the Civil War, on union activism, on the war against Spain in 1898, and on the Mexican Revolution. As with many other countries, a turning point came during World War I, when the local Church hierarchy was allowed, and even pushed, to show unconditional patriotism as soon as the United States declared war on Germany. But that realignment did not prevent the Church from jealously defending its autonomy over the years, taking clear distance from Washington time and time again. This was the case during World War II, when it contested the US alliance with the Soviet Union. It was also the case after World War II, when, despite the Cold War, Pope Pius XII reiterated the Church's condemnation of the American way of life, which was often considered more "materialistic" than the Soviet way of life. And it was again the case at certain critical junctures, including the Vietnam War in the 1960s and 1970s, the arms race in the 1980s, and the Gulf wars of 1991 and 2003.

Indeed, the United States and the universal Catholic Church have very rarely found themselves on the same path. There was the thunderous clash about the war in Iraq in 2003, and even today, on the subjects of Palestine, Europe, and Latin America their positions collide. When it comes to other important international issues, such as relations with China and Southeast Asia, with the Indian subcontinent, with Russia, and with Africa, the strategies and the purposes of the Catholic Church and the United States differ strikingly. Similarly, their opinions differ considerably about some hot domestic American issues, such as immigration, education, the death penalty, gun control, abortion, contraception, stem-cell research, and even the climate issue.

THE "CATHOLICIZATION" of the United States of America is a recent phenomenon. Some observers say that its emergence began under Ronald Reagan; others say that it was at the time of George W. Bush, a Protestant, whom Rick Santorum nonetheless called "the first Catholic president, much more Catholic than Kennedy."[5] What is certain is that, until February 2016, out of the six current Catholic justices in the Supreme Court, two were appointed by Ronald Reagan, one by George H. Bush, and two by George W. Bush.

The trend toward the overrepresentation of Catholics among America's politically elite became patent, however, during Obama's administration. Not only did he appoint the sixth Catholic justice of the Supreme Court, but, for six years, more than one-third of the members of his administration were Catholic, whereas nationwide only about one in four (or in three, depending on the sources) Americans is Catholic. In the same period, also Catholic were the vice president, Obama's second-term chief of staff, his national security adviser, his homeland security adviser, the three successive speakers of the House of Representatives (Democratic from 2008–12, and Republican after November of 2012), the Democratic leader of the House, the director of the CIA, the director and the deputy director of the FBI, and the army chief of staff (a position that changes frequently, but Obama has appointed two chiefs of staff, both Catholics), the commandant of the Marine Corps, and the chief of staff of the US Air Force.

One can wonder if there will be another Catholic president. In this book I will explain why the Catholic Church itself does not seem keen on this possibility. Before the 2016 presidential election, however, many potential Catholic candidates were gathering, so we cannot simply dismiss this eventuality. Out of the sixteen Republican candidates listed in five or more major independent nationwide polls at the end of the summer in 2015, six were Catholics (Jeb Bush, Marco Rubio, Chris Christie, George Pataki, Bobby Jindal, and Rick Santorum). And the only potential Democratic candidate who seemed in a position to challenge Hillary Clinton's nomination was the Catholic Joe Biden.

Here, too, we are witnessing a trend. In 2004, one candidate for the presidency was Catholic, and in the last three presidential elections, in 2008, 2012, and 2016, all the candidates (Republican and Democratic) for the vice presidency were Catholic (we will see why—from a Catholic point of view—Sarah Palin should be considered Catholic). The Democratic and Republican conventions of 2012 were opened by the speeches of two Catholics—Rubio and Castro, respectively—and concluded with a prayer led by the then president of the US Bishop's Conference, the archbishop of New York, Cardinal Timothy Dolan. It is curious that only once before was the president of the American bishops invited to both conventions: this was in 1972, at the time of the first presidential election in which the Catholic vote massively shifted toward Republicans.

Speaking of shifts, I will conclude this overview by naming some high-ranking bipartisan conversions to Catholicism: from Jeb Bush to Newt Gingrich to the governors of Louisiana and Kansas, respectively, Bobby Jindal and Sam Brownback; from the mayor of Nashville, Karl Dean, to Representative Hansen H. Clarke (D-Michigan) to General Wesley Clark. For a while a rumor circulated that even George W. Bush was tempted to follow in the footsteps of his brother and of his former ally Tony Blair.

Surprisingly enough, this overabundance of Catholics at the forefront of the American political scene has gone almost unnoticed. The only case about which there has been a public debate is that of the Supreme Court. In this debate statistics were advanced to emphasize that, in the entire history of the Court, there have been only thirteen Catholic justices and that five of them sit there simultaneously today (before the death of Antonin Scalia there were six). Because the Supreme Court plays such an important role in American politics, it is more than understandable that this debate arose. But, since observers noticed the outsized role played by Catholics in the Supreme Court and failed to notice the outsized role played by Catholics in other key American institutions, we seem to have been blinded to the forest by the trees.

ONE CAN ARGUE that the presence of all these Catholics at the pinnacle of American politics is merely a coincidence. But, as Agatha Christie allegedly said, one coincidence is a coincidence, two coincidences are a clue, and three coincidences are a proof. In this case we have far more than three coincidences, so, we might argue, we have a proof. But a proof of what?

First of all, we have the proof that this trend is real, and it deserves at least to be acknowledged. Once we have identified the trend, though, we are bound to provide some hypotheses about its causes and its possible perspectives. Even if, hypothetically, this overrepresentation of Catholics in the American elite were a peculiarity of the Obama era, and even if it were to end with the end of that era, it would deserve an attempted explanation, and it could at least be useful to have a better understanding of it.

The first possible explanation could be *disorientation*. Disorientation and uncertainty are the main characteristics of our long post–Cold War era. After the fall of the Berlin Wall history sped up, and it became very difficult for everybody—states, governments, intellectuals, and laypeople— to keep up with it. This is particularly true for the United States, whose affluence and whose global leadership were until very recently not only taken for granted but also perceived as everlasting. In the final decade of the twentieth century, Americans were told that they had won the historical struggle against the "evil empire," that their economic system had triumphed, and that they were the only remaining superpower. At the beginning of the new century the worst form of evil hit Americans on their own soil, their economic system faced a deep crisis, and a multitude of new and old superpowers started contesting American global leadership in effective ways. Since the beginning of the new century, the dominant feeling in the United States has gone from a relaxed optimism to a gloomy sense of distress.

In fact, the troubles of the first years of the new century are not merely temporary setbacks. They are the first tangible signs of the beginning of a new era in which the United States is doomed to lose its global leadership. Even though American excellence continues in some key areas—such as research and development, education, freedom of discussion, armament, energy, and immigration—it is nonetheless indisputable that the economy of many US competitors is growing faster. This means that the American share of the global market is dramatically shrinking.

The relative decline of the American economy is the main feature of the new era, and it has heavy geopolitical consequences. In his celebrated

The Rise and Fall of the Great Powers (1987) Paul Kennedy drew this "valid conclusion" from his historical analysis: "There is a causal detectable relationship between the shifts which have occurred over time in the general economic and productive balances and the position occupied by individual powers in the international system."[6] Elsewhere in his book Kennedy stated that the "uneven economic growth rates of countries" leads "ineluctably to the rise of specific powers and the decline of others," that is, to "shifts in the world's political and military balances."[7] For the United States, any shift of power means—ineluctably—that its global hegemony is weakening; and if its global hegemony is weakening, many of the benefits that accompanied it are doomed to fade away.

More than twenty-five years after Kennedy's book, Robert J. Samuelson wrote that the US economy is going to be forced to deal with a "new economic norm," characterized by a prolonged slow growth "that threatens to upend our political and social order."[8] The risk of undermining the political and social order is serious enough in every country that, in the past, has drawn a material advantage from its privileged position in the world. It is of even greater seriousness for the United States, whose brief history is the only one that has been characterized almost entirely by sustained growth and by the expectation of continuous improvement. Paradoxically, the most important exception to its history—the Great Depression—greatly contributed to this feeling, insofar as after that crisis Americans enjoyed their most prosperous decades, drawing the (obviously mistaken) conclusion that any crisis, even the deepest, could be but momentary.

In the United States a panoply of optimistic philosophies has arisen over the centuries to encourage, feed, or merely depict the rise and the country's successes; but the United States is philosophically unequipped for its decline. It is therefore understandable that it has new needs for solid anchors. With the current international situation the traditional reference points are vanishing: they are losing their material and ideal substance and, therefore, their political effectiveness. Everywhere in the world traditional religions are increasingly filling some voids left by states and their secular ideologies (for instance, certain varieties of "civil religions" or some social services). This is why many states (and not only the United States) are looking for new and more solid points of reference—not necessarily in order to *replace* their civil religions but possibly to strengthen them with other more reliable and better-tried contents.

Since the Catholic Church is the oldest, most centralized, and most widely established institution in the world; and since the Catholic Church is currently—whether one likes it or not—the most authoritative, and the most flexible, provider of moral principles, it is possible to argue that any link with Catholicism can help improve the steadiness of a nation. If this is the main reason for the overrepresentation of Catholics in the upper echelons of the US government, it is very likely that this trend will continue, even though not necessarily as overwhelmingly as it appeared during Obama's two terms. A decrease in the numbers of Catholics occupying influential positions under the next president would indicate that the Obama era was particularly poor[9] in terms of "inner" ideas, motivations, projects—in a word—benchmarks and thus that it was particularly eager to find "external" ones.

Another crucial consequence of the relative decline of the United States is its reduced influence on international affairs. Paul Kennedy covers this issue as well: "Decision-makers in Washington must face the awkward and enduring fact that the sum total of the United States' global interests and obligations is nowadays far larger than the country's power to defend them all simultaneously."[10] Kennedy was writing in 1987, but twenty years later, the US National Intelligence Council confirmed empirically that "owing to the relative decline of its economic, and to a lesser extent, military power, the US will no longer have the same flexibility in choosing among as many policy options" on the international stage.[11] In these circumstances, which substantiated Barack Obama's strategy of retrenchment, a solid connection to an institution with multiple antennae (from nunciature to parishes) in many countries of the world can only be beneficial. The mediation of the Vatican between the United States and Cuba, which has allowed the reestablishment of diplomatic relations between the two countries, may be considered a dress rehearsal for other possible initiatives.

There is another possible explanation for the increased role of Catholics in American political life that, although simpler, is no less plausible: today, average American Catholics are more knowledgeable than average Americans. In a brochure published in 1924 a theologian lamented the lack of a political Catholic leadership in the United States (the fact that that very same year the governor of New York had tried to become the first Catholic candidate to the presidency was an exception). In fact, in the 1920s Catholics still mostly represented the lower strata of the working class, and, at the same time, the Church was not extremely keen on promoting an educated, mature, independent, and judgmental laity. At that time the only field in which Catholic laypeople had practiced their organizational skills was that of the trade unions.

After World War II many American Catholics moved from blue-collar to white-collar jobs and from the cities to the suburbs. Their social ascent changed their relationship with the clergy: laypeople tended to be much more educated and to participate more actively in the life of the parish, becoming increasingly involved in the management of one of the more experienced and better-rooted organizations in the world and, at the same time, more demanding. Labor unions first, then parishes, and finally universities and colleges were sites where a new political Catholic leadership formed and trained itself. In the 1950s a text by another theologian revealed that Catholics were finally a noticeable component of the American political class, even though still slightly underrepresented in Congress. A half-century later, they are a slightly overrepresented component of Congress (around 30 percent, whereas Catholics would represent—depending on the source—between 22 percent and 25 percent of the American population, even though, from a Catholic point of view, they are closer to 30 percent than to 25 percent).

This almost exact equivalence between the percentage of Catholics in the population and the percentage of Catholic members of Congress is surprising given the much greater proportion of Catholics in Obama's administration, the Supreme Court, or the military and security leadership. This peculiar difference leads to another implication: the overrepresentation of Catholics in the American political landscape is much more a top-down phenomenon than bottom-up. As we can see, with the exception of governors, all the offices in which Catholics are heavily overrepresented are appointed, not elected, ones. In other words, this is the result of a deliberate choice by the president, or by staff close to him, either because

Catholics are more knowledgeable or because they are linked to a solid institution with even more solid points of reference, or both.

THE ROLE OF CATHOLICS in American politics is unique, despite the fact that they are not the only religiously identified group to be overrepresented in this specific field. Jews and Mormons—who respectively represent approximately 2 percent of the American population—are, as well. In fact, the followers of the Church of Jesus Christ of Latter-day Saints are not only overrepresented in the political system (where they can play other precious cards, such as their unswerving optimism, honesty, and family values) but also hold a disproportionate number of top jobs at several major companies. But the political importance of Mormons falls off geographically: it is very high in Utah, their center of influence; higher than their average numbers in Washington, DC; and nil in the rest of the world.

The overrepresentation of Jews among cultural, artistic, economic, scientific, and political elites, and not only in the United States, has been largely studied, interpreted, and also dreadfully misinterpreted. There is, however, a crucial difference between the political overrepresentation of Catholics and Jews. Jews are overrepresented in the Supreme Court (one-third) and also in Congress (12 percent of the Senate and 5 percent of the House), fairly represented in Obama's cabinet, but underrepresented as mayors, governors, potential candidates to the presidency, military and security leaders, and so on. The other big difference is that Catholics are incomparably more numerous (around eighty million vs. six million).[12] And, last but certainly not least, Jews do not have behind them a structure as powerful as the Catholic Church. Jews embody a history, a tradition, and a centuries-long tragedy, but they are not members of an organization that is also an institution and happens to be *the* most ancient and *the* broadest in the world, as well as one of the more centralized and more powerful.

A FINAL THING that should be considered when speaking of the role of Catholics in American politics is the phenomenon that Robert C. Christopher has called "the de-WASPing of America's power elite."[13] In this process (which started after WWII but became universally noticeable more recently) other non-WASP groups—notably Jews—played an important role: it suffices to go back to the example of the Supreme Court, where, since the retirement of the Protestant John Paul Stevens and the appointment of Elena Kagan, who is Jewish, for the first time in the history of the institution, there is no WASP among the justices.

Since the first decades of the nineteenth century, Catholics have represented the largest religious denomination in the United States. It is therefore not surprising that many observers link the "de-WASPing" process to the increasing numbers of Catholics. Some recent studies state that in the near future America will be more and more Catholic *because* of the importance of Latino immigration. According to some demographic projections, by the mid-twenty-first century there will be one hundred million Catholics in the United States; others believe that, by that same time, they will represent half of the American population. These hypotheses are largely debatable, if only we consider that at least one-third of Latino immigrants do not describe themselves as Catholics. But, whatever its actual dimension, any increase in the numbers of Catholics would necessarily have repercussions on their political relevance: if Democrats or Republicans are able to draw a large majority of Catholics into a future coalition (as did Franklin Roosevelt and Ronald Reagan), they can enormously improve their chances of winning any electoral competition.

But this is speculation. Neither of the two major parties today seems able to build such a coalition, and in any case it is highly unlikely that the Catholic Church, as far as it is able to steer the Catholic vote, would be willing to put all of its eggs in one basket. Since the Democratic Party ceased being a Christian Democratic party in the 1960s, the Catholic Church behaves toward the two major parties as a child does toward his or her parents when they argue with each other: it tries to take advantage of their quarrels in order to obtain more from both.

But this book is about American Catholic political leadership, not about the number of Catholics in the United States. The emergence of a political leadership among Catholics is not an immediate result of the numbers of Catholics living in the country. It took decades for Catholic immigrants from Ireland and Germany, then from Italy and Poland, to transform their numerical quantity into political quality. Today, there are already clear signs of a future Catholic Latino leadership, for instance—see the cases of Justice Sonia Sotomayor or even of Marco Rubio and Julian Castro—but it always takes time before the population of more recent immigrants produces new political leadership.

THE RISE of a new political leadership is not only a question of time but of social advancement and, above all, of organization. Organization requires a group of individuals who want to implement clear goals and who can count on a reliable and authoritative leadership, a structure, cadres, and activists. According to Arnold Toynbee (as paraphrased by Joseph Ratzinger), "the fate of a society always depends on its creative minorities"[14] or, to be more precise, on "organized minorities." As some political theorists (including Gaetano Mosca, Lenin, Elmer Schattschneider, and Mancur Olson) have asserted, organized minorities can easily defeat a larger, disorganized opposition. Political parties, unions, lobbies, syndicates, religious denominations, and so on, all constitute minority groups that struggle against other minority groups to achieve their goals. And in this struggle, as political scientist Seth Masket puts it, "the key is not persuasion, but organization."[15] And while cadres, structure, and leadership are of course indispensable, the key to success is unity and clarity of purpose.

Jesse Jackson once said that "in politics, an organized minority is a political majority."[16] But it is important to underline that being a minority is a *state*, whereas joining or forming an organization is a *choice*, or a *skill*. In other words, the secret to political success does not lie in being a minority; the secret lies in being better organized than other minorities. The Catholic Church today is a minority even in the most Catholic of countries, but it is less of a minority and better organized than any other contending organization. When people say that "only" one-third (or even one-tenth, or one-twentieth) of Catholics regularly attend church, they do not consider that no other existing organization on Earth is able to mobilize, on a purely voluntary basis, so many people so often. In their self-alleged "greatest rally in the last twenty years," in October 2010, French labor unions were able to mobilize between one-sixth and one-half (depending on the sources) of the people that the French Catholic Church mobilizes every week, without having to broadcast. And this is in one of the most secularized countries in the world.

As I will attempt to demonstrate in this book, this is the fundamental reason why Catholics are influencing, and will likely continue to influence, American politics much more than evangelicals do. And it is why the fear (or hope, depending on one's point of view) of the political role of evangelicals in the United States is largely misplaced. Politics cannot be measured in terms of decibels but in terms of organization. It is not the most colorful, the most boisterous, the most theatrical, or even the most violent of political actors who are actually important but those who are able to reach, or to influence, power. The Catholic Church is a single global institution with centuries-long accumulated experience in managing and influencing power; evangelicals, conversely, are divided into a myriad (according to some sources, more than thirty thousand) of small churches, or even nano-churches, with different and at times even opposite points of view on political, social, and even theological issues. When most of them are united with respect to some goal, they can influence some movement of opinion, but they are not able to have a steady impact on political power. During the last thirty years they have not even been able to reach their goal with respect to ending the availability of abortions. The last real political leader close to their sensibility was Jimmy Carter; in more recent times their closest wannabe political leader, who did provoke great dreams, was a baptized Catholic, Sarah Palin.

In the eyes of the Catholic Church the overvaluation of evangelicalism is a good thing. Although it has fed the need—so typical in a mass society—to put forward charismatic leaders capable of stirring the passions of the crowds, it is not thanks to such a superficial and ephemeral approach that the Catholic Church has established its success. Its success is based, rather, on a common identity made up of precepts, rituals, and shared ethical horizons. It is grounded in a network of parishes, schools, hospitals, and missions, all brought together via a centralized, disciplined organizational structure. It is based on that "actual organized, visible and religious society, with all the powers of a perfect and sovereign society, with its own laws, with its own authority, with its own means and ends."[17] This "actual organized society" works deep within the folds of society more broadly, and the more the spotlight is turned elsewhere, the better its hold.

Even while maintaining its low profile, the Catholic Church in 2014 was directly managing almost 5,400 American elementary schools, 1,200 secondary schools, and 225 universities and colleges, for a total of more than six million students and more than two hundred thousand teachers and professors. In the health care system it controlled a network of 550 hospitals serving, in 2013, approximately ninety million patients, not to mention nursing homes, retirement homes, halfway houses, and many other charitable institutions, which, in total, served more than nine million people in 2013.[18]

The Church is, in a nutshell, the second-largest social network in the country after the federal government. In the era of the "new norm," in which Americans will have to learn to live with economic growth rates about one-third lower than in the decades prior to the 2008 crisis, the network of social services and the army of several millions of volunteers that the American Catholic Church is able to mobilize are proving extremely valuable, perhaps indispensable.

EVEN SO, according to conventional wisdom, all this social capital, as well as the overrepresentation of Catholics in the American political elite, is meaningless, because the Catholic Church is undergoing a deep and possibly irreversible crisis. We are insistently told that the numbers of priests, nuns, seminarians, and practitioners are falling dramatically; that the numbers of religious weddings and baptisms are also decreasing rapidly; that parishes are closing, and many churches are being transformed into shops, cafés, warehouses, or even evangelical venues; and finally, that the pedophilia scandal has definitively destroyed all confidence in the Church. Moreover, the Church is said to have been losing its salient characteristics, becoming less and less "Catholic" (that is, etymologically, "universal") and less and less "Roman," as its center of gravity shifts toward the Global South (with the election of an Argentine pope as Exhibit no. 1). An enemy of relativism, the Catholic Church would paradoxically be "relativizing" itself on the doctrinal, organizational, and even geographical levels.

There is a striking consensus around this thesis of the Church's decline. Some of its traditional enemies (Protestants as well as secularists), as we might expect, firmly believe it or, at least, eagerly hope for it. Yet the stauncher partisans of this thesis are found among Catholics themselves; we could even say that this is the only point on which almost all Catholics agree. For conservatives, this supposed crisis proves that the Church is too open to profane influences, that it is loosening its links to tradition, or, in a word, that it is becoming Protestantized. For liberals it is exactly the other way around: this supposed crisis proves that the Church is unable to grasp "the signs of the times," that it is spending too much energy in trying to impose the outdated moral standards of just a few overzealous traditionalists, and so forth. Finally, the hierarchies, whatever they really think about the state of the Church, very much endorse the "decline thesis," not only because it perfectly embodies the Catholic quasi-Pavlovian propensity for victimization but especially because, as in the case of the overestimation of evangelicals, it greatly justifies the Church's traditional low-profile policy. And the more the influence of the Church rises, the more the low-profile policy is needed.

All the factions within the Catholic Church are able to use the "decline thesis" against each other because many of the pieces of evidence commonly used to prove it are indisputable. The fact is that those pieces of evidence still don't prove much. They only show that the Catholic Church is no longer what it used to be and that the world is no longer what it used to be—which, in hermeneutical terms, means nothing. Some people tend to spontaneously compare the current situation of the Church with the era of Christendom, during which religion and society were linked by "osmosis and interpenetration" (in the words of René Rémond);[19] but the problem, as Joseph Ratzinger himself admitted, is that "a universal Christian atmosphere no longer exists"[20] and that this has been so for at least two centuries.

Others compare the current situation with that existing before the Second Vatican Council, which is equally an anachronism, because in the last fifty years society has changed profoundly, and the Church has changed perhaps more profoundly still.

The Vatican Council was called precisely because the Church had big troubles in recognizing "the signs of the times" and was trying not to lose touch with a society no longer permeated by religiosity. Cardinals, bishops, and priests debated intensely and sometimes ruthlessly for three years, and as soon as the debate came to a close and the documents were voted upon, a new crisis exploded within the Church, possibly its worst since the Reformation or the French Revolution. What happened is that, following the Council, everyone left Rome with his own idea about what had been decided, and the hesitancy of Pope Paul VI was of little help. On the contrary. In short, the Church had lost its unity of purpose, and for a while it became a kind of loose confederation of small, independent Catholic republics, often governed by a single bishop or even a single priest or theologian. Among the consequences of this crisis, to mention but one, around one hundred thousand priests in the world (and possibly even many more nuns) resigned between 1970 and 2000, according to the Italian Vaticanist Sandro Magister—that is to say between 20 and 25 percent of the global numbers of priests. The remaining pastors, curates, and nuns lost a great deal of their social prestige, which led to a rapid decline in the "vocations." After that tsunami, instead of being surprised that so many churches have been transformed into warehouses, we should be surprised that the majority of them are still open for business.

AND WE SHOULD BE even more surprised by the fact that the majority of them are thriving. In fact, as Charles Morris put it, "the 'spirit of Vatican II' intersected with the cultural upheavals of the 1960s and 1970s, a time of rudderless yawing for almost all established institutions."[21] The social ascent of Catholics, under way since the end of World War II, together with these social upheavals, radically changed the relationship between the Church and its flock.

When John Paul II and Joseph Ratzinger swept away "the detritus of the post–Vatican II confusion"[22] (Deal Hudson), and the Church recovered its unity of purpose and its identity, there certainly were fewer priests, nuns, parishes, practitioners, and so on. At the same time, people who kept going to church did so not because they felt socially compelled, or because everybody else did, but because they *chose* to do so. Consequently, they were much more involved in the life of the parishes: the recruitment of permanent deacons started to grow at an exceptional rate, especially in the United States, to the point that today, more than 40 percent of all the permanent deacons in the world are Americans. Even in the harshest years of the pedophilia scandal, between 1995 and 2005, their numbers increased by 50 percent. Besides the permanent deacons, laypeople in many parishes started to take on—often as voluntary workers—management positions as liturgists, catechists, religious directors, accountants, and community organizers, as well as to become volunteers in charities and social services. In a series of parishes that Charles Morris surveyed in the 1990s, between one-fifth and one-third of parishioners were actively involved in some sort of parish work.

This does not mean, of course, that the Church is no longer interested in recruiting priests or that it is ready to place priests and active parishioners, or even priests and permanent deacons, on equal footing. But even after the post-Council crisis the situation appears far from desperate. The only country in the world in which there are more priests than the United States is Italy: roughly fifty thousand vs. forty-five thousand midway through the first decade of the new millennium. The United States is home to around 7 percent of all Catholics and 12.5 percent of all priests. The ratio of priests to citizens in the United States is lower than in Europe but higher than in the ensemble of the American continent, more than four times that of Africa, more than eight times that of Asia, and almost double that of Brazil, the most populous Catholic country in the world. The risk of "desertification" of the parishes remains remote.

WITH THE ELECTION OF POPE FRANCIS the American Catholic Church has taken a new step in the long process of the universal Church's "conquest," a process begun in 1891. Before that year, in which Pope Leo XIII published his *Rerum novarum* encyclical, the "social question" had long been under discussion among bishops in the United States, where rapid industrialization had confronted an essentially Catholic working class with a series of problems with which the Church had never dealt. The successful battle some American bishops fought in Rome to be allowed to organize labor unions opened the doors to the very official Catholic "social doctrine," one of the most important turning points in the relationship between the Catholic Church and "modernity." Since then, the influence of the American experience on Rome has been steadily growing. And this is not only because the United States had, since the end of the nineteenth century, become the single largest contributor to the universal Church's finances.

Many of the principles accepted by Vatican II—in particular, religious freedom and freedom of conscience—came primarily from the American experience. Today, faced with the widespread trends of secularization, flock disaffection, and competition from other religions, even in traditionally Catholic lands, the Vatican has come to accept what might be called the entrepreneurial mind-set of the "American model": competition among different denominations to ensure favors and offerings from believers. This "free market of faith" is often considered one of the main factors behind the religious exuberance of Americans, in contrast to the monopolistic dominance of Catholics in southern Europe (and in Latin America), Protestants in the North, and Orthodox in the East, which is said, on the contrary, to have greatly contributed to the decline of religious life on the Old Continent. In addition to having already proven its worth, the "American model" offers the Catholic Church another prospective advantage: in theory, in any system based on free and open competition, the best-equipped competitor has the greatest odds of success.

In Latin America the Catholic Church experienced failure in its attempt to win the evangelical competition with only the traditional tools of anathema. Jorge Mario Bergoglio brought from Buenos Aires to Rome the theory—and practice—of a Catholic Church that "goes forth," "permanently in a state of mission," "to the outskirts of its own territory or towards new sociocultural settings."[23] This Church learns to do what evangelicals do and to compete with them on the same field—with the incomparable advantage of being much better-equipped. In the years of Latin American *desarrollo* evangelicals were successful mainly among the nonpracticing baptized, who were overlooked by a Church too institutional or too fatuously subversive. They aroused them and brought them back to religious practice. But evangelicals have neither the unity of purpose nor the experience to transform this success into a durable organization and, eventually, into a political machine. Only the solid and well-established organizational machine of the Catholic Church can do so, provided that it gives up a part of its privileges, of its institutionalized role and all its subversive temptations, and that it "goes forth."

The experience of American Catholicism taught the universal Catholic Church the advantages of religious pluralism, the kind of pluralism that forces such a going forth. As Pope Leo XIII feared when he condemned "Americanism," American Catholicism has been, inevitably, pervaded by environmental pluralism, giving rise to a unique diversity of sensitivities and accents, further multiplied by the social rise of the faithful after the Second World War.

It should be mentioned, however, that the Catholic Church has been able to resist, for better or worse, all the historical storms it has ever had to suffer before it ever saw the birth of its American branch. And one of the reasons for its resilience lies precisely in its internal pluralism. For most of its history the Church has rested on several pillars: it suffices to remember how much Franciscans, Dominicans, and Jesuits, to mention but a few, have been in harsh competition with each other in the promotion of the greater glory of God. In the twentieth century many new movements, currents, and tendencies, comprising essentially laypeople (for instance, Catholic Action and Opus Dei), were added to the traditional religious orders, enriching the capacity of the Church to extend its reach into any folds of society. The clergy, too, had become specialized: from army chaplains to pacifist priests; from Monsignori close to the Roman Black Nobility to working-class priests and liberation theologians; from clergymen responsible for unspeakable violence (in Croatia, Ireland, Latin America, and Rwanda) to missionaries in charge of healing the effects of this same violence.

In 1923 the Catholic Carl Schmitt explained "some of this diversity and ambiguity—the double face, the Janus-head, the hermaphroditic nature" of the Church in essentially political terms: "In the tactics of political struggle, every party with an established world-view can form coalitions with the most disparate groupings." From this argument Schmitt drew his famous saying: "The Catholic Church is a complex of opposites, a *complexio oppositorum*. There appears to be no antithesis it does not embrace."[24] Pluralism within the Catholic Church is not an accident but one of the very conditions of its achievement: "With every change in the political situation, all principles appear to change save one: the power of Catholicism."[25]

The Roman Catholic Church is one and many, not only for tactical reasons but also because within it there are multiple voices, cultural inflections, and material interests. There has always been, at least in the last centuries, a competition—at different levels of intensity—between the pope and the curia, between center and periphery, between the Propaganda Fide[26] and the local bishopric, among local bishops themselves, and so on. This cacophony is rarely heard in public, where a symphonic unity prevails. When it can be heard, it means that this unity is in crisis, as happened when Pope Benedict XVI resigned. That decision brought to light a "singular tribal structure . . . a long chain of conflicts, maneuvers [and] betrayals in the shadow of the Dome of St. Peter's . . . a legacy of hostility, of personal grudges, of factional struggles [and] of economic vendettas with legal implications," according to Massimo Franco's vivid description.[27] But such crises represent a momentary rupture of an equilibrium that, although delicate, does prevail; indeed, they represent the pathological degeneration of a physiological condition.

THE UNIVERSAL CATHOLIC CHURCH thus owes a lot to American Catholics and also to the United States as a country. As of August 2015, fifteen American cardinals[28] are proof of this. These cardinals represent not only the second single largest national contingent but also the largest American contingent ever within the College of Cardinals. Given their far-from-negligible role in the election of the first "American" pope, in 2013, they are at the same time the witnesses and the interpreters of the current stage of the progressive "Americanization" of the universal Catholic Church.

"Americanization," though, means that the universal Church has been able to draw the best from the experience of the American Church, from its point of view and in order to achieve its own goals. It does not entail any particular link, any special relationship, with the United States. It is important to remember that the Church *does not* rely on the United States, or on any other political or economic power, to strengthen and advance its status on the global stage. The Church does not refuse any help—material or political—as long as its total and unconditional freedom of action is guaranteed.

Because we are speaking of humanity's oldest enduring institution, we can well assume that its leaders know, and practice, the virtues of pragmatism and compromise to the highest degree of refinement (even more so since the current pope is a Jesuit). But it is the Church's autonomy that is one of the key factors behind its successes and its credibility. In fact, the more the Catholic Church criticizes consumerism, the American way of life, the death penalty, anti-immigration legislation, abortion, "moral relativism," and the Iraq War, the more popular and appealing it becomes in the United States. The Catholic Church has its own politico-spiritual agenda, which does not match the agenda of any other power: its purpose is "the normative guidance of human social life," as Schmitt wrote in 1923.[29] Transposed to the international level, the goal becomes—in the words of Benedict XVI—the realization of "a *true world political Authority*, as my predecessor Blessed John XXIII indicated some years ago": namely, an authority that is "a postulate of the moral order and derives from God."[30]

From the American side it seems implausible that, in Washington, someone set out deliberately to affect the current shift in global power by filling the Supreme Court, the administration, and the military leadership, not to mention the ranks of presidential candidates, with Catholics—all the less so because this Catholic political leadership does not speak for the Church. Neither Joe Biden, John Kerry, John Boehner, Sonia Sotomayor, nor Joseph Dunford are official—or informal—representatives of the interests, policies, and goals of the Church. Still, they personify a very noticeable trend: as if, in this historical moment, the coupling of the return of religion to the public stage and the relative economic decline of the United States have increased the need to open as many lines of communication with the Catholic Church as possible—that is, with an institution that is simultaneously a solid moral and psychological anchor, with a wide social base, and a network of relationships with close ties to the ruling classes of most of the world's states.

IN 1978, at the funeral of Paul VI, President Carter sent his mother as the official American representative. In 2005 the funeral of Pope John Paul II was attended by the incumbent president, George W. Bush, his two immediate predecessors, Bill Clinton and George H. W. Bush, and Secretary of State Condoleezza Rice (in addition to a nonofficial delegation including John Kerry, Edward Kennedy, Michael Bloomberg, George Pataki, the Senate Republican leader Bill Frist, and the White House chief of staff Andrew Card). For many commentators a delegation so influential, led by three presidents, was intended to pay a tribute of gratitude to the man who, along with Ronald Reagan, had decisively contributed to the fall of the Soviet "evil empire." There were, no doubt, fundamental geopolitical considerations to that tribute. But my guess is that it concerned not only the parallel paths followed by the United States and the Catholic Church in the past but also, and perhaps more importantly, the parallel paths they will follow in the future.

CHAPTER I

Catholics in the United States

"The Greek in the Midst of Troy"

TOWARD THE END OF THE FIRST WORLD WAR, to the demand of including the Vatican in future peace negotiations, US Secretary of State Robert Lansing answered: "We are a republic, and like France, Switzerland and other republics we do not wish to set up relations with the Holy See, whose objectives are openly in contrast to the democratic ideals of America."[1]

This statement indicated a structural—not a temporary—incompatibility between the two sides: the objectives of the Roman Catholic Church and those of the United States government were physiologically divergent.

Today we know that Lansing was wrong. After meeting with Pope Francis in March 2014, Barack Obama declared that "there is a potential convergence" between the pope's intentions and "what policymakers need to be thinking."[2] The gap between an "open contrast" and a "potential convergence" is huge, so we cannot blame Lansing for not having foreseen it. It is true that almost a century has passed since the declarations quoted above. But America's hostility and mistrust toward Catholicism, particularly toward the Catholic Church, were so profound that they survived for many more decades—at least, according to a prevailing opinion, until the 1980s, when Ronald Reagan succeeded in becoming the center of a coalition overturning Lansing's perception of irreconcilable difference, a change for which the arrival of millions of Catholics on American shores was a crucial factor.

Robert Lansing was perfectly in line with the anti-Catholic tradition that for two hundred years had been consubstantial to the very nature of the United States. The history of this tradition can be divided into four phases: (1) the period extending from the arrival of the *Mayflower* up to the Declaration of Independence, which is characterized by a theological and political ostracism; (2) the first decades of life of the United States of America, characterized by a legal quarantine; (3) the period from the great Irish immigration to World War I, characterized by the expansion of the Catholic community; and (4) the period extending from the 1920s to the 1980s, characterized by its laborious integration into the American national life and by the exhaustion of the Protestants' traditional hostility.

OSTRACISM

The Puritans who sought refuge on the eastern coast of North America as they fled the Church of England's persecutions were animated by a double anti-Catholic feeling: against blatant "popery," both theological and institutional, and against what they considered a kind of "popery of a second degree," represented by their Anglican persecutors. In fact, apart from some doctrinal divergences (e.g., the denial of the Immaculate Conception and Purgatory), the Church of England had inherited most of the characteristics of the Church of Rome, actually changing only its head—the king instead of the pope. With the tendency toward autonomy of national churches in the countries thrust into new colonial conquest in the sixteenth and seventeenth centuries, Anglicanism represented a middle way between the total—theological and organizational—rupture of North European Protestant churches and an attempt by Spanish and French monarchies to nationalize local episcopacies without completely separating from Rome.

As a result of the religious conflicts raging in Europe, English territories in America experienced a constant influx of colonists belonging to a wide range of religious affiliations: Anglicans, Presbyterians, Calvinists, Lutherans, Baptists, Congregationalists, Quakers, Catholics, and even a few Jews,[3] in addition to Puritans who had opened the way.

Initially, the various New World Christian confessions continued Old World practices. In 1565 the first contact between Christians of different denominations was the massacre, by the Spanish in Florida, of a colony of French Huguenots who had been accused of "scattering the odious Lutheran doctrine in the province."[4]

In that case, however, political considerations were more weighty than religious ones. In actuality, the Spanish intended to chase the French, no matter what their religion, from a region they wanted for themselves. Religious motivation was a useful—but completely instrumental—excuse for stirring up passions. This much is clear not only because they were ignorant of the form of worship practiced by the French colonists (Huguenots were Calvinists, not Lutherans) but also by the fact that the Huguenots' massacre was avenged three years later by a French aristocrat, a Catholic, who murdered all the Spanish in the garrison snatched from the Huguenots.

Conversely, in Massachusetts—the British colony that was considered by Alexis de Tocqueville to be a prototype of American democracy—discriminations and persecutions were based on theocratic motivations totally unfamiliar to the Spanish. The conviction that they had founded the evangelical "City upon a Hill"[5] stimulated Puritan colonists to establish a "Bible Commonwealth" from whose rulings the followers of other Christian confessions were obviously excluded. Its norms were draconian: the obligation to participate in religious services; prohibition of music, dancing, theater, tobacco, gambling, and even of celebration of the Nativity and Resurrection; and the proscription of Quakers, Jews, and Catholics. Two laws, those of 1647 and 1700, contemplated capital punishment for Catholic priests who returned to Massachusetts after having been expelled. This climate of exacerbation of religious sentiment provoked the mass hysteria that led to the notorious Salem Witch Trials (1692–93), as a result of which nineteen people were hanged and four more died in jail (at least one under torture and one by stoning); two dogs were also executed for their complicity with witches.[6]

Many of those persecuted in Massachusetts found shelter in neighboring and more hospitable Rhode Island. Catholics were not tolerated there either, however. According to Albert West, "It is said that in 1680 there was not one Catholic in the colony." In 1739, West continues, there were thirty-three churches (twelve Baptist, ten Quaker, six Presbyterian, and five Episcopalian) but not one Catholic. The first one was built a century later, in 1837.[7]

The situation was not very different in the other colonies. In New Hampshire, Catholic colonists from nearby Quebec were expelled when, in 1641, the territory was brought under the jurisdiction of Massachusetts. The new 1679 law limited itself to excluding them from public office. In Connecticut "the spirit of antagonism to all things Catholic was everywhere," James O'Donnell writes, and "proscription of Catholics was officially taught as a duty."[8] In other colonies (New Jersey, South Carolina, Georgia) freedom of worship was guaranteed to all "except papists."

Considering its particular and growing importance, the New York colony echoed for a long time the events that took place in the motherland. Dutch governor Pieter Stuyvesant's decision to authorize only Calvinist worship was invalidated by the West Indies Company, and freedom of worship was confirmed by the English as early as 1664. At the time when the British Crown was swaying once again toward Catholicism, New York had no less than two Catholic governors: Anthony Brockholls (1681–82) and Thomas Dongan (1682–88). After the Glorious Revolution of 1688, however, the limits on and persecutions of Catholics of other Crown territories were introduced in New York as well: Catholic priests and teachers were expelled, and in 1741 an elementary schoolteacher and preacher was hanged under the charge (probably false) of being a "Popish priest." When independence was proclaimed, there were about two hundred Catholics (out of a total population of about 340,000) in the province of New York; considering that between three hundred and four hundred Jews were living in the city of New York alone, we can get an idea of the especial hostility toward Catholicism.[9]

Catholics enjoyed relative freedom only in Maryland and Pennsylvania. The Maryland (or *Terra Mariæ*) colony was founded by a Catholic baron, Lord Baltimore, in 1634 and became a safe haven for the Catholics persecuted in England. But being the first Catholic territory to declare religious liberty, Maryland also became a refuge for Anglicans persecuted by Puritans and for Puritans persecuted by Anglicans, which soon reduced Catholics to a minority. The English Revolution of 1649 caused a Puritan coup in the beginning of the 1650s, which entailed the abolition of religious liberty, with particular hostility against Catholics, whose churches were set on fire. The Toleration Act promulgated by the Catholic governor was definitively abolished in 1692 following the Glorious Revolution. In 1704 the local legislative assembly passed *An Act to Prevent the Growth of Popery Within This Province* that resulted not only in expulsion of "Popish bishop, Priest, or Jesuite" but also in the progressive expropriation of Catholic landlords, whose lands went from 25 percent of the total in 1688 to 5 percent in 1776.[10]

Many Catholics sought refuge in the North, in the region that in 1681 took the name of Pennsylvania. The Quakers who had founded the new colony intended to make it a safe haven for all religiously persecuted people, provided that they recognized "Jesus Christ [as] the Savior of the World." Although Catholics were de facto, if not de jure, excluded from public office, as they were considered loyal to a foreign sovereign (the pope), Pennsylvania was nevertheless the only colony where they were never, or almost never, persecuted.

The colonists' anti-Catholic zeal fed on a profound aversion to the pope, who was not only regarded as the Antichrist but also as the head of a foreign power, certainly hostile to England and therefore inclined to conspire and ally against it. We should not forget that only fifty years before the voyage of the *Mayflower*, Pope Pius V pronounced Queen Elisabeth I "to be a heretic and favorer of heretics," absolving her subjects "from any duty arising from lordship, fealty and obedience" (bull *Regnans in Excelsis*, 1570).

In the land of America, political aversion to "popery" was not only the result of local reflections of the English wars but also of the special geopolitical position of the thirteen colonies, virtually encircled as they were by two Catholic superpowers—France and Spain—with whom the English were far from having definitively settled past accounts. Although the Catholics in the colonies constituted a meager and insignificant minority of a few thousand people in the second half of the eighteenth century, the passions unleashed by the Seven Years' War (1756–63) gave rise to outright pogroms against them, as they were once again regarded as a foreign body and, under the circumstances, as a potential fifth column of the French.

Events relating to the Revolution determined two opposing attitudes. On the one hand, the Quebec Act—enacted in 1774 by His Majesty's Government to prevent a potential conjunction of the restless francophone Catholics in Quebec and the insurgents in nearby Massachusetts—provoked a new outburst of antipapist feeling in the thirteen colonies. On the other hand, the support of France and Spain for the American insurrection, in 1778, provoked considerably more restrained feeling, closer to the revolutionary leaders' positions, widely favorable to religious freedom for all. But the hopes nurtured by independence and the Constitution were mostly dashed.

LEGAL QUARANTINE

The delegates of the Philadelphia Convention of 1787 represented almost all the thirteen colonies, with the exception of Rhode Island, and almost the entire range of religious denominations. Thanks to Frank Lambert's research, we know that twenty-eight of the delegates were Anglicans (or Episcopalians, as they had been called since independence), eight were Presbyterians, seven Congregationalists, two Dutch Calvinists, two Lutherans, two Methodists, and two nonaffiliates.[11] And there were two Catholics as well: Thomas Fitzsimons, a merchant and banker from Philadelphia, and Daniel Carroll, a major plantation owner in Maryland, who was the cousin of Charles Carroll, one of the signers of the Declaration of Independence, and brother of the Jesuit John Carroll, the founder of Georgetown University (1789) and the first American Catholic bishop (1790).

Neither Fitzsimons nor the Carrolls ever suffered persecution or discrimination of any kind—not even before independence. It must be said, though, that the former was at the head of one of the biggest companies engaged in commercial traffic with the East Indies, whereas the latter, with his sixty thousand acres of land (in spite of ongoing Catholics' expropriation in Maryland that had started in 1704), was one of the wealthiest men on the continent. Furthermore, these two delegates represented the two most tolerant colonies when it came to religious matters. Nevertheless, their presence at the convention gave the country's Catholics, at that crucial moment, a political representation considerably higher in proportion to their weight in the rest of society: 3.6 percent (two delegates out of fifty-five), against about 1 percent of the total population of the new country in 1776.[12]

The living conditions of almost all of that 1 percent continued for a long time to be very different from those of the two rich Catholics sitting in Philadelphia. Popular sentiment against them, their religion, and above all their pope did not, in fact, change substantially with the revolution or independence. And their legal situation actually remained the same, despite the voting in favor of the Federal Constitution and, later, the First Amendment.

This amendment prohibited Congress's officially acknowledging a religion and, at the same time, impeding its free exercise; nevertheless, almost all new states preserved the laws or regulations that favored this or that religion. Even after the approval of the Fourteenth Amendment (1868), concerning equal protection of citizens, North Carolina and New Hampshire had to wait until 1875 and 1877 respectively for all religious references to be removed from their constitutions.

The First Amendment broke with a long tradition of established churches enjoying an exclusive relationship with political power. That had been the rule for quite a while in nine colonies out of thirteen: in Massachusetts, New Hampshire, and Connecticut this privilege was granted to the Congregational Church; in the province of New York and in Virginia, Maryland, North Carolina, South Carolina, and Georgia to the Anglican Church. Only in Rhode Island, New Jersey, Pennsylvania, and Delaware was there no official church.

All the states had written the principle of religious freedom into their new constitutions; but, as John K. Wilson writes, "The vagueness of these provisions, and the lack of a mechanism to enforce them, suggests that they rarely affected the actual treatment of religious groups in any of the states." And, in any case, "many states required tests to keep non-Christians or in some cases Catholics out of public office."[13] Practicing the Protestant faith was required, according to Wilson, in Massachusetts, New Hampshire, New Jersey, both Carolinas, and Georgia, while in Pennsylvania, Maryland, Delaware, and Vermont, public officials had to acknowledge the Trinity dogma (which excluded Jews but not Catholics).

In some states the rule—that obliged public officials to "abjure and renounce all allegiance and subjection to all and every foreign king, prince, potentate and state in all matters ecclesiastical as well as civil" (as per the 1777 Constitution of the State of New York)—remained in force, where "foreign king, prince, potentate and state" clearly indicated the pope and his state.[14]

Although in New York the law restricting Catholics' rights of citizenship had been abolished in 1806 (twenty-nine years after the Constitution was voted in), in other states adjustment periods were different: from Rhode Island, where the limitations were removed as early as 1783, to North Carolina, where the "Protestant Test" remained in force until 1868.

The permanence of anti-Catholic dispositions resulted from the inertia of a popular sentiment that, as I have already mentioned, was consubstantial with the very existence of the colonies. Frank Whelan points out that "to an average 18th-century [American] Protestant, Roman Catholics were regarded with the same horror as Germans during World War I or radicals in the Joe McCarthy era."[15] A direct testimony of that feeling was transmitted by the historian Thomas Jones (1731–92), who posited New York's "Golden Age" as the 1750s, when "Presbyterians, Moravians, Seceders, Lutherans, German Calvinists, those of the French Reformed Church, the people called Quakers, and even the very Jews lived in perfect peace and harmony."[16]

The absence of Catholics in Jones's list smacks of *damnatio memoriæ*. Actually, what contributed to keeping alive the memory of the "papist threat"—all through the eighteenth century—was Guy Fawkes Night (November 5), the festival in memory of the 1605 failed Catholic conspiracy to kill King James I. On this day a carnival pageant ended with the burning of the pope's effigy and launching of fireworks symbolizing "popish spirits coming from below." Regardless of George Washington's 1775 decision to prohibit "that ridiculous and childish custom of burning the Effigy of the pope" (in the hope of conquering Canadian Catholics' hearts, "whom we ought to consider as Brethren embarked in the same Cause"),[17] the practice continued in some states into the 1880s, particularly in New Hampshire and Massachusetts.

Washington's pronouncement shows that anti-Catholic feelings were still present during the years of the fight for independence. In fact, in some cases they became an element of propaganda on both sides. Following the Quebec Act, the patriot leader Isaac Low stated that "the King is a Roman Catholic, nay, a Roman Catholic tyrant . . . [who] had established the popish religion in Canada." In contrast, at the moment of France's entrance into the war (1778), it was loyalists who accused patriots of serving the "popish King of France."[18] And the fact that few Catholics of the thirteen colonies participated in the war on both fronts made them objects of contempt on both sides.

Things changed a little after the American Revolution. Victorious fervor, gratitude toward France and Spain, the calming of political tensions and clashes, as well as the sparse number of Catholics in the country, contributed to the temporary appeasement of traditional antipapal feeling.

In the first thirty years of the new republic, immigration to the United States was sparse (in 1830 immigrants made up hardly 1.6 percent of the population), and within this immigration Catholics were a minority. Up to the 1830s, as Charles Morris writes, two-thirds of Irish immigrants were Protestants; furthermore, the lack of places of worship forced Catholics to go to Protestant venues to attend Mass. But above all, most of the Catholics who arrived in the first decades of the new century represented a "self-improving bourgeois elite . . . quietly adapting to a Protestant country." Therefore, as Morris concludes, "Catholicism was gaining intellectual and social cachet," to the point that Congress chose a Catholic chaplain for its session of 1832.[19]

In reality embers smoldered beneath the ashes. And they flared up following the turbulent changes of those very years. The country's territory doubled with the annexation of the Northwest Territory (1789), Louisiana (1803), and Florida (1821); in that same period the population grew two and a half times, almost exclusively owing to natural growth; and a new war was fought against Great Britain (1812–14). The severest tensions, though, derived from impetuous economic development and from the division among an industrious and industrial North; an agricultural, commercial, and financial Center; and a South dominated by expansive plantations, especially cotton plantations, which became particularly profitable after the invention of the cotton gin.[20] The epic of the West had begun in New England, as had industry, navigation, and fishing. The first big strike of maritime workers took place in New York in 1802, and it was legally prosecuted as a "conspiracy."[21]

As often happens in moments of crisis and transition, this period of turbulence was favorable to the manifestation of a new wave of religious fervor, known as the Great Awakening. Dozens of preachers traveled back and forth across the country urging crowds to return to lost values, contesting the institutionalization of religions and insisting instead on individual conversion, regeneration (or rebirth), and the gifts of the Holy Spirit. This awakening of religious passions, exclusively Protestant, also brought about a new wave of tensions among different denominations, tensions whose principal victims were again Catholics.

The violence of the 1830s inaugurated a century of militant hostility during which "Natives"[22] did everything they could to exclude or subdue Catholics. But they were not able to prevent Catholicism from becoming the most important confession of the United States nor Catholics themselves from becoming, a century later, an essential component of American domestic and international politics.

EXPANSION

American Catholicism's physiognomy altered radically after the 1830s. The major reason lies in the successive waves of immigration that brought millions of people to the United States, mostly from European Catholic countries: first the Irish, then Germans, Italians, Hungarians, and Poles.[23]

Aroused by a determined desire for redress, many of these immigrants became the protagonists of an unprecedented activism, which manifested itself on a number of fronts: trade unionism, politics, editorial activity, and education, to name a few. For the Catholic Church the Civil War eventually became the first case of institutional involvement in domestic and international politics of the United States (and the Confederacy): a sort of a field promotion, regardless (or rather because) of its, to say the least, ambiguous position both on slavery and on secession.

The more Catholics became visible, and occupied the space that until then had been an exclusively Protestant prerogative, the more, in the Protestants' opinion, a papal plot to take control of the United States seemed to become a reality.

During the first decades of the nineteenth century, traditional mistrust was stirred up by ethnic hostility, which fed on ferocious competition in the labor market. Attracted by the immense project of constructing the Erie Canal (1817–25), the first immigrants gathered in nearby Massachusetts, where anti-Catholic feeling had its deepest roots.[24] In Boston the number of Irish rose from two thousand (4.6 percent of the total population) in 1820 to seven thousand (11.4 percent) in 1830, and to thirty-five thousand (26 percent) in 1850. As so often happens, in taking the place of workers on strike and accepting inferior wages, immigrants contributed to the reduction of salary and qualification levels of the local working class, which up until then had consisted essentially of Puritan "Yankee plebeians."

In 1823, 1826, 1828, 1832, and 1833 Catholic neighborhoods in Boston and the surrounding area were attacked by groups of Protestant workers. In August of 1834 the Ursuline Convent, on the outskirts of the city, was set on fire. And in 1837 a large part of the Catholic neighborhood was destroyed again. Clashes between Catholic and Protestant gangs took place on an almost daily basis in New York, Louisville, St. Louis, Detroit, and Philadelphia. The names of some Irish Catholic gangs in Philadelphia— Killers, Bouncers, Rats, Skinners, not to mention the famous Dead Rabbits from New York's Five Points (whose symbol was a dead rabbit impaled on a spike)—speak volumes about their belligerent spirit. Some of those fights turned into bloody riots, such as those in Bangor (Maine) in 1833 and Boston in 1834.[25]

Between 1830 and 1850 the number of immigrants to the United States multiplied by twelve, increasing from 1.6 percent to almost 10 percent of the population (almost all concentrated in the Center and in the North, where the percentage was therefore much higher). Between 1841 and 1860 about 1.7 million Irish immigrants arrived, fleeing the Great Potato Famine, and about 1.4 million Germans, about half of whom were Catholics (see table 1). In the early 1860s a quarter of the New York population had been born in Ireland, and a sixth in Germany.

The country's social and ethnic composition was thus substantially transformed, and tensions between communities intensified. In Philadelphia in 1844, two consecutive riots, in May and July, caused dozens of casualties; several churches and a seminary were set on fire and numerous homes were destroyed.[26] Other conflicts took place in 1853 in Cincinnati, Boston, Baltimore, and Brooklyn and again in 1855 in Cincinnati, Bath (Maine), and Louisville, all ending with burned churches and homes and often with numerous victims.

After the Philadelphia riots, New York archbishop John Hughes warned publicly that if even one New York Catholic church was burned, "the city

TABLE 1. *Irish and German immigrants living in the United States, 1820–1900*

	1820–1830	1831–1840	1841–1850	1851–1860	1861–1870	1871–1880	1881–1890	1891–1900
Irish	54,338	207,381	780,719	914,119	435,778	436,871	655,482	388,416
Germans	30,000[a]	130,000[a]	434,626	951,667	787,468	718,182	1,452,970	505,152

SOURCE: US Census Bureau, Senate Documents, 61st Cong., 3rd Sess.: Statistical Review of Immigration, 1820–1910.
[a] Estimation.

would become a second Moscow." In an article published in the diocesan journal, this same archbishop boasted that "there is not a [Catholic] church in the city, which was not protected with an average force of one to two thousand men—cool, collected, armed to the teeth—and with a firm determination, after taking as many lives as they could in defense of their property, to give up, if necessary, their own lives for the same cause."[27] According to these numbers, "Dagger John" (as Hughes was nicknamed) had at his command a real army of at least twenty-five thousand men for the defense of the seventeen existing Catholic churches in Manhattan in 1844. A large majority of them were Irish, as he was, but there were also many Germans (five churches were German) and French (who were parishioners of St. Vincent de Paul).

After the first waves of Irish immigration the clashes between different communities took a political turn as well. Against Catholic aliens—considered deprived, ignorant, strike-breaking, heavy-drinking, and violent (even the papal delegate Gaetano Bedini, who visited the city in 1853, noted with apparent uneasiness that in the United States "they form the idea of Catholicism as the Religion of the poor")[28]—"Nativists" began to organize on a political basis. Their party, the Know-Nothing Party,[29] became the main political force in Chicago, Boston, Philadelphia, and Washington in the mid-1850s and won the governor's office in states like Massachusetts and California. In 1854, 121 members of Congress declared themselves Know-Nothings.

But in that same period Catholics began to get organized as well. At first they organized through neighborhood gangs, then through shelters for the newly arrived immigrants clustered around parishes and embryonic unions, and finally, in New York, through affiliation with the powerful Democratic political machine Tammany Hall, of which they became an extremely active and often reckless militant base (the least immoral of its illegal activities was the practice of ballot-box stuffing).[30] In 1854 Tammany Hall managed to have its own candidate, Fernando Wood, elected mayor of the city.

Leaning on those Irish Catholics who had already succeeded in moving up the social ladder and had become lawyers, judges, bankers, financiers, merchants, and entrepreneurs, Bishop Hughes conceived a project that many initially considered senseless and unattainable but that, for New York's and for all US Catholics, became a source of great pride: the construction of the imposing new St. Patrick's Cathedral on Fifth Avenue. Soliciting Irish pride had, according to Morris, a more ambitious objective: to "turn the American church away from its assimilationist path and forge a culturally and ethnically cohesive Catholic state-within-a-state."[31] The main instrument of this operation was the creation of an educational Catholic network against which the Nativists concentrated their fire.

As an alternative to public schools, which provided a Protestant education,[32] Catholics in the 1820s founded a network of parochial schools, not always reserved for Catholics alone. At the first Boston Catholic school, for example, 90 percent of the students came from the families of wealthy Unitarians, a Christian anti-Trinitarian movement that split off from mainstream Puritanism. In one of his texts Pastor Lyman Beecher—father of thirteen children, of whom Harriet Beecher Stowe was the most famous, and an implacable enemy of Unitarianism and disestablishment of the Congregational Church—clearly implied that Catholics bestowed "such cheap and gratuitous facilities of education on Protestants" in order to conquer the young republic from the inside: their schools were "the Greek in the midst of Troy."[33] His fiery speech "The Devil and the Pope of Rome" lit the fuse of the attack on the Ursuline Convent in August of 1834.

The issue of parochial schools showed the extent to which the Catholic hierarchy was able to control the New York Democratic Party in 1840. When a group of Democrats voted against the proposal to extend public financing to Catholic schools, Bishop Hughes made a list of "unfaithful" candidates who were not reelected. In the new legislature, as Morris writes, "Democrats meekly fell in line on the school bill."[34]

The Catholic educational network continued to develop throughout the century in spite of fierce Nativist opposition, until a decision taken by the Baltimore Council in 1884, which made attending parochial school almost mandatory for the Catholic flock.

But it is the position, ambiguous, to say the least, taken by the Church and the Catholics during the Civil War that offered the Nativists the incontrovertible evidence that popery was alien, impossible to assimilate, and potentially subversive.

When a part of the black population that had flooded northward began to be exploited in the same way that the Irish themselves had been exploited vis-à-vis the Yankee plebeians—as scabs for workers on strike who would thus bring down wages—the Irish reacted the same way the Yankee plebeians had. The government's decision to enforce a compulsory draft in the same year of the Emancipation Proclamation led to the New York riot of the summer of 1863, "the most lethal riot in American history," according to Morris.[35] Being sent to likely death so as to free those the Catholic *Freeman's Journal* called "ugly black niggers,"[36] that is to say, masses of future rivals on the labor market, was considered pure self-injury. What made it even more unbearable was that the cause of emancipation of the slaves was supported by rich and arrogant Puritans who, among other things, could avoid the draft by paying $300 (an average year's salary) to whoever replaced them. The explosion of popular anger was directed mainly against the black population of New York: the four-day riot was suppressed by members of the army recalled from the front. According to the official figures, about a hundred people died, among them half a dozen blacks who were lynched, hanged, and burned.[37]

Several years later, in 1875, speaking against the public financing of private schools, President Ulysses S. Grant still had in mind the behavior of the majority of Catholics during the Civil War. According to him, the future dividing line would not be between the North and the South "but between patriotism and intelligence on one side, and superstition, ambition, and ignorance on the other."[38]

Yet it was in that exact situation that Catholic Church hierarchies were recognized for the first time as major political interlocutors. And this occurred on both fronts of the Civil War, despite the fact that the percentage of Catholics in the population of the South was one-third the size of that in the North: President Abraham Lincoln sent John Hughes to Rome, and President Jefferson Davis sent Charleston's bishop, Patrick Lynch; each was supposed to convince Pope Pius IX to endorse his own cause.

This was the first such event; furthermore, it occurred at a time when the majority of Americans still expressed the most open hostility toward Catholicism, and when, in Rome, the thousand-year-old power of the king-pope was on the wane. But as would happen again, a domestic and international political crisis made Washington (and in this case, even Richmond) seek support in Rome.

INTEGRATION

Roger Aubert writes that one of the results of "the enthusiastic adhesion of Catholics to the [Great] War" was "to reintegrate them into the nation in which, on the eve of 1914, they were internal migrants, especially in France and Italy."[39] Aubert should have added Germany and, to a certain extent, the United States.

It is true that, at that time in the United States, the dominant feelings were those expressed by Lansing in 1918 and that the years immediately following the conflict saw a resurgence of anti-Catholic hostility. But it is also true that during the war Catholics redeemed their reputation as dubious citizens, loyal to a foreign authority and therefore inclined to stab the American nation in the back. After all, during the War of Independence, the War of 1846–48 against the Catholic Mexico, and obviously, during the Civil War, Catholics offered overt evidence of ambiguity, bordering on treason. If to these examples we add the uneasiness about the war against Spain in 1898 and an openly favorable Catholic attitude toward the Central Powers at the beginning of the Great War, we can understand the skepticism that greeted the 1917 statement of the Bishop of Peoria, John Lancaster Spalding, according to whom the Catholic "record for patriotism [wa]s without blot or stain."[40]

Yet those eighteen months of the war were enough to trigger a turnaround of the tendency, although not immediately, of course. Two great turning points—the New Deal and the Reagan coalition—had to take place before the path of "integration into the nation" was completed, but the most important step was taken in April 1917. The bishops immediately silenced their hesitations and divisions and supported the duty of "absolute and unresolved obedience to [the] country's call," giving birth to the National Catholic War Council, "to do whatsoever is in us to do, for the preservation, the progress and the triumph of our beloved country."[41] Dioceses were invited to underwrite war bonds and organize prayers for victory, but, most important, Catholics "constitute[d] perhaps 35 percent of the New Army,"[42] as Secretary of War Newton Baker declared, at a time when they represented around 15 percent of the American population.

Between 1860 and 1900 the number of Catholics had quadrupled, reaching twelve million: half were in the Northeast and a third in the upper Midwest; 30 percent were concentrated in five dioceses: New York, Brooklyn (the two boroughs alone accounted for 16 percent of all American Catholics), Chicago, Boston, and Philadelphia. In 1900 there were twelve thousand priests, fifty thousand nuns, and more than twelve thousand parishes and missions spread over ninety-three dioceses.[43]

The changes between the end of the Civil War and World War I were impressive not only for Catholics, of course, but for all of American society. During the Gilded Age the country was transformed from a midlevel agricultural and commercial power into the world's leading industrial power: the growth was so intense that between 1860 and 1890 real wages increased about 60 percent *despite* the influx of at least ten million new immigrants.[44] Catholics, at the bottom of the social ladder, were the group primarily responsible for both the country's economic success and the challenges to it: they dominated the first trade unions, which gave a markedly interclass character to demands that could (and partly did) lead to revolutionary outcomes.

The decision of the American Catholic hierarchy to recognize the most important trade union organization at that time, the Knights of Labor, and to support its cause in Rome before Pope Leo XIII in 1888, deserves to be considered in all its implications. It was the first example of "Americanization" of the universal Catholic Church, because many of the arguments presented to the pope were adopted in the *Rerum novarum* of 1891. This encyclical enabled the Catholic Church to establish its credibility with workers, to whom it often became indispensable, offering them comfort and protection; but it established just as much credibility with employers, offering them a trade union that was bold and belligerent but opposed to the class struggle and, most important, to socialism. The action of the Knights of Labor allowed them to keep the white proletariat in the Democratic Party's camp, defeating any attempt to create an alternative Labor Party, even at the cost of chasing the recalcitrant out of the Church.[45] Last but not least, it allowed them to recruit a broad mass of cadres for the Church from within the proletariat: all American cardinals in office after World War I, writes Morris, were children of manual laborers.

In the Gilded Age two other fundamental decisions put the American Church in a position to collect, channel, and represent some underlying social trends: the renewed attention to education and the relative softening of ethnic tensions between Catholics in general.

With regard to the first point, the 1884 Baltimore Council's decision and the increase in immigrants (chiefly Poles, who would play a decisive role)[46] determined a very rapid development of the Catholic education network—especially between 1900 and 1920, when the number of parochial schools rose from 3,300 to 6,550, and high schools from a hundred or so to more than fifteen hundred.[47]

The second point proved to be much thornier and was solved (or at least attenuated) only by the intervention of Rome. Following the mass migrations of the 1840s, the American Catholic Church became substantially "Irishized."[48] The first tensions arose in the 1850s, when the Irish progressively forced out the French; then it was the turn of the Germans, who sent their allegations of discrimination to Rome; and finally that of the Italians, Poles, and Ruthenians. Rome thus decided to impose its authority, rejecting "the request to establish national blocs within the American hierarchy."[49] This forced reconciliation did not, however, succeed in preventing the persistence of tensions: some Polish, Lithuanian, and Ruthenian clergy separated from Rome and founded three minuscule national churches in 1897, 1914, and 1938 respectively.[50] The subsequent disagreements, especially between the Italian and Irish, ended up having major political repercussions, as we will see later.

Those disagreements, aggravated by bitter animosity within the episcopacy, were one of the main reasons for the controversy at the end of the century about so-called Americanism, that is, the trend toward an even greater assimilation of Catholics in American society. We will see how this controversy, resolved by Leo XIII's authority in 1899, acted as a screen for other hot issues concerning the European policy of the Holy See, the relationship between the Vatican and the American hierarchy, and, as I have already mentioned, internal rivalries within the local episcopacy.

World War I marked the final establishment of the United States as the first world power, not only from the point of view of industrial production but also in financial, political, and military terms. For many Americans of the time, however, it represented only a violent upheaval of the social order, one whose responsibility fell doubly on Europe: first, for having forced the United States to go there to reestablish order and, second, for having sent to the United States its "more sordid and hapless elements," as Woodrow Wilson said in 1902.[51] The results of this postwar resentment were partial closure of the border to immigrants, isolationism, and the birth (or rebirth, as in the case of the Ku Klux Klan) of virulently anti-Catholic movements.

The drastic slowdown of immigration was probably the factor that, more than any other, enabled the Church to consolidate its structures, those that in previous decades had been overstretched by the constant flow of Catholic immigrants. A permanent body of Episcopal consultation, the National Catholic Welfare Conference (NCWC) was created, not without difficulty; the existing structures were extended, especially in education (between 1921 and 1931, ninety-one parishes, eighty-nine schools, three high schools, fourteen colleges, a girls' school, and a seminary were inaugurated in Philadelphia alone); Catholic University was opened to laity; trade union activity was intensified to the point that "priests across the country [including the archbishop of Detroit, Edward Mooney] in the 1930s encouraged their parishioners to join unions," and some of them "served on regional labor boards and played key roles in workplace negotiations;"[52] and finally, a program was launched—the Catholic Conference on Industrial Problems—with the more or less open intention of making the United States a "laboratory" of the social doctrine of the Church (the experiment failed because of the withdrawal of business executives).

And, of course, there was greater involvement in the political life of the country. The theologian John Ryan, head of the NCWC Department of Social Action, wrote a booklet in 1924 entitled *A Question of Tactics for Catholic Citizens*, which demonstrated two fundamental shortcomings of Church action: the lack of Catholic political leadership and the lack of universities capable of teaching it. That same year, a Catholic, Governor Alfred Smith of New York, ran for the first time for the Democratic nomination. Beaten by John William Davis, Smith was able to impose himself as a candidate of the party in 1928. His defeat at the 1924 convention and especially his crushing defeat in the elections of 1928 by Herbert Hoover (58.2 percent to 40.8 percent, and winning only eight of forty-eight states) confirm that the leadership was not truly ripe.

To make Catholics a cornerstone of a government coalition, what was needed was an Episcopalian New Yorker, a Democrat in conflict with the Tammany Hall system: Franklin Delano Roosevelt. From Roosevelt on, Catholics were a constant component of American political life, and a Catholic political leadership gradually began to take shape, whose most symbolically significant moment was John F. Kennedy's victory in 1960. Finally, in the 1980s, the Reagan coalition sanctioned the Catholics' separation by mutual consent from the Democratic Party, a symbiosis that had already clearly been in crisis since the time of Richard Nixon.

The Church obviously contributed its support to Catholic integration into the nation. But the decisive factor was the quantitative and qualitative transformation of Catholics themselves between the end of World War II and the Reagan years.

In the early 1950s Catholics made up about 23 percent of the American population and, more important, their average social status was no longer that of the penniless immigrants of the past. "Younger Catholic families in places like Los Angeles," writes Morris, "were as likely to be headed by accountants or engineers as blue-collar workers."[53] Their social ascent, and their move to the suburbs, not only altered their relationship to parishes and religious practice, as well as their relationship to the faithful of other religions, but it also altered their relationship to society as a whole and therefore to politics. It was the beginning of the era of "the de-WASPing of America's power elite," as Robert C. Christopher called it;[54] other groups presented themselves as candidates for new elites.

Between 1950 and 1990 the gross national product in the United States grew by two and a half times, and per capita income grew 120 percent. And as the number of university students was rising in the same period from 2.4 to 13.7 million,[55] Catholic parents increasingly "did not scruple to choose a public school for their kids if it seemed educationally superior."[56]

Processes of this magnitude always produce more or less contradictory outcomes, sometimes seemingly mysterious ones. In this case it is perhaps even truer: the social ascent of the average Catholic American brought with it a crisis in the traditional role of the parish, the decrease of religious practices, but also, *and for the same reasons*, the birth of a true national Catholic leadership—that leadership whose absence was lamented by John Ryan—the same leadership that under the Obama presidency occupied a large number of positions at the highest level of responsibility in Washington, DC.

CHAPTER 2

The Catholic Church and the United States

The Discovery of America

WHEN SPEAKING OF THE CATHOLIC CHURCH in the singular, we generally imply an abstraction—just as in defining a law of physics, we ignore friction. In the case of the Church we ignore all the frictions that, at every level, go through the universal body: between the pope and the curia, within the curia, between Rome and local bishops, and, finally, between the different currents and sensitivities of the different local episcopates.

This is also, and perhaps especially, true for the relationship between the Catholic Church and the United States. This relationship involves a multiplicity of actors: on the American side the federal government, the states, and the widest array of instances of local authorities; on the Catholic side the pope, various Roman institutions, representatives of Rome in the United States (the Congregation de Propaganda Fide),[1] apostolic delegates, nuncios, and of course cardinals and local bishops. The latter also represent different perceptions (of the relationship with the society and politicians, for example), interests, tastes, and personalities but also, as we have seen, ethnic origins. What completes this picture is the Catholic laity, which is exceptionally varied as it has been nurtured simultaneously by the pluralistic tradition of the Church and that of the United States.

In other words, to quote Peter McDonough, " 'The church' is shorthand for a medley of beliefs, devotional practices, and ministries that coexist in doubtful syncopation. . . . The outward formalism of Catholicism both expresses and obscures a chambered complexity. The precise expressionism of Alfred Hitchcock, a student of the Jesuits, gets this right."[2]

So the Church is an abstraction but an abstraction that, like certain laws of physics, allows easier access to the understanding of reality; in fact, thanks to its centuries-old experience, the Catholic Church has had the opportunity to learn not only how to manage its internal contradictions but sometimes even to benefit from them. This prerogative, accumulated over time, gives it a definite advantage compared to all other institutions and human organizations.

This is what Carl Schmitt noticed in 1923, when he called the Church a *complexio oppositorum*: "There appears to be no antithesis it does not embrace," wrote the German thinker.[3] It is not surprising that Schmitt came to that conclusion in the wake of World War I, during which the Church had regained its prestige and credibility precisely by managing to be patriotic, warmongering with various national episcopacies, and at the same time presenting itself as a universal and pacifist Church of the Roman center.

Confronted with the unprecedented experience of World War I, the American Catholic Church developed the art of *complexio oppositorum* at the highest level and took full advantage of the "uncertain syncopation" of such a dialectic. Despite and by virtue of public opinion's protracted suspicion, despite and by virtue of an elusive and sometimes confrontational relationship with Rome, and despite and by virtue of its internal fault lines, it has gone from being a foreigner with respect to the rest of the body of society to a political actor of the first order: directly, with the proclamations of its episcopate on various topics, and indirectly, through a *Catholic political leadership*, by now massively present in all the nerve centers of the life of the country. And, more important, it has become the model according to which the universal Church has been eventually reshaped.

THE AMERICAN ENIGMA

Conventionally, the Treaty of Tordesillas of 1494 is considered the first formal act of division of the world into spheres of influence. Sanctioned by papal authority, that treaty was based on three postulates that history would be charged with proving wrong: that the only two powers authorized to carve up the world were Spain and Portugal, that the conquered territories were *terræ nullius*, and that one day the entire planet was destined to become Catholic.

The first postulate was contested by France, the Netherlands, and England, unwilling to see their access to new lands precluded by a pope's decree. Their insubordination seriously undermined Roman authority, especially since shortly thereafter, it was accompanied by the contesting of the second postulate: the territories conquered by England and the Netherlands would not become Catholic but Protestant.

Catholic missionaries followed (and sometimes preceded) Spanish, Portuguese, and French colonial expeditions. But soon the political authorities of those countries took things in hand, and missions became one of the instruments for controlling these new lands. The Church therefore had to compete on two fronts: on the one hand, against the Catholic powers in an attempt to preserve its autonomy; on the other, against the Protestant powers who denied access to Catholic missionaries, who were seen as agents of the enemy.

The colonial questions were evidently in the exclusive competence of the European chancelleries, and it was with them that the Church—a power among powers but with an additional claim to universality—had to negotiate its role. Starting at the beginning of the seventeenth century, Rome flanked the loyal Jesuits, already at the forefront of the movement,[4] with a specific army to be deployed directly in the new overseas territories: the Congregation de Propaganda Fide, created in 1622 to preside over the conversion activities of the natives in the colonies. The implicit goal was to create an on-site loyal army that would be able to influence the decisions of colonial administrations.

But the heart of the contest for the colonies was beating in the Old Continent: in the eyes of the Church the Seven Years' War (1756–63) was essentially a European war between Catholicism and Protestantism. And this attitude did not change during the American Revolutionary War, seen once again as a conflict between Catholic France and Spain on one side and Protestant England on the other. For Rome the colonists who settled in the British territories of America were, and would remain for a long time, little more than "exotic peoples to be converted," as Massimo Franco writes, halfway between proper Europeans and the local natives.[5] This view of them was ultimately not very different from the way the British of that time regarded the same people, with the political consequences that we know.

At the time of the founding of the United States, the patriot Charles Carroll's cousin, John Carroll, a Jesuit from Baltimore and a friend of Benjamin Franklin's, was at the origin of a "declaration of independence" of

American Catholics from the Apostolic Vicariate of the London District, under whose jurisdiction they had previously been placed. To avoid getting caught in the web of the Congregation of Propaganda Fide, which, as Franco writes, "was attempting to place land owned by the Church across the Atlantic under its protective umbrella,"[6] John Carroll asked that a local bishop be appointed, using a politically "strong" argument: "No authority derived from the Propaganda Will ever be admitted here. . . . The Catholick Clergy and Laity here know that the only connexion they ought to have with Rome is to acknowledge the Pop as Spirl. Head of the Church," he wrote in 1783.[7]

These words comport extraordinarily with the statement that John Adams had made to Congress a few years earlier, in August of 1779: the United States "will be too wise ever to admit to their territories . . . a Catholic legate or nuncio . . . or, in other words, an ecclesiastical tyrant."[8] Therefore, from the earliest years of the United States' existence, local clergy already counted on the *local* political authorities to guarantee to themselves ample space for maneuver with respect to Rome.

As Francis Rooney affirms, "Rome did not initially embrace the concept of a semi-autonomous American Church, much less grasp the concept of 'America.' "[9] It was not until 1789 that the pope approved John Carroll's appointment as the first bishop of the United States, after having entrusted the administration of US Catholics to the Archdiocese of Quebec for six years.[10] But the second part of Rooney's statement is even more interesting: not only did Rome not approve of the concept of autonomy, but it could hardly grasp "the concept of 'America.' "

There are two fundamental reasons for this. The first is that, beginning that same year, 1789, the Church in Europe found itself dragged into one of the most violent upheavals of its history. Fewer than ten years after Carroll's appointment, Pope Pius VI was deposed and arrested by the French; he died in captivity shortly after. His successor, Pius VII, was himself arrested by Napoleon in 1809 and remained a prisoner until 1814. One can imagine that, in similar circumstances, the problems connected with the United States' existence were overshadowed by "real" problems, that is, those that were upsetting the European chessboard. The second reason is the absence of precedents: never before had Rome dealt with a Catholic

Church in a non-Catholic country, one not under legal restrictions and not controlled by the state.

As early as 1790, John Carroll observed "the justice and political advantages of not only a free toleration, but of extending equal rights to the professors of all religions."[11] For Rome and the rest of the Catholic world of the time, those words sounded quite alien and clearly smelled of sulfur. Nevertheless, Carroll was not condemned, partly because Americans continued to be seen as "exotic peoples" with eccentric customs and traditions to whom concessions had to be made to avoid repeating the fatal mistake made a century earlier of condemning the "Chinese rites"[12] and partly because, beginning exactly in 1790—the year the Civil Constitution of the Clergy was ratified in France[13]—the Church could no longer afford unilateral breaks with anyone.

In 1797 President Adams—who eighteen years before had said that the United States "will probably never send a minister to his Holiness"— appointed a consul in Rome. The US commercial fleet had become one of the collateral victims of the new round of European wars in the late eighteenth century: between July 1796 and June 1797, writes Robert Moskin, the French seized 316 US merchant ships, and the British, besides seizing vessels, "were stopping American merchantmen on the high seas and kidnapping seamen for their navies."[14] In this context the State Department gave birth to a large consular network, especially in European port cities; and the two main ports of the Papal States, Civitavecchia and Ancona, allowed double access, Tyrrhenian and Adriatic, to the peninsula. Moreover, adds Moskin, Americans considered Rome a useful "listening post," in this or any future situation of international turmoil.

The Papal States, restored by the Congress of Vienna, only sent its first consular representative to the United States thirty years later, in 1826. This decision met resistance not so much from the political class or from Protestant public opinion as from the same American Catholic hierarchy, jealous of its own autonomy. This reaction was not specific to America; in general, the stronger and more nationally legitimate an episcopate feels, the less it is inclined to accept a papal envoy on a permanent basis. It was no coincidence that it was the Polish and the Irish bishops who most vehemently opposed the opening of diplomatic relations between their countries and the Holy See.[15] In the United States (but also in Canada), whenever a rapprochement between Washington and Rome came into view, the bishops manifested their opposition. Gerald P. Fogarty relates that in 1891, in an attempt to break that resistance, Leo XIII went so far as to propose to the archbishop of Boston, Denis O'Connell, the possibility of a nunciature in Washington to combat Propaganda Fide's interference in the affairs of the American Church: in short, a Roman institution (the nunciature) would guarantee the autonomy of the US episcopate against another Roman institution (Propaganda Fide).[16] Conversely, for the archbishop of Baltimore, James Gibbons, the most likely risk was that Rome would use its possible contacts in the federal government to interfere with the affairs of the American Church.

If we consider that the American bishops themselves were divided on this, and many other issues (the archbishop of New York, Michael Corrigan, in favor of a closer relationship with Rome, was allied with German bishops to slow down assimilationist tendencies), then we have all the pieces of the puzzle before us: Romans against Romans, Americans against Americans, Romans allied with Americans against other Romans or against other Americans, and so forth—not to mention that even the US federal and local governments often had an interest in interfering with the complex web of relationships and rivalries. As one can see, the "pluralism" with which American Catholicism is imbued was nurtured by many sources.

Actually, it was often the US government that took the initiative. It did so, as we have seen, in 1797; it did so again in 1848, when the Senate voted to install an American *chargé d'affaires* in Rome. In 1831, after yet another political blaze in Europe,[17] the American consul to the pope, Felix Cicognani, highlighted the need to strengthen this valuable listening post; but the Papal States, one of the most backward and obscurantist states in Europe, did not arouse any sympathy in the United States. It did not help that the newly elected Pope Gregory XVI publicly defined liberty of conscience as "insanity" and freedom of press as "harmful and never sufficiently denounced," also condemning the separation of state and church (encyclical *Mirari vos*, 1832).[18] Completing the outline of positions antithetical to the American spirit, Gregory XVI wrote in his apostolic letter *In supremo apostolatus* (1839) "that the slave trade should at least cease amongst Christians."[19]

Pius IX, elected in 1846, inaugurated his pontificate by liberating political prisoners and promoting a series of economic reforms. In 1847, on the wave of his extraordinary popularity, he proposed a step forward in diplomatic relations with the United States. The US Senate discussed his request a year later, in the wake of the February revolution in France, and at the height of the insurrections in Milan, Vienna, and Budapest; the question of the listening post was decisive in the debate: for Senator Edward Hannegan, Rome was "the emporium of the intelligence in Europe," and an aspiring great power could not fail to have a presence there.[20]

The motivations of the United States were clear and indicated a precise and insurmountable limit: "to carefully avoid even the appearance of interfering in ecclesiastical questions," as Secretary of State James Buchanan instructed;[21] that is, never give the impression that the country had established a relationship with the head of a religion rather than a head of state.

The Church's motivations were expressed by Pius IX to the new American *chargé d'affaires* Jacob Martin when the pope congratulated himself on firming up relations with "so great a nation, especially with one in which the Catholic Church has nothing to fear from the Government nor the Government from the Church."[22] The possibility of expanding the outreach of Catholicism in the United States without having anything to fear from the government was a pleasing novelty that, by now, had breached even the Vatican walls.

Whether or not the US government had anything to fear from the Catholic Church had yet to be proven. Throughout the nineteenth century the Church of Rome always sided against the United States on major issues of foreign and domestic policy; the most sensational case was the Civil War, at the end of which Washington decided to suspend diplomatic relations with the Holy See. Those relations would be reestablished only 117 years later, in 1984.

A CENTURY OF DIVERGENCES

Rome was surprised and upset by the withdrawal of the American delegation in 1867, a reaction that says a lot about the difficulty Rome had, at the time, in grasping the real balance of power in the international arena. One could not expect much more from Pope Pius IX, who was persuaded that "what they call modern civilization" was "a system manufactured on purpose to weaken and perhaps even to destroy the Church of Christ" (Encyclical *Iamdudum cernimus*, 1861).[23] But looking at the relationship with Washington more generally, the fact that before, during, and after the Civil War, and until World War I, Rome had never sided with the United States in anything of crucial importance to its political circumstances, one is pressed to consider those few years of halting diplomatic relations between the two countries a miraculous exception rather than a desirable norm.

There are apparently no stances adopted by the Vatican on the War of 1812, but at that time Rome was part of the French Empire, the pope was a prisoner, and the universal Catholic Church functioned, so to speak, on autopilot. From Timothy Byrnes we know that John Carroll "deprecated some of the policies that led to the War of 1812"; but once hostilities broke out, "he was unswerving in his defense of the American cause," aware that American Catholics were forced to counterbalance the hostility and distrust to which they were subjected with a surplus of patriotic fervor.[24]

Although the War of 1812 was a conflict between two Protestant countries, Carroll's deprecation is understandable, and it is easy to guess for which side the heart of universal Catholicism was beating: it suffices to take into consideration that, for Americans, the conquest of Canada (only "a matter of marching," according to Jefferson) was supposed to be the cornerstone of the military operations to follow. The idea that Quebecois Catholics, protected by the 1774 law, could end up under the rule of the United States, so hostile to popery, must certainly have pleased neither the imprisoned pope nor Carroll and even less so the Canadian clergy. It is also important to keep in mind that, at the time, Great Britain was the main enemy of the Church's main enemy: Napoleonic France.

During the Mexican-American War the American clergy remained remarkably discreet. The Sixth Council of bishops, under way during the first days of the conflict, discussed three issues: the choice of the Virgin Mary as the patroness of the United States, the duties of missionary priests toward their ordinaries, and the observation of the banns of matrimony. There was no mention of the war. Blanche Marie McEniry, author of a 1937 study of the issue, called the lack of editorials on this subject in Catholic newspapers "astounding."[25]

On the contrary, this silence speaks volumes. In contrast to what happened in 1812 and 1898 the members of the American Catholic hierarchy *did not* support their country, but they had no reason to support Mexico either. There were several reasons for this. First of all, they did not want to appear as a Mexican fifth column, which would have fueled the ongoing Nativist campaign; second, President James K. Polk had made some decisions favorable to American Catholics, in order to prevent the conflict from turning into a religious war;[26] and ultimately, the Mexican Republic, especially during the previous decade, had begun to "strip the Church of its wealth and its privileges, and loosen its ties with Rome."[27] Some Protestant Americans expressed fear that the conquest of Mexican lands could even strengthen the Catholics, and it cannot be ruled out that some of the bishops thought the same way, obviously with opposing feelings.

Nevertheless, a few hundred Irish soldiers deserted and went over to the Mexican side, giving birth to the famous and brave *Batallón de San Patricio*. Within a year their ranks were swelled by other Catholic deserters—German, Canadian, French, Italian, Polish, Scottish, Spanish, and Swiss—and, according to James Callaghan, by some runaway slaves from the United States. For American Protestants it was the confirmation of Catholics' natural propensity for betrayal.[28] This propensity would seem to be widely confirmed by the attitude adopted during the Civil War, which we will revisit in more detail.

As soon as the war against the Confederates had been victoriously concluded, the focus shifted back to Mexico, where Napoleon III, taking advantage of the American Civil War, had established in 1862 a puppet empire, supported by the local clergy. As Giacomo Martina writes, when the United States intervened to restore the liberal government of Benito Juárez in 1867, Pius IX did not abandon the "wait-and-see" position adopted throughout the period of the French occupation.[29] Less cautious were the pope's condemnation of the reforms adopted by Juárez in 1854 (allocution *Numquam fore*, 1856) and of "the most unjust laws against the power of the Catholic Church" (Secret Consistory of September 30, 1861), namely, the Constitution of 1857.[30] The difference from the "wait-and-see" attitude toward the imperial government was likely due to the fear that a failure of the Mexican adventure could weaken, at home and abroad, its instigator, Napoleon III, who had been the last bastion of temporal power.[31] Considering that those were the years in which Pius IX was sending messages of comfort to Jefferson Davis and Washington was closing its offices in Rome, it is not hard to guess the pope's real feelings about US intervention in Mexico in favor of Juárez and against his French protector.

The Vatican was yet again obliged to assume a position of cautious neutrality in 1898, at the time of the Spanish-American War, but only after having played all its cards in an attempt to avoid it. Everything leads me to believe that no one in Rome had read the works of Alfred Mahan, the American rear admiral who, since 1890, had hypothesized the war, or rather, its geopolitical inevitability. The Church most likely would not have been able to act otherwise in any case: it would not have been able to refuse its support to Spain, one of the few European countries remaining (circumspectly) close to the papacy once it lost its temporal power. But in politics a stance dictated by awareness, even in the case of failure, almost always manages to achieve a few results, if only with regard to the future. In this case, however, Rome managed to lose on all fronts: in Washington, where it confirmed the image of an inherently hostile papacy; in Madrid, where its authority and credibility emerged severely weakened; and even in Paris, where Leo XIII's *Ralliement* policy—which we will examine further on—suffered a dizzying loss of support.

Once again, the Holy See reacted with irritation to defeat. Castagna reports that in 1901, "mindful of the intransigence demonstrated by [the US president William] McKinley in 1898, the Vatican Secretary of State Rampolla prohibited the Apostolic Delegate and other members of the Episcopate to attend the funeral of the assassinated president and any other commemoration ceremony."[32]

All through the twentieth century and in the early twenty-first, as we will see, the divergences between the Holy See and the United States would continue to be numerous and even particularly acute at times. But these divergences would take on a very different character from those of the previous century, because they were, quite often, the result of a gradual realization by the highest Catholic authorities that international relations had finally and irrevocably changed since the days when the Church permeated all of society and was an undisputed authority among all Christian princes, since the days when the Church had at its disposal a state with all its inherent prerogatives. That awareness, though painful, would enable the Church to deal with the issue of *Catholic interest* in a much more profitable way.[33]

But before it was to reach that stage of awareness, the Church had lost almost all its battles on the international stage. The major ones had been lost in Europe, but the one lost in the United States between 1861 and 1865 would leave deep and lasting wounds in the relationship between Rome and Washington.

THE CIVIL WAR

The Civil War merits a separate discussion, not only because of its importance in the history of the United States but also because it represents one of the rare times when the feelings of the majority of American Catholics, the majority of its bishops, and even the pope coincided. And those were feelings of hostility toward the war against the South and, more important, to freeing the slaves.

A renowned New England intellectual who converted to Catholicism, Orestes Brownson wrote in 1863 that "no religious body in the country stands so generally committed to slavery and the Rebellion, or as a body have shown so little sympathy with the effort of the Government to save the unity and life of the nation as the Catholic."[34] According to Albon P. Man, the only ecclesiastical dignitary openly opposed to slavery was the archbishop of Cincinnati, John B. Purcell;[35] Charles Morris adds that "the Church followed the normal practice of segregating its institutions" and that "several bishops owned slaves."[36] Furthermore, in his textbook *Theologia moralis*, published in 1841, the future bishop Francis Kenrick explained that "in accord with Catholic teaching, slavery is not opposed to natural law," provided that the owners treat their slaves with humanity."[37] At the same time, the bishop of Charleston, John England, explained to President Martin Van Buren's secretary of state that in the letter *In supremo apostolatus*, "Pope Gregory XVI had condemned the trade in slaves, but that no pope had ever condemned domestic slavery as it had existed in the United States."[38]

Between 1861 and 1862 John Hughes, archbishop of New York, once again confronted the matter from the doctrinal point of view. It is true, he affirmed, that the Church is opposed to slavery "but only in the sense that she is opposed to the calamities of human life, which she has no power to reverse." It is certainly sad that the state of slavery is hereditary, the prelate continued, but that is part of the human condition in general: "Original sin has entailed upon the human race its consequences for time and eternity. And yet the men who are living now had no part in the commission of original sin."[39]

Of the twelve avowedly Catholic newspapers, writes Man, only two supported the war unconditionally. The March 28, 1863, *Metropolitan Record*— which, for the *New York Tribune* was the "Official Organ of the Most Rev. Archbishop of New York"—defined the emancipation of the slaves as a decision "vile and infamous," adding, "Never was a blacker crime sought to be committed against nature, against humanity, against the holy precepts of Christianity." The other New York Catholic newspaper, the *Freeman's Journal*, challenged its readers to find "one precept of Pope, of Council, or of Catholic Doctor, who exhorted masters to manumit their slaves" (April 4, 1863). James A. McMaster, editor of the *Freeman's Journal*, supposedly said, according to Man, that "Negroes . . . that migrated to New York from the South were to be driven away, imprisoned, or exterminated."

This last recommendation was taken literally by the rioters who, as we have seen, devastated New York and massacred dozens of blacks between July 11 and 16, 1863. Man writes that "the Catholic clergy's power over the rioters was shown by the success of priests in dispersing them"; but the archbishop's invitation to "the men of New York, who are now called in many of the papers, rioters," did not arrive until July 17. "Hughes urged that the disturbances be stopped, for the sake of religion and the honor of Ireland. And they did stop," concludes Man, "though perhaps more from the fact that their fury had already been spent."

Hughes's position on the war was very different. Up until the Emancipation Proclamation, the archbishop of New York was on the same wavelength as Abraham Lincoln: the nation's unity had to be maintained at all costs. But that was supposed to be the only purpose of the war: "We Catholics, and a vast majority of our brave troops in the field, have not the slightest idea of carrying on a war that costs so much blood and treasure just to gratify a clique of Abolitionists in the North."[40] In the autumn of 1861 the president had therefore sent Hughes to Rome to gain the pope's support of the cause of the Union, a move made even more urgent by the fact that Jefferson Davis had already sent there the bishop of Charleston, Patrick Lynch, with the same mission for the Confederacy.

But it seems that Rome had already made its choice. Pius IX had replied to a letter from Davis calling him "the Honorable President of the Confederate States of America" and attaching his autographed photograph. For General Robert E. Lee, as well as for many of the Union's policy makers, that letter and picture were as good as official recognition (which in reality never was granted). Historians are also inclined to believe that the pope somehow was in sympathy with the Confederacy. Giacomo Martina writes that the papers that were considered the unofficial voice of the pope, such as the *Osservatore romano* and the Jesuit *Civiltà cattolica*, "manifested in numerous articles their benevolence and support of the cause of the South." Beginning on October 9, 1863, the *Osservatore* published a series of articles by the bishop of Louisville, Martin J. Spalding, in which he stated that "the war could only end with the recognition, by the northern states, of the Confederacy of the southern states as a separate, fully independent state." The dream of a great State of North America, Spalding wrote, would prove illusory, just as had happened in South America.[41]

Besides, the position of Pius IX on slavery was the same as that of Kenrick and of England, as he demonstrated by countersigning the instruction of the Holy Office of June 20, 1866, which stated that "slavery itself, considered as such in its essential nature, is not at all contrary to the natural and divine law."[42]

Pius IX's sympathy toward the South did not end with the end of the conflict. In his letters from prison Jefferson Davis recalls that "a voice came from afar to cheer and console me in my solitary captivity. The Holy Father sent me his likeness, and beneath it was written, by his own hand, the comforting invitation our Lord gives to all who are oppressed."[43] In contrast, the pope did not comfort Archbishop Hughes, guilty of having supported Lincoln, and actually "punished" him by denying him the cardinal's hat (which he granted instead to his successor, John McCloskey in 1875). In short, writes Martina, "Pius IX sided with history's losers, not its winners."[44]

Complicating the relationship between Washington and Rome was the discovery that one of those suspected of Abraham Lincoln's assassination, a Catholic, just like the murderer John Wilkes Booth, had managed to evade justice owing to the protection of the prelates and religious institutions in Canada and in England, and he managed to get as far as Rome, enlisting as a Papal Zouave in 1866.

The final blow to the American legation to the pope was the news—false—that the (private) religious ceremonies for the Protestant personnel posted to Rome had been forbidden. But that was only a pretext. By then, few in the United States saw any reason for maintaining a diplomatic relationship with the Holy See. The attitude of American Catholics and of the Church during the Civil War (and after) was certainly decisive. Yet it was not the only cause: when Congress withdrew funding for the legation in January 1867, the Papal States had already lost nearly three-quarters of its territory, which was annexed to Italy, and Rome resisted only because it was protected by the French army. Its precariousness reduced its value as a *listening post.*

Moreover, three years earlier, Pius IX had published the *Syllabus of Errors*, a summary of propositions that amounted to an absolute denial of American values: after ruling out Protestantism as a Christian religion and condemning freedom of speech, the press, and religion as well as the separation of church and state, the document concluded with the commitment to never accept or "come to terms with progress, liberalism and modern civilization." What a delight for all those who, in the United States, had always stressed the absolute incompatibility between Catholicism and the American way of life! "Pope Pius is about to go out of business," wrote the *New York Tribune* in the days when Congress was cutting funding to the Roman legation. "All the better for him, and the world."[45]

THE DISCOVERY OF AMERICA

John Pollard writes that "if Christopher Columbus discovered America in 1492, then it could be argued that the Holy See only 'truly' discovered

American Catholicism four hundred years later,"[46] that is to say, during Leo XIII's pontificate.

Pius IX's attitude before, during, and after the Civil War would seem to indicate that for him and his staff the United States continued to be a strange and mysterious thing and not very relevant from the point of view of Vatican geopolitics. The Church's accumulated experience, as we have seen, is its most remarkable asset, but, at times, relying on experience can prove to be the most remarkable obstacle to the perception of novelty. Pope Pius IX proves this in a most masterly manner.

In the late nineteenth-century Church's view the world was divided into pagan (or non-Christian) countries, which were to be evangelized; non-Catholic Christian countries, where evangelization was forbidden; and Catholic countries, where secularization was reducing its possibilities for action. For a long time the United States had been considered as belonging to the first category—like the rest of the American continent since 1492—rather than the second. A Protestant country "in which the Catholic Church has nothing to fear from the Government" was a source of bewilderment and, essentially, of incomprehension.

The other obstacle, perhaps more important, was Eurocentrism. The only path to converting the entire world to Catholicism was the path the Church had always taken: whether it was Godfrey of Bouillon, John of Montecorvino, Hernán Cortés, or Matteo Ricci, the radiating center of Catholicism had always been Europe; it could not be imagined otherwise. In the previous centuries, however, half of Europe had become Protestant; the Church's attention was therefore focused on the other half that remained nominally Catholic and where an attempt to stop the gradual marginalization of its authority was of the essence. Finally, under Pius IX Italy became a nearly exclusive obsession; its process of unification would bring an end to the Papal States and the abolition of their temporal power. For several decades relations with other states were calculated only on the basis of whether they were in a position to support the cause of the pope against Italy.

It is noteworthy that David Kertzer, in his detailed study of the diplomatic initiatives of the Vatican before and after the Italian conquest of Rome, did not once mention the United States.[47] It is equally significant that Luca Castagna, referring to a period fifty years later, under the pontificates of Benedict XV and Pius XI, notes that most of the attempts at diplomatic contact between the Holy See and Washington revolved around the "Roman Question."[48] In between, there was the "discovery of America," as Pollard calls it, but the status of the Holy See remained the Vatican's fixation.

The Vatican's "American policies," Morris writes, "were mostly the thoughtless backwash of European power-jockeying and were rarely pursued with force or conviction."[49] It can be asserted that the first of the two main reasons (we will deal with the second one before long) for Leo XIII's "discovery of America" was his desire to make it one of the instruments of his "French policy," a keystone of the Church's anti-Italian geopolitics in the last years of the nineteenth century.

In 1870 the old world noisily collapsed. Rome was conquered by the Italians, and the pope's temporal power was wiped out, along with the Vatican's best European ally, the France of Napoleon III. The center of the Continental political stage was now occupied by a new creation: the German Empire; and its "Iron Chancellor," Otto von Bismarck, had launched a campaign of cultural homogenization—the *Kulturkampf*—designed to eliminate the influence of the Church and make the peripheral Catholic regions (Bavaria, Baden-Württemberg, the Rhineland, Alsace, Lorraine, and Silesia), of dubious loyalty, toe the line. The alliance of 1882 between the anti-Catholic Germany of Bismarck and anticlerical Italy pushed the Church, after several years of hesitation, to bet on Germany's traditional European rival: France.

The trouble was that in republican France, born after the disaster of 1870, Catholics were fierce monarchists. To facilitate an agreement with Paris, it was thus essential to calm the French faithful by forcing them to suspend hostilities against the country's institutions. This was the reason for the development of the early 1890s *Ralliement* policy, which was Leo XIII's invitation, issued in a May 3, 1892, letter to the French bishops, to accept, respect, and submit to the republic "as if it represented the power derived from God."

The American example was instrumental to this new pro-French policy. It was used to show the reluctant French faithful that accepting republican rules could even be advantageous for the development of Catholicism and to show the authorities of Paris that the Church and republican institutions could coexist peacefully and maybe even support each other.

That policy failed on all three fronts: in France it divided the faithful without obtaining any tangible results and finally came crashing down as a result of the "awkward behavior of Catholics in the Dreyfus affair";[50] in Germany it displeased everyone—bishops, faithful, and government; in the United States it exacerbated the divisions within the episcopate and ended, paradoxically, with Leo XIII's condemnation of Americanism, the current of thought most favorable to peaceful coexistence with the republic.

That sentence, pronounced in 1899, concluded a phase in which the same Leo, writes Aubert, had urged "Catholics to use with opportunism constitutional freedoms in the service of their cause."[51] And it opened another phase, based on the Vatican's attempt to repair the relations with the Germanic world, an attempt for which the American example was no longer of any use.

The dispute around Americanism is usually presented as a harsh confrontation within the American Catholic hierarchy between "conservatives" contrary to assimilationism and therefore, in theory, closer to Rome, and "liberals" willing to shape the Church in the United States around American values and therefore, in theory, more reluctant to accept papal interference. The matter is actually much more complex and cannot be understood without considering at least three other factors: the instrumental use of the issue for a French context, which I talked about above; the severe personality clash among some US bishops; and the unquenched desire of Rome to place the American Church under its direct control. This wish was supported by the fact that each side (complete with nuances) hoped to play the Roman card against the other.

Paradoxically, it was the archbishop of Saint Paul, Minnesota, John Ireland, considered the leader of the "liberals," who brought the first apostolic delegate, Francesco Satolli, to the United States, thus provoking the wrath of the rival party gathered around the archbishop of New York, Michael Corrigan: "We, school-children of the hierarchy, will again receive a lesson in our Catechism from another Italian sent to enlighten us," wrote the bishop of Rochester, Corrigan's supporter.[52]

After sending Ireland to Paris to hold conferences on the virtues of the republic, and after delegating to him the mediation between Washington and Madrid at the time of the Spanish-American War of 1898, Leo XIII did not hesitate to dump him when the geopolitical priority of the Vatican was no longer Paris but Berlin. In 1899 he wrote the encyclical *Testem benevolentiae nostræ* condemning "those views which, in their collective sense, are called by some Americanism,"[53] a tendency, writes John T. Ellis, that seemed to be "an American version of Gallicanism."[54] As we can see, France continued to be the standard of measurement.

Corrigan then went back to being pro-Roman and "publicly thanked Leo XIII for saving the Church from heresy,"[55] whereas Ireland was accused by French Catholics of causing the break with the state and by German and Spanish Catholics of failing to prevent the war of 1898. The purge of "Americanists" resumed in 1907, when Pius X condemned modernism, a phenomenon considered, once again, a "French disease."[56] The *New York Review*, "the most intellectual magazine of the American Church," was suppressed, and priests suspected of having "an inclination for culture"[57] were relieved of their responsibilities.

Only three years after the encyclical against Americanism, however, Leo XIII addressed another letter to the US bishops—*In amplissimo*—with no trace of censorship. On the contrary, the pope wrote, "While the changes and tendencies of nearly all the nations which were Catholic for many centuries give cause for sorrow, the state of your churches, in their flourishing youthfulness, cheers Our heart and fills it with delight." The encyclical illustrated in detail all the reasons for his delight, concluding with what was likely the most important one: "the liberality with which your people are endeavoring to contribute by their offerings to relieve the penury of the Holy See."[58] And it is in that liberality, in all probability, that we need to look for the second most important cause of Leo XIII's "discovery of America."

Pollard writes that "after 1870, America made an increasingly large contribution to Peter's Pence."[59] Count Edward Soderini, who had the pope's ear, recalls that during the pontificate of Leo XIII, "there was a considerable increase in the St. Peter's Pence by the Catholics of the United States," which was supposed to compensate for the decline of offerings from the "nations which were Catholic for many centuries."[60] Besides, the growing role of the American contributions induced Rome to look with much more indulgence on the rivalries within the American Episcopate; in fact, Morris writes, "since a good Peter's Pence performance translated directly into influence at Rome, bishops in the larger dioceses competed hard to head the league tables and pushed their flocks correspondingly hard."[61]

In 1917, in the words of Benedict XV himself, "the bulk of the offerings [Peter's Pence] come from the United States,"[62] a dominance that would be consolidated at the end of the war. A few years later, Odo Russell, British ambassador to the Holy See, reported the rumors that "American gold had something to do with the promotion of the two archbishops," that is, with the simultaneous appointment to the cardinalate of George Mundelein and Patrick Hayes in March 1924. Actually, Russell went on, the Catholics in Chicago and New York, cities where the two new cardinals were archbishops, "are by far the largest contributors to Vatican funds."[63]

The argument that the political axis of the Church had shifted in response to the growing weight of American financing was later revived several times: for example, by Germany during the Second World War and then again by Britain and the Soviet Union in the postwar period. It would be inaccurate to say that this shift of the financial axis did not cause any change in the internal balance of the Vatican. But we will see that this influence did not actually affect the independence of judgment or the behavior of the Church.

On the contrary, for a long time those substantial cash flows failed even to dispel the sense of haughty superiority that Romans had toward Americans: in an institution that for centuries had considered *pecunia stercus diaboli*, this feeling was reinforced by the ease with which American bishops handled and distributed money (according to Morris, the archbishop of Philadelphia, Dennis Dougherty, had brought to Rome $1 million on the occasion of his appointment to the cardinalate in 1921). With regard to that time Pollard recalls the dominant feeling of "disdain and dislike of Americans in Roman ecclesiastical circles," relieved, however, by a disenchanted awareness that "US Catholics were paying a lot of the Vatican's bills."[64]

That ability to pay "a lot of the Vatican's bills" finally made of the United States something still a bit exotic yet concrete and indispensable. The "discovery of America" was completed just as the United States asserted itself as the first global power on all fronts. From that time on, it became, in the eyes of the Church, a parallel and competing empire.

CHAPTER 3

The Catholic Church and the United States

Parallel Empires

THE EXACT DATE of the rupture between the Church and France can arguably be fixed at August 26, 1789. On that day the Constituent Assembly ratified the Declaration of the Rights of Man and of the Citizen, a text establishing principles valid not only for France but for the entire world. From that moment on, revolutionary France set out on a path that was parallel to that of the Church; and, like all parallels, the two paths were bound to meet only at infinity.

UNIVERSAL VALUES AND PRAGMATISM:
WORLD WAR I

The Church considered—and still considers—itself to be "the sole holder of laws inscribed by God into nature"[1] (Daniele Menozzi); therefore, its monopoly of "universal values" did not allow for competitors. Pius VI characterized very early (1790) the rights included in the text voted on in France as "monstrous rights," and he condemned them again in *Quod aliquantum* (1791) as contrary "to the right of the Creator," and once again in *Adeo nota* (1792) as "contrary to religion and to society."

Nevertheless, as Menozzi conveniently recalls, Pius VI had not condemned the contemporaneous explicit references to the *natural* rights of man, present in the American Declaration of Independence, nor the statements of 1790 by the bishop of Baltimore John Carroll in favor of the institutions of his country and even of freedom of worship. The fact that France was putting itself in competition with the Church from the same Christian "heartland" can explain this double standard. What was worse was that it seemed well able to impose itself in the wake of revolutionary enthusiasm. The United States of Carroll's time, on the contrary, was still a mysterious object of little importance; moreover, it was dominated by Protestants. Even the idea of Manifest Destiny, which was developed later, did not provoke any reaction from Rome, despite its messianic inspiration, and in all probability, at the time of its formulation (the mid-nineteenth century), even passed unnoticed.

Only in the aftermath of World War I did the Church realize that the United States, too, claimed its own universalist vocation, more precisely, when Woodrow Wilson's Fourteen Points were incorporated into peace treaties. If, in Europe, human rights on the French model had severed "the link between political affiliation and religious affiliation,"[2] the League of Nations risked burying the traditional ambition of the Church: that of representing "the highest moral authority in the world" (as the Vatican Secretary of State Pietro Gasparri wrote to the apostolic delegate in Washington in January of 1916).[3] What made the threat even more insidious was the overwhelming force with which the United States had imposed itself on the world: before the war in economic terms, during the war in military terms, after the war in financial and—as demonstrated by the Treaty of Versailles—in political terms. This was nothing like the vain French ambitions of 130 years earlier.

In other words the United States and the Catholic Church became, writes Massimo Franco, "the only two Western realities capable of geopolitical projection on a world scale,"[4] although with obviously different and often incompatible approaches, means, and purposes: "parallel empires," according to Franco's own apt phrase. And for this reason they were bound, let me repeat myself here, to meet only at infinity.

Between 1914 and 1915 three more serious reasons for friction between Rome and Washington accumulated, aggravated by President Wilson's blatant intolerance of Catholics: the increasingly manifest inclination of Wilson to go to the rescue of the Allies, the Vatican's attempt to drag the United States into the settlement of the Roman question, and Washington's recognition of the Mexican government of Venustiano Carranza, who continued his country's long-standing policy of secularization. The last issue inevitably ended up subordinate to the other two, and both the Vatican and the United States used it as a pawn to play on the chessboard that was by far the most important: the world war. On that front, writes Castagna, "the clash between Benedict XV and Wilson became more or less total, since the latter considered pontifical diplomacy inappropriate interference by a spiritual leader" in international affairs.[5]

It should be added that the pope, in turn, judged the diplomacy of states as inappropriate interference in a field—that of international relations—to which only the moral authority of the Church could bring order and peace. In his first encyclical, *Ad beatissimi apostolorum principis*, published in November 1914, three months after the outbreak of the war and two months after his election, Benedict XV was explicit: "For ever since the precepts and practices of Christian wisdom ceased to be observed in the ruling of states, it followed that, as they contained the peace and stability of institutions, the very foundations of states necessarily began to be shaken." The only way "to get rid of . . . the causes of serious unrest pervading the whole of human society," he continued, was "by again bringing Christian principles into honour."[6]

At that time the relationship between the two "parallel empires" was particularly unbalanced: the United States was an emerging power with unstoppable dynamism, while, according to Stewart Stehlin, "By the first decades of the twentieth century, it appeared as if the Vatican might become a *quantité négligeable* in world affairs." Subsequently, Stehlin continues, "by the First World War, it appeared to many observers as if the Papacy for the Christian world, like the Caliphate for the Moslem world, was on the way out."[7] It is thus understandable why the American Catholic hierarchy did not hesitate to embrace the national cause as soon as the United States declared war on Germany in April 1917. Benedict XV had in some way "authorized" national bishops to support the war effort of their respective countries in order to avoid the risk of schisms and the birth of patriotic Catholic Churches;[8] but the American decision of April 1917 was seen as an unjustified defection from the front of the neutral countries, and the rapid conversion of the local clergy to warmongering was received in Rome with an icy silence, as demonstrated by "the almost total absence of communication, from March to July 1917, between the Secretary of State, the Apostolic Delegation, and Cardinal Gibbons."[9]

After the war the frustration of the Church caused by American competition on the terrain of moral authority (and, above all, by its political implementation) reached its climax. In an encyclical of 1920, *Pacem, Dei munus pulcherrimum*, Benedict XV alluded to the League of Nations, founded five months earlier, although he mentioned it only as a desirable eventuality: "It is much to be desired . . . that all States, putting aside mutual suspicion, should unite in one league, or rather a sort of family of peoples."[10] The pope was actually convinced that it was "necessary that Jesus . . . should lay His hands upon the wounds of society . . . this work, *this duty the Church claims as her own* as heir and guardian of the spirit of Jesus Christ" (sec. 12). Then, supposing that others could take the initiative, the pope set out his condition: "The Church will certainly not refuse her zealous aid to States united under the Christian law in any of their undertakings inspired by justice and charity, inasmuch as *she is herself the most perfect type of universal society*" (sec. 18, my emphasis).

The League of Nations was obviously not founded "under the Christian law," and Benedict's successor marked its distance from it even more clearly: "No merely human institution of today," wrote Pius XI in an encyclical in 1922, "can be as successful in devising a set of international laws which will be in harmony with world conditions as the Middle Ages were in the possession of that true League of Nations, Christianity."[11]

Between the two wars the Church was almost completely preoccupied with bringing together all European countries, to prevent the risk, expressed by the Catholic thinker Richard Coudenhove-Kalergi, that the Old Continent might end up divided into two spheres of interest, one Anglo-American and the other Russian, with the Rhine as the border.[12] When speaking of European unification, we must always bear two things in mind: (1) that at the origin of that plan there was a will—explicit or implicit—to restrain, counteract, or even fight American supremacy and (2) that at the origin of that plan there was, above all, the Catholic Church. In other words European unification was probably one of the most important issues for which the Church and United States had competing, if not divergent, geopolitical objectives.[13]

Yet this very competition over Europe offered the Church the chance to put its rediscovered pragmatism to the test. In fact, after a failed attempt to obtain a peace settlement that would be less burdensome for Berlin, the Vatican took advantage of Washington's shared interest in redressing the balance of power in Europe to make an intervention that was likely to revive the German economy. After two summit meetings (1921 and 1922), Vatican Secretary of State Pietro Gasparri, together with Jack P.

Morgan, laid the foundations of what, according to Stehlin, would become the Dawes Plan of 1924.[14] Although the strategic aims were opposed, the Holy See took advantage of this first window of opportunity for its tactics to converge with those of Washington. And it did so without remaining inflexible on matters of principle—as had been the case with the League of Nations—which was inevitably going to be frustrated by an unfavorable balance of power.

PRAGMATISM AND UNIVERSAL VALUES: WORLD WAR II AND THEREABOUTS

A lot has been written on the attitude of the Church toward the coalitions formed on the eve of and during World War II, and in some cases opinions vary considerably. It is possible, however, to affirm that, despite a number of compromises and distressing silences, the Vatican managed to preserve its autonomy and to pursue its goals, even when they differed from those of the United States.

The first example concerns hostility toward Soviet Russia.[15] "In the 1930s and in the 1940s," writes Morris, "the Vatican's foreign policy and the Church's obsessive anticommunism led to continuing friction with the Roosevelt administration."[16] Even before the newly elected president assumed his office in January of 1933, Vatican Secretary of State Eugenio Pacelli (the future Pope Pius XII) condemned the president's decision to establish diplomatic relations with the USSR as seriously damaging "the cause of civilization [and] the social and political cohesion of this republic [the United States]."[17] And on December 16, when the agreement was reached, he sent a harsh note of disapproval, which sounded like a disavowal of the albeit timid attempts at justification by some American bishops.

Dominic Tierney says that in November 1938, in the final stages of the war in Spain, the Holy See (which had already recognized the Franco government in May of that year) dodged President Roosevelt's attempt to involve it in his effort at mediation. And in December it contributed to the failure of a shipment of 250,000 barrels of flour to Spain, fearing it might end up in the hands of the Republicans.[18] But according to Michael Barone, it was Roosevelt himself who persisted in his policy of nonintervention in Spain in order to avoid, as he said to his adviser, antagonizing the Catholic hierarchy and losing "the support of every Catholic voter in the 1938 elections."[19]

In December of 1939 Roosevelt decided to bypass the predictable domestic protests against the opening of a diplomatic mission to the Holy See by appointing a personal envoy to the Vatican. The decision had three purposes, obviously related to the outbreak of hostilities three months earlier: (1) reactivating a listening post that was more than ever essential under the circumstances, (2) trying to prevent Italy from entering the war, and (3) trying to make the Vatican more accommodating to Moscow. The practical results were meager, starting with Italy, which declared war on France and Great Britain just a little more than three months after the arrival of Roosevelt's envoy.

According to Morris, "His [Pius XII's] diplomacy and America's were constantly at cross purposes during the war." When Germany attacked the Soviet Union, "Pius XII steadfastly refused to endorse Roosevelt's program of aid to the Soviets."[20] In March 1942, when the Vatican decided to establish diplomatic relations with Japan only three months after the attack on Pearl Harbor, the US State Department believed, writes Charles Gallagher, that "Pope Pius XII was lining up the Holy See on the wrong side of the wartime equation. . . . President Roosevelt," continues Gallagher, "took the development as a personal insult."[21]

During the war, recalls Cardinal Domenico Tardini (at that time "foreign minister" of the Holy See), the Church was strongly opposed to the principle of unconditional surrender demanded by Washington, one of the keystones of the conflict.[22] Nor did the Holy See approve the decisions made at Yalta and Potsdam, in particular the division of Germany and Europe. According to Jacques Maritain, French ambassador to the Vatican at that time, Pius XII spoke in October 1945 in "defense of the unity of Germany in the best interests of Catholicism."[23] The Vatican consistently refused to recognize Polish sovereignty over Silesia and Pomerania until 1972, the year when the two German states established diplomatic relations; only then did the Holy See reorganize its diocese at the junction of the German Democratic Republic and Poland according to the "new" borders.[24]

As might be expected, the decision to give birth to the United Nations was also met with hostility. In his first encyclical, in September of 1939, Pius XII confirmed the reluctance of his two predecessors regarding an international forum that was not founded on "Christian law": when "the cruel strifes of the present have ceased," wrote the pope, "the new order of the world . . . must rest no longer on the quicksands of changeable and ephemeral standards . . . [but] on the unshakable foundation, on the solid rock of natural law and of Divine Revelation" (*Summi pontificatus*, sec. 82). In 1944, in the Christmas radio message, Pius XII made a favorable allusion to "responsible leaders of nations, [that] meet for talks, for conferences, to determine the fundamental rights and duties" (without ever mentioning the United Nations); yet, according to Italo Garzia, this was only because Americans had almost forced him to do so.[25]

In return, writes the Jesuit Joseph S. Rossi, the United States allowed some delegates of the American episcopate to participate as consultants to the US delegation at the United Nations Conference on International Organization (UNCIO), in charge of drafting the UN Charter. Despite "UNCIO's failure to mold the United Nations in the spirit of the Pope Pius XII and his predecessor Benedict XV," the American bishops maintained an office at the UN until 1972. Their work, says Rossi, helped the Church as a whole "to move from a public stance of antagonism toward the UN to one of cautious and unanticipated endorsement."[26] This was one of the cases in which the American Church acted as a "pioneer" in the transformation of the universal Church.

In 1947–48 another case of complete divergence between the Holy See and the United States arose—the creation of the state of Israel. The Church had been resolutely opposed to the creation of a national home for the Jews in Palestine ever since the end of World War I. In March of 1919 Benedict XV had stated that "it would be a terrible grief for us and for all Christians if infidels in Palestine were placed in a privileged and prominent position; much more if those most holy sanctuaries of the Christian religion were given into the charge of non-Christians."[27] In July 1921 the pope received for the first time a Palestinian Arab delegation, and on January 15, 1926, the Catholic magazine *Raqib Sahyun* published the first Arabic translation of *The Protocols of the Elders of Zion*.[28] In the spring of 1943 Vatican Secretary of

State Luigi Maglione wrote to the apostolic nuncios that "if Palestine were to belong exclusively to the Jews, Catholics would feel wounded in their religious feelings and therefore, would fear for their rights."[29]

Less than a year after the birth of the state of Israel, Pius XII issued three encyclicals on the matter;[30] in the last one the pope, who had never mentioned the fate of the Jews during the war, expressed his sorrow for the "concentration camps" in the Middle East, where "numerous refugees" lived as "prey to destitution, contagious disease and perils of every sort." In May 1949 *Fides*, the news agency of the Propaganda Fide, went so far as to defame Zionism as "the new Nazism."[31]

Although the American Catholic Church, unlike the universal Catholic Church, had expressed—since November 14, 1942—its "revulsion against the cruel indignities heaped upon the Jews in conquered countries,"[32] at the time of the creation of Israel the positions of Rome and of American clergy again coincided. American Catholic journals rallied unanimously, and Cardinal Francis Spellman, archbishop of New York and the leading figure of political Catholicism, tried to convince Truman to withdraw his support for Israel at the United Nations: "The traditions and interests of millions of Christians of the United States and of the entire world, who look to Palestine also as their Holy Land, must be articulated . . . by your representatives." Later, Spellman condemned "the effrontery of a member of the United Nations, the state of Israel, which has . . . tried to make the 'new city' of Jerusalem its capital."[33]

There is no doubt that the convergence of the United States and the Soviet Union concerning the creation of the state of Israel could only amplify the consternation of the Church in those very years when, with the beginning of the Cold War, the United States seemed at last to be converted to the word of anticommunism that the Catholics had spread for decades.

FROM "THIRD-FORCE-ISM"
TO "THIRD-WORLDISM"

With the beginning of the Cold War the American Catholic Church thought that its big moment had (finally) arrived—the moment when Americans would finally have to acknowledge that the alliance with the Soviet Union had been a mistake and that Catholics had always been right. According to

Morris, this was "arguably, the first time that a national political consensus had come to track closely a long-held and identifiably Catholic view."[34]

In those years there was the conviction, which some try to revive today, of an identity of interests between the Holy See and the United States on the international stage. There was indeed an identity, although only tactical and temporary, regarding the need to prevent the Soviet Union from going beyond the boundaries laid out by the Yalta division, especially in Italy: to avoid the nightmare of "Cossacks watering their horses at the fountains in Saint Peter's square" (a cliché of the anticommunist campaign of the time), Pius XII bent, though reluctantly, to the American decision to put all its eggs in the Christian Democrat basket (but then supported it unreservedly in subsequent electoral campaigns).[35]

Nonetheless, the views of the Vatican and Washington on strategic goals were far apart. The pope was clear about this: "Our position between two opposing camps," he said in his 1947 Christmas radio message, "is exempt from any prejudice, from any preference for this or that people, for this or that block of nations, as it is foreign to any sort of temporal consideration. To be with Christ or against Christ, that is the whole question." On the eve of General Marshall's visit to the Vatican (October 20, 1948), the editor-in-chief of L'Osservatore romano, Giuseppe dalla Torre, wrote two articles to support Italian neutrality, a position that influenced wide sectors of Christian Democrats themselves, long hostile to the country's accession to NATO. In June of 1948 the pope had already stated that the alternative was in those "clairvoyant and courageous spirits" who were striving to build a Europe intended "to restore a sincere spirit of peace among nations," and, as he said more explicitly in November 1948, a "united Europe."[36]

In brief, Pius XII had never been, as some of his friends and enemies claimed, the "chaplain of the Atlantic Alliance." His resistance "to aligning the Church with the Western or Atlantic bloc," writes Francis Traniello, "reflected, in cultural terms, an idiosyncratic view in opposition to the American way of life."[37] According to Peter Hebblethwaite, the pope considered the practical materialism of the American way of life to be only slightly better than the theoretical materialism of the Soviet Union.[38] Dorothy Day, one of the leading figures of American social Catholicism, explained to her readers in 1955 that the definition of "a cancer on the political body" given by *L'Osservatore romano* referred to "our industrial capitalistic system."[39]

In its unfailing support of the country's policy in the 1950s and 1960s, the American Catholic hierarchy once again diverged from the Vatican, just when the illusion of a perfect concurrence was at its peak. This illusion faded at the time of the Vietnam War. The attention that Rome devoted to American intervention in Korea and later in Vietnam could not be unrelated to the presence of substantial Catholic communities in those two countries. In particular, the Church's support for the regime of Catholic Ngo Dinh Diem—who had dedicated South Vietnam to the Virgin Mary, making the Church the first landowner in the country and provoking a massive repression of Buddhism—was unconditional. But in 1963, when John F. Kennedy decided to get rid of Diem, who had become the main obstacle to the resolution of the conflict, the Vatican's attitude changed radically. Paul VI condemned the war repeatedly; in particular, his speech at the United Nations in October 1965 focused entirely on the rejection of the war in general and was followed by a meeting with President Johnson, during which the latter was confronted with the problem of the ongoing war in Vietnam. Three months after that meeting, Cardinal Spellman, who had called US intervention in Indochina a "war for civilization" and "Christ's war,"[40] decided to spend Christmas holidays with the troops: although Spellman was far from representing the totality of the American clergy, it is impossible to imagine a more patent demonstration of the divergence of opinions.

The reasons the Church had been obliged to seek a "realistic" compromise with the United States during the aftermath of World War II no longer existed in the 1960s. Ennio di Nolfo, who bases his argument on documents from American sources, reports that the first signs of reciprocal attention between the Vatican and the Soviet Union date back to 1952.[41] In March 1956 there were even hypotheses of a forthcoming Concordat with Moscow; the Vatican secretariat of state, however, even if he was "extremely sensitive" to such a possibility, considered it premature, as the Italian ambassador informed his government.[42] In August of the same year, after a meeting in Rome between the Soviet *chargé d'affaires* in Rome and the nuncio to Italy, Polish archbishop Stefan Wyszyński and Hungarian archbishop József Mindszenty were granted amnesty and placed under house arrest (both would be released the following month in the wake of workers' insurgencies in Poland and Hungary).

Yet the direction the Church took with the most determination at the international level was not that of approaching Moscow but that of Third-Worldism, far more congenial to its vocation as the "world's leading authority" and therefore, necessarily, *super partes*. Third-Worldism was born of the disintegration of colonial empires and became the instrument for all those who, for one reason or another, had an interest in contesting the balance of power that emerged from World War II. Exploited in turns by Japan, China, India, and France, and even by the Soviet Union, Third-Worldism never translated into a coherent political trend, with the exception of a shared anti-American slant. Here again the Church, never siding with any of the international political actors, enjoyed a relative advantage.

In the mid-1950s Pius XII developed a public reflection on the responsibilities of the European powers in the outbreak of the anticolonial wars (and, simultaneously, inaugurated a policy of appointing cardinals from the so-called Third World).[43] At the same time, a number of bishops and Catholic intellectuals (mainly—and significantly—francophone) began to take up "the challenge of underdevelopment and lack of infrastructures in a large part of the world," with a "much more rapid [awareness] compared to the nineteenth-century workers' issue."[44] And it is true that "Third-Worldism" can be regarded as the "international version" of the social doctrine of the Church—but with one major difference: the social doctrine owed much to American influence, whereas Third-Worldism owed much to French influence in an audibly anti-American tone.

The theoretical crowning moment of Third-Worldism is represented by the encyclical *Populorum progressio*, dated 1967, in which Pope Paul VI developed an antithesis that became classic: "hungry nations" versus "peoples blessed with abundance."[45] In the text the pope expressed criticism of "a type of capitalism" that "has given rise to hardships, unjust practices, and fratricidal conflicts" (sec. 26), of the "widening gap" caused by the "the harsh economic realities of today" (sec. 8), of free trade that should be subordinated to the principle that "every man has the right to glean what he needs from the earth" (sec. 22), of private property that "is not absolute and unconditional" (sec. 23), and so on.

No wonder the text was greeted by a storm of criticism in the United States. The *New York Times* (March 29, 1967) defined it in an editorial as "strongly leftist, even Marxist in tone"; for the *Wall Street Journal* (March 30, 1967) it was "souped-up Marxism"; for *Time* magazine (April 7, 1967) it had "the strident tone of an early 20th-century Marxist polemic." In addition to revealing that their authors had never read a line of Marx, those critics—which is much more important—highlighted that, in a little more than twenty years, the parties were reversed: in the early 1940s the Church accused the United States of plotting with communists behind its back, while at the end of the 1960s it was the United States that accused the Church of secretly plotting with communists.

The anxiety that circulated in American ruling circles about the Church's Third-Worldism could not be related mostly to the Soviet Union, which, beyond ideological campaigns, could not present a real geopolitical threat; the anxiety essentially involved Latin America. The first practical effect of Catholic Third-Worldism could cause vibrations potentially threatening the very foundations of the Monroe Doctrine and could make the Church of Rome the bridgehead of a massive European penetration into Washington's proverbial backyard.

Those concerns revealed the United States' sense of insecurity, which had not existed only ten years earlier. During that decade there had obviously been the Cuban Missile Crisis, but, more important, there had been the war in Vietnam, and there had been the Japanese and German economic miracles, which gave the two powers defeated in World War II increasingly large shares of the global market, until then dominated by the Americans. At the end of the decade, writes Henry Kissinger, "the age of America's nearly total dominance of the world stage was drawing to a close."[46] Following the relative decline of the first world power, a new phase of international relations was about to open, in which the relations between the United States and other political actors on the world stage would be profoundly modified. This included US relations with the Catholic Church.

Even for the Church, however, the 1960s represented a watershed: those were the years of the big *aggiornamento* of the Second Vatican

Council and, especially, of the convulsive crisis that followed that council, a crisis that would decrease, within a few years, the number of priests and faithful and lead to a drastic loss of the Church's influence and credibility. Not until the pontificate of John Paul II would the Church resume its dynamic expansion and return to its role as an international political actor of the first order.

When, in the 1980s, Ronald Reagan and the pope met and resumed diplomatic relations after a freeze that had lasted 117 years, the two "empires" had very different characteristics compared to those of a few decades earlier. But they would continue to be "parallel," that is, bound only to meet at infinity.

CHAPTER 4

Catholics and American Politics

The Rise and Fall of the New Deal Coalition

EACH AMERICAN PRESIDENTIAL ELECTION tells a different story. In some cases—as with Roosevelt in 1936, Nixon in 1972, and Reagan in 1984—it is the scale of the victory that makes history; while in other cases—as with Kennedy in 1960 and Bush Jr. in 2000—it is the minimal margin of success that is likely to cast a dark shadow long after the election.

Hence the historical significance of John F. Kennedy's victory in 1960 deserves reconsideration, particularly taking into account that "the dirty tricks that helped defeat Nixon were more devious than merely the ballot-stuffing of political lore," according to an inquiry published by the *Washington Post* fifty years later.[1] Nevertheless, history chose to reduce those "dirty tricks" to a little footnote in the story of a president whose mysterious death turned him into a myth and who is remembered for being the first (and only) Catholic elected to the White House.

There is no doubt that for American Catholics Kennedy's election had a powerful symbolic impact, comparable to the symbolic impact of Barack Obama's election on the African American community almost half a century later. But as in the case of Obama, it was essentially no more than a symbol. The real situation of American blacks has not changed much since Obama's election, just as the relationship of American Catholics to politics did not change much with Kennedy's election.

This relationship, in fact, had changed earlier and would change even further, but it did so for reasons largely independent of the Kennedy presidency. The presidents who actually contributed to this change were three Protestants: Franklin Roosevelt, Richard Nixon, and Ronald Reagan. The first and last managed to build broad coalitions, in which the weight of the Catholic electorate probably had a decisive role.

Nixon, by contrast, cleverly took advantage of the Democratic Party's metamorphosis in the second half of the 1960s, which cut the party's roots with the South and the working class and led to the most resounding defeat in the party's history in 1972, as well as its long-term exclusion from power, lasting from 1968 to 1992, with the exception of Jimmy Carter's inglorious parenthesis.

The social rise of American Catholics is the flip side of this evolution. It began in the aftermath of World War II and is still under way, if we consider the contribution of subsequent waves of Catholic immigration—Asian and especially Latin American. It has produced a new Catholic political leadership that throughout both of Barack Obama's terms came to occupy an extraordinary number of key posts in the political elite of the United States of America.

FROM THE GREAT WAR TO THE GREAT DEPRESSION

As we have seen, during World War I American Catholics earned full recognition of citizenship. Their disproportionately high involvement in the conflict greatly contributed to the fading away of the tinge of strangeness and disloyalty that had clung to them since before the republic was born. Also contributing to their acceptance was their participation in workers' struggles after the war, judged subversive by many at its beginning, but which, on the contrary, served to counterbalance and weaken the revolutionary spirit triggered by the war and the Bolshevik example.

That phase of social disorder of the postwar period had two distinct consequences: on the one hand, the widespread need of a return to "normalcy," which Warren Harding exploited in his election campaign of 1920: the need to close as soon as possible the parenthesis of World War I and to reestablish an imaginary WASP golden age. On the other hand, there were the laws limiting immigration; anticommunist raids, organized by Attorney General A. Mitchell Palmer and his right-hand man, the young J. Edgar Hoover (head of the Alien Enemy Bureau); and the use of justice as a political tool, exemplified in the famous trial of Nicola Sacco and Bartolomeo Vanzetti. One can add Prohibition to these products of the climate of that time. Another fallout of these dominant protectionist and xenophobic sentiments was the comeback of the Ku Klux Klan, whose membership, according to some sources, reached five million in 1923.

The second consequence of the crisis was the social engagement of the American Catholic Church. One of the first decisions of the National Catholic Welfare Conference, created in 1919, was to make public a "Bishops' Program for Social Reconstruction" that, according to Charles Morris's summary, envisaged "a legal minimum wage, government-sponsored health and old-age insurance, strict child-labor laws, tougher anti-monopoly enforcement, and equal wages for women."[2]

The author of this text, John Ryan, later became the main liaison of Franklin D. Roosevelt to the Catholic world, and he even earned the ironic nickname of "Right Reverend New Dealer." There is indeed a striking harmony between the principles he articulated in 1919—in an era characterized by *laissez-faire* rather than by state interventionism—and those launched by the New Deal president more than ten years later in the midst of the most devastating economic crisis ever experienced by the country.

The reason for this anachronism resides in the Church's conception of the capitalist system. Although it ultimately has recognized the system as a matter of objective fact, the Catholic Church has remained steeped in its essentially pre- and anticapitalist tradition. It has come to a historic compromise with the idea of money creating value (having transformed itself into a leading figure of capitalist economy, especially in the financial sector), but its roots are still firmly planted in feudalism. The Church is quite familiar with the current organization of society (against which it has been fighting hard for several centuries) and is able to predict and anticipate all its shortcomings; and when no longer able or willing to fight it, it proposed a "social doctrine" to alleviate these shortcomings.[3] While bourgeois economic theories are, in brief, free-market in times of growth and interventionist in times of crisis, the "social doctrine" of the Church is almost always interventionist, corporatist, and solidarist. In other words it is a doctrine for the crisis of capitalism, both during and in the absence of any crisis, because anyhow, sooner or later, a crisis will occur.[4]

For Catholic leaders and theorists, this underlying pessimism about the fate of capitalism is a reason for profound optimism about the future of the Church. In March 1917, in the midst of the war and at the outset of the Russian revolution, the dean of cardinals, Vincenzo Vannutelli, said that "history teaches us that Providence uses great social unrest for the good of Its Church."[5] Vannutelli died just a few months after the outbreak of the crisis of 1929, before all its terrible consequences became apparent, but there is no doubt that he would have found ample confirmation for his theory.

In fact, the crisis inaugurated a new phase in the relations between the Church and US politics; Francis J. Lally described it as "a new kind, almost a new level, of association, provoked by both depression and war but also indicating a change in the 'official' American attitude toward the Church, and equally important, in the Church's disposition toward the government."[6]

CATHOLICS AND THE ROOSEVELT COALITION

The majority of the 12.8 million unemployed Americans in 1933 (sixteen times more than in 1926, almost a quarter of the working population) were Catholic. In one of his speeches of the 1932 presidential campaign, Franklin Roosevelt called the social encyclical of Pius XI *Quadregesimo anno*, published the year before, "one of the greatest documents of the modern times."[7] In particular, he quoted the condemnation of "the unlimited freedom of struggle among competitors . . . which lets only the strongest survive . . . those who fight the most violently, those who give least heed to their conscience."[8] Roosevelt's comment smacks of campaign tactics, but there was also evidence of common views on the regulatory level that the state must attain in times of crisis.

This encyclical made clear reference to fascism, which, since the Roman Question had been resolved, could be pointed to as a model: "Anyone who gives even slight attention to the matter," wrote the pope, "will easily see what are the obvious advantages in the [corporate fascist] system. . . . The various classes work together peacefully, socialist organizations and their activities are repressed, and a special magistracy exercises a governing authority" (sec. 95). Praising the *Quadregesimo anno*, Roosevelt winked at Italian Americans[9] but also at the Catholic supporters of the "third way," of the appeasement of class struggles and the elimination of social injustice through the re-equilibrating intervention of the state and "the laws of strictest justice—commutative justice, as it is called—with the support, however, of Christian charity" (sec. 110). He addressed *all* Catholic supporters of the "third way," including its pro-Fascist wing, whose best-known representative was the radio broadcaster Charles Coughlin, founder of the periodical *Social Justice*; and its left wing, whose best-known representative was Dorothy Day, the ex-anarchist social activist and the founder of "hospitality houses" and the *Catholic Worker* newspaper.

The coalition set up by Roosevelt was one of the largest and longest-lived in the political history of the United States. But the main difficulty in gaining the vast majority of Catholic voters (according to various estimates, between 70 and 80 percent of Catholics did eventually vote for him in 1932) did not consist in bringing together Coughlin's and Day's supporters, who all opposed the free market as strongly as they invoked the "third way." The main difficulty was imposing himself on a party that, as a "Catholic political party,"[10] had no chance whatsoever of succeeding in the United States as a whole. The loss of the Catholic governor of New York State Alfred Smith in the 1928 presidential election had eloquently proved it.

In the opinion of the Italian ambassador of the time, Giacomo De Martino, the Smith coalition appeared as a "strange alliance of southern landowners with newcomers, Irish workers, Italians, Germans, Slavs, who introduced to the party the interests of minor classes and urban working masses." It was, continued De Martino, "similar to the beginning of a revolution." But, in fact, it was only the beginning: the "strange alliance" did not take root; the historical heart of the Democratic Party—"the slaveholders, landowners and Southern Protestants"[11]—did not join in. In comparison with the results John Davis achieved in 1924, Smith lost Virginia, North Carolina, Tennessee, Texas, and Florida—that is, 72 out of the 136 electoral votes won in the South in 1924. With the exception of Tennessee (lost by Cox in 1920 but gained back by Davis in 1924) those states had remained loyal to the Democrats all through the five presidential elections lost between 1900 and 1924 (see maps 1–6).

For his part, Democrat Al Smith won Rhode Island and Massachusetts; he won the twelve most populous cities in the United States and brought the majority of Catholic female voters to the polls for the first time since women's suffrage had been granted in 1920, all shifts that would later be successfully exploited by Franklin Roosevelt.

Smith had been caught in the crossfire of the Republicans and all the anti-Catholics in the country, including those in the Democratic Party; the most moderate of them were convinced that Catholicism and democracy

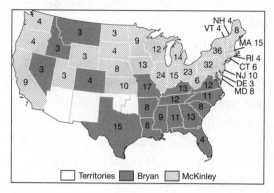

MAP 1. *Presidential election, 1900.*

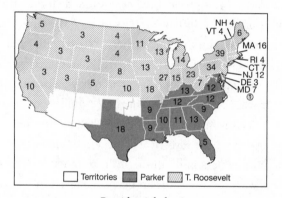

MAP 2. *Presidential election, 1904.*

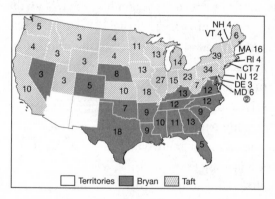

MAP 3. *Presidential election, 1908.*

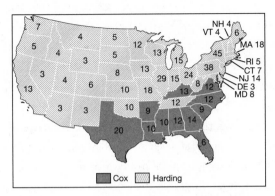

MAP 4. *Presidential election, 1920.*

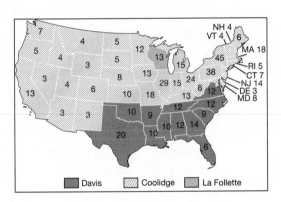

MAP 5. *Presidential election, 1924.*

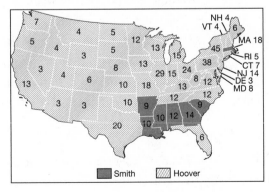

MAP 6. *Presidential election, 1928.*

were incompatible, and the most hostile believed that the country could end up under the indirect (or even direct) control of the pope. In short, if Catholics wanted to enter the halls of power, they had to rely on a non-Catholic, who—helped by the crisis, of course—would close the circle of the "strange alliance" of which Ambassador De Martino had caught sight.

The leaders of the Church were the first to understand this. Beginning in 1931, the year of Pius XI's encyclical and the launch of Roosevelt's presidential campaign, the bishops claimed a convergence of the analysis, language, and objectives of Roosevelt's policies and the social doctrine of the Church. The episcopate spoke in favor of the introduction of a minimum wage and a more equitable distribution of profits, a series of public works programs, greater government control of business, an income tax, a tax on annuities, and, finally, a system of unemployment benefits. According to Castagna, the "forums in which the various segments of American Catholicism expressed the bitterness they felt at *the failure of the capitalist system* and the obstinate nonintervention policy of the Hoover administration" proliferated.[12] Castagna also recollects that in April of 1933 the archbishop of Boston, William O'Connell, called Roosevelt "a man sent by Providence";[13] curiously, the same words had been used by Pope Pius XI in 1929 to describe Benito Mussolini.

Thus the first signs of a Catholic political leadership at the national level appeared under the Roosevelt administration. In September 1934 John Ryan wrote: "There are more Catholics in public positions, high and low, in the Federal Government today than ever before in the history of the country."[14] Among them were Thomas Walsh, appointed attorney general;[15] James Farley, the true soul of the election campaign, appointed postmaster general; Joseph Kennedy, president of the Securities and Exchange Commission and later ambassador to the United Kingdom; Frank Murphy, appointed governor of the Philippines, then attorney general, and, finally, a Supreme Court justice; and Robert Hayes Gore, appointed governor of Puerto Rico.

The weakening of the political influence of the Tammany Hall machine in New York City thus passed through various stages: Al Smith's defeat at the Democratic convention in Chicago in 1932; the promotion of Roosevelt's most faithful supporters in New York (such as Farley, Kennedy, and Edward Flynn); the agreement with the Republican Fiorello H. La Guardia, "promoted" to mayor of the city, and with Herbert Lehman, who was "promoted" to governor of the state (succeeded by La Guardia himself in 1946).

Of Italian descent, with a Catholic father and a Jewish mother, although he became an Episcopalian, La Guardia embodied an alternative to the Irish-dominated Tammany Hall; he was a bridge to New York's increasingly important Jewish community, of which Lehman was a prominent political representative (as well as heir to the financial dynasty of Lehman Brothers). In short, it was a sort of an informal Italian-Jewish coalition, supervised by "imported" Irish, that was nevertheless based on a historical matter of fact: "a tradition of hostility toward Jews existed in Catholic America that for decades had led to assaults on Jewish children and adults by Irish youth in New York, Boston, Pittsburgh, Jersey City, Philadelphia and other cities,"[16] but this hostility was "much more between Irish Catholics and Jews than between Italian Catholics and Jews."[17]

Another key element of Roosevelt's Catholic coalition on the national level was the world of trade unions. The Committee for Industrial Organization, founded in November of 1935, organized, on an industrial basis, unskilled workers, who had previously been excluded from the traditional craft union, the American Federation of Labor. Its first president, John L. Lewis, an isolationist, broke with Roosevelt in 1940; he was then replaced by Philip Murray, the first Catholic to head a national union. The CIO then became an actual transmission belt of the Democratic Party, advancing political demands (civil rights, universal health coverage, public works), supporting war efforts, and, in 1943, constituting the first Political Action Committee in US history to direct workers' votes to the Democratic Party. In 1945 the union could count on six million members in more than two thousand workplaces.

In addition to the unions, the New Deal coalition included the traditional southern base, big business, heavy industry, big northern cities, civil servants, intellectuals, and other ethnic and religious minorities, such as Jews and African Americans. Owing to their weight in the big industrial cities and in the union, Catholics had a decisive role in determining the coalition's success, at least until the 1948 elections. Since that time—

with the exception of 1960 and 1964—the "Catholic vote" has become a "swing vote," partly because of the social ascent of American Catholics and partly because this electoral flexibility provides a bigger margin of negotiation for the American Episcopate (see table 2).

FROM THE GREAT DEPRESSION
TO THE GREAT EUPHORIA

The "politics" of the Catholic Church actually consists of two separate policies: one is directed inward, the other outward. The first—the principles, organization, and relationship with the faithful—is the condition for the second: the Church can have an influence on the external world only if it appears to be an institution that is capable of having an influence on a country's internal affairs. In terms of the subject at hand, the Church had to prove that it was a firm and influential benchmark for millions of Americans in order to become a part of American politics. And in virtue of that solid relationship of trust, "anxious to attract Catholic voters, exploit Catholic resources, and apply a religious gloss to their own partisan programs, can-

TABLE 2. *Catholic Vote, 1948–2012*

Election year (prevailing party)	1948 (D)	1952 (R)	1956 (R)	1960 (D)	1964 (D)	1968 (R)	1972 (R)	1976 (D)	1980 (R)
Dem. Catholic vote	65	53	47	80	78	57	43	56	43
Rep. Catholic vote	35	47	53	20	22	43	57	44	48
Majority of Catholic vote	D	D	R	D	D	D	R	D	R

Election year (prevailing party)	1984 (R)	1988 (R)	1992 (D)	1996 (D)	2000 (R)	2004 (R)	2008 (D)	2012 (D)
Dem. Catholic vote	44	49	47	54	51	47	55	51
Rep. Catholic vote	56	51	34	36	47	52	45	49
Majority of Catholic vote	R	R	D	D	D	R	D	D

SOURCE: Approximate averages from various sources. When a column does not total 100%, it is because there was a third-party candidate in that election year.

didates and party leaders have sought the bishops out, engaged the bishops in political discussion, and highlighted the bishops' moral agenda."[18]

Although Al Smith did not have to put a great deal of effort into attracting the votes of his fellow Catholics, Roosevelt was the first to "plan" the conquest of the Catholic electorate. In the process of their integration into American society, Catholics had gradually taken hold of local institutions: municipalities, counties, law courts, trade unions, and police and fire departments, besides parishes and their various structures. Roosevelt made sure to convey part of this local responsibility to the national level, and this was facilitated by the decision of the American Catholic Church to strengthen its national structures in the years following the First World War.

In addition to the aforementioned National Catholic Welfare Conference, a number of organizations of the faithful, affiliated by profession, by social and leisure activities, and so forth, also saw the light. These organizations served purposes both defensive (creating a sort of a "parallel society" capable of resisting the pressure of an anti-Catholic environment) and offensive (being present and recognizable in each segment of society).[19] As a whole, the Church could also count on the powerful array of mass media (newspapers, publishing houses, radio and film companies) gravitating toward dioceses and parishes. It even went so far as to decide to recruit teachers to send to *public* schools.

The main goal of the Church was not to bring Catholics into politics. That might be a side effect, as Ryan stated in his pamphlet of 1924, but it was not the fundamental objective. In the Church's view, influence on political life is actually just one possible consequence, and certainly not the most important one, of an investment actually made to strengthen its position (the means) so as to *catholicize* the entire society (the end).

From the point of view of the political class, obviously, the opposite is true: politicians are largely skeptical or indifferent to the catholicizing of society; they essentially see the Church as one tool for achieving power. As Walter Mondale's 1984 campaign manager said to Timothy Byrnes, "If you are a bishop, you've got some pretty substantial organizational capabilities. . . . You've got a lot of people, you've got money, places to meet. . . . You've got a lot of things that any good politician would like to have at his disposal."[20]

The end of the New Deal coalition also marked the end of the Democratic monopoly on the Catholic vote. But it was not until the 1960s and 1970s that in the two major parties a machine for the conquest of that particular segment of the electorate was set in motion.

As a result of World War II the United States had strengthened its economic hegemony to the point of single-handedly producing half of all manufactured goods in circulation in the world. The "Fabulous Fifties," during which everything seemed possible, marked the peak in secularization of American society. According to Jacques Berlinerblau, "the years 1925 to 1973 might be described as the Golden Age of American Secularism."[21] The two dates refer respectively to the year of the Scopes Monkey Trial—the trial in which the literal interpretation of the Bible was publicly ridiculed—and the year of the Supreme Court verdict in *Roe v. Wade*, which legalized abortion, "the zenith of a secular political and judicial worldview that had gradually become an orthodoxy in the half-century since Scopes."[22]

But secularization is not limited to its political and legal aspects alone;[23] another aspect is the decreasing importance of religion in daily life. From this perspective the success of secularization in the United States is recognized to have been less remarkable than in any other industrialized society. What is more, it looks different, or at least out of sync, whether we speak of Catholics or Protestants. In broad terms—and relying on opinion polls, whose results are only approximate—it can be argued that this phenomenon of religious disaffection was manifested first among mainline Protestants and then, with a twenty-or-thirty-year time lag, among Catholics. A Gallup poll shows that in 1955, 75 percent of Catholics attended religious services weekly, compared to 42 percent of Protestants; in the mid-1990s the percentages were almost the same (46 to 43), and they became identical (45 percent) in 2005.[24]

Of course, the causes of a greater or lesser bond with religion may be numerous, and attendance at services might be one, but certainly not the only, indicator of this bond (however much more significant for Catholics than for Protestants). But the fundamental reason for the tendency toward religious disaffection is the phenomenon Max Weber called "disenchantment of the world": mystical explanations of a phenomenon are abandoned as soon as it can be explained scientifically. Similarly, the attempt to solve any problem by resorting to heaven is abandoned as soon as the problem can be solved by earthly means. So there is an undeniable link between improving the material conditions of existence (income and social security) and a weakening of religious sentiment.[25]

At the end of World War II the living conditions of Catholics were still below average, and in particular much lower than those of mainstream Protestants: as estimated by Liston Pope, 66 percent of Catholics were classified as "lower class," compared to 56 percent of the total American population and 42 percent of Episcopalians; while 9 percent of Catholics were considered "upper class," compared to 13 percent of the total population and 24 percent of Episcopalians.[26] From that moment on, at the approach of the 1950s, Catholics began their rapid rise in the society: "In twenty years," writes Morris, "from 1950 to 1970, the rate of Catholic socio-economic advancement was faster than that of any other religious subgroup except the Jews."[27] Already in 1964, according to a Roper and Gallup poll, Catholic income was on average higher than that of Protestants. And Andrew Greeley points out that in 1987 and 1988, "Catholic income [was] 14 percent higher than [white] Protestant income," adding that "if one includes blacks in the Protestant category, the Catholic advantage goes up."[28]

The social rise of the 1950s and 1960s certainly did not involve Catholics alone. Already in 1944, when only 1.2 percent of the labor force was unemployed, less than in 1926, the situation was one of virtually full employment; the US population grew by more than fifty million people between 1950 and 1970, and income increased by 50 percent, net of inflation; college students, who constituted 7 percent of their age group in 1940, increased to 12 percent in 1950 and 32 percent in 1970. A statistics series proposed by Lewis Perry allows us to follow the process of secularization in a particularly important segment of society, that of higher education: in 1900 there were seventeen religious ministers (of all denominations) in the United States for each university professor; the ratio became 3:4 in 1950 and 3:5 at the end of the 1970s.[29]

Specialists are still divided over the exact date when the New Deal coalition was exhausted: for some the end correlates to the death of its architect in 1945, and for others its last display was in the elections won

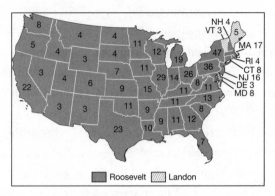

MAP 7. *Presidential election, 1936.*

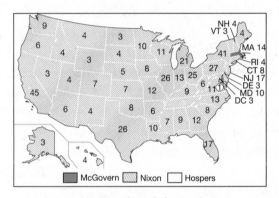

MAP 8. *Presidential election, 1972.*

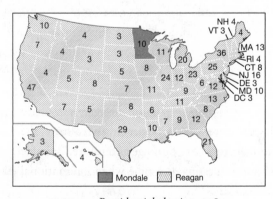

MAP 9. *Presidential election, 1984.*

by Lyndon B. Johnson in 1964. Even without going into details, it is clear that in the 1960s the social conditions that had led to the New Deal not only no longer existed, but they were, so to speak, reversed: even if they still had "to include the excluded" (according to a famous Roosevelt slogan), the United States had passed from the "great depression" into the "great euphoria." And it was in this climate that the constituency of the two major parties was reversed: whereas in 1936 the Democratic Party had triumphed with virtually no competition (see map 7), from the 1968 elections forward, the Republican Party became more and more the party of the owners of the South and the white working class of the North, a kind of reversed New Deal coalition that triumphed in 1984 with Ronald Reagan (see maps 8 and 9).

BURDEN AND BLESSING:
JOHN FITZGERALD KENNEDY

In the midst of ongoing secularization President Dwight "Ike" Eisenhower decided to insert the words *under* God in the pledge of allegiance to the flag and to adopt the new motto "in God We Trust." Yet Patrick Reardon asserts that this was an era when presidents "didn't trumpet their faith."[30] In fact, there seems to be no contradiction: even those who say that "in religion, as in so much else, Ike was far more sophisticated than commonly realized" also acknowledge that "Ike probably intuited that Judeo-Christian civil religion was a unifying moral force that was infinitely preferable to most of its likely alternatives."[31] In short, he wanted to provide the United States with an additional ideological weapon during the harshest phase of its confrontation with the Soviet Union.

As Congressman Charles Oakman stated when introducing the proposal for the new oath (February 1954), "one of the most fundamental differences between us and the Communists is our belief in God."[32] Eisenhower—the first president to be baptized *after* the beginning of his term—explained that the choice of reference to God served to reaffirm "the transcendence of religious faith in America's heritage and future."[33] In fact, it revived the concept of Manifest Destiny at a time when international circumstances imposed on the country a strict moral cohesion that had to be protected by all means, including the spectacular political processes of McCarthyism.

There is a huge difference between the God of the 1950s—chosen by Eisenhower as the armigerous deity of the United States in the Cold War— and that of the new formalism that emerged in the second half of the 1970s. And if John Fitzgerald Kennedy had not been Catholic, religion would probably never have been mentioned in a US presidential campaign until Jimmy Carter chose to ride the rising wave of popular religious revival.

When Kennedy was chosen as a candidate, inflexible antipapists raised their voices again, digging up paranoid, and by then definitely outdated, accusations of a possible control of the United States by the pope. A series of Gallup polls shortly before the 1960 election revealed that about a quarter of Americans would never vote for a Catholic candidate, which also meant that, for the remaining three-quarters, the nomination of a Catholic did not pose a problem.[34]

In his memoirs, Richard Nixon translated this simple mathematical calculation into a simple political one: "The pockets of fundamentalist anti-Catholic prejudice that still existed were concentrated in states that I stood to win anyway. But many Catholics would vote for Kennedy because he was Catholic, and some non-Catholics would vote for him just to prove they were not bigoted."[35] The fact that there remained only "pockets" means that the clearing of Catholics by Roosevelt, and especially their social ascent, had contributed significantly to undermining that "fundamentalist anti-Catholic prejudice." Kennedy's victory undermined it even further: in August 1961 the percentage of Americans opposed to a Catholic candidate had dropped to 13 percent in the Gallup poll; fell below 10 percent at the end of the 1960s; and continued falling to 5 percent in 2003. Thus on the eve of John Kerry's candidacy the "fundamentalist anti-Catholic prejudice" had virtually disappeared.

Kennedy's victory was proof that a Catholic political leadership was possible, but it was the proverbial swallow that does not make a summer. In 1955 John Tracy Ellis had published an article in the Fordham University quarterly *Thought* in which he complained, like Ryan in 1924, about the lack of a Catholic intellectual elite; Ellis emphasized that "in the entire history of the country there have been only five Catholic members of the Supreme Court of the United States and fourteen members of the presidents' cabinets out of a total of 301 men since 1789, and ten of these have been appointed since 1933."[36]. The tendency seemed to continue under Kennedy: in his first administration there were two Jews but only one Catholic (his brother Robert), while two other Catholics were appointed later (Anthony Celebrezze in 1962 and John Gronouski in 1963). Kennedy appointed an Episcopalian and a Jew to the Supreme Court (thus interrupting the series of Catholic justices inaugurated by Roosevelt and carried on by Truman and Eisenhower). At the time when Ellis was writing, ultimately only 14 percent of House representatives and 10 percent of senators were Catholic, compared to a percentage of Catholics in the American population exceeding 20 percent.

From the point of view of the Church, then, the experience of the first Catholic president of the United States was quite disappointing. The popular sanction of the full citizenship of American Catholics was an extremely valuable result: in fact, no longer having to prove their loyalty at every step, bishops felt authorized to take more independent, if not critical, positions against the policies of the United States. Without that victory, a distancing at the time of the Vietnam War, as well as the condemnation of the two Gulf wars, would have likely been more problematic and more subtle.[37]

Yet the Church was definitely disappointed in Kennedy's inflexible secularism, which so perfectly suited a character so far from being a Catholic role model. From a wealthy Bostonian financial dynasty, an alumnus of two schools of the traditional Massachusetts Puritan establishment (Choate and Harvard), mundane, liberal, a womanizer and an occasional drinker, Kennedy was a pure product of New England and secularization. Some even believe that his behavior contributed to secularization's progress: according to John Neuhaus, a Lutheran pastor who converted to Catholicism, "Whatever his intentions may have been, then Senator Kennedy was widely perceived to be saying that Catholicism posed no serious threat, because he was not a very serious Catholic."[38]

At the time, however, what caused confusion in the Church hierarchy was not so much his lifestyle as his 180-degree turn from the positions that he had supported as Massachusetts' eleventh-district congressman (1947–53), when he had managed to find federal funds for books, canteens, and doctors' offices in Catholic schools. Once Kennedy became a candidate for the presidency, he declared his resolute opposition to any form of public funding, even indirect, of religious schools, as well as to a possible opening of diplomatic relations with the Holy See. During the campaign he wanted to let people know he believed "in an America where the separation of church and state is absolute."[39]

Massimo Franco reports that when a stunned Cardinal Spellman asked a common acquaintance "what the devil Kennedy was planning to do, the answer was: exactly what he says."[40] After that, Spellman, who was a longtime friend of Kennedy's father, and who had celebrated the marriage of John's two brothers, Robert and Edward, decided to support Richard Nixon's candidacy. Spellman's case was not isolated: according to Theodore White, "In many of the most important dioceses of the nation, it was known in 1960 that if the Catholic Church had any silent inclination, it leaned to Richard M. Nixon rather than to John F. Kennedy."[41] Even Rome was bewildered: according to Eric Hanson, "John XXIII never understood the strong secular tone of the Kennedy administration," and "the Texas Protestant Lyndon Johnson proved much easier for the Vatican to deal with than the Irish Catholic Kennedy from Massachusetts."[42]

Kennedy's experience clarifies why the Church does not seem to be at ease with the idea of a Catholic president. Every American presidency is a window on the world; it is therefore understandable that, if the president is Catholic, the Church expects to be provided with a public image of the president's religion that is as close as possible to what Rome wants to convey (and of course with a guarantee of a number of the Church's interests). However, and though they may move in the same direction on certain specific issues, the United States and the Church have different purposes; it is therefore impossible for an American president, whatever his or her religious inclination, to follow the Vatican's agenda. So it is much better for Rome to avoid adding the complication of an unfaithful faithful to every other possible difficulty: it suffices to imagine how many more problems would have arisen if the president responsible for the attack against Iraq in 2003 had been a Catholic. Or, for there is no need to imagine scenarios, it suffices to remember the "friendly fire" that, in 1984 and then in 2004, rained down respectively on the Catholic candidates Geraldine Ferraro and John Kerry. As Jonathan Beale wrote, being a Catholic president is "as much a burden as a blessing."[43]

Kennedy's victory had cooled the Church but heated electoral strategists of the two parties: the idea of adding up the votes of Catholics and those non-Catholics who wanted to prove they were not bigoted appealed to everyone. For three elections in a row, at least one of the two parties nominated a Catholic to the vice presidency: the Republican William Miller (1964) and the Democrats Edmund Muskie (1968) and Sargent Shriver (1972). In 1972 several Catholics (including Ted Kennedy, Edmund Muskie, Kevin White, and Gaylord Nelson) rejected George McGovern's proposal, whose choice then fell on the Catholic Thomas Eagleton, later replaced by another Catholic, the very devout ambassador Sargent Shriver (also Kennedy's brother-in-law). This frantic search did not stop the Catholic electorate from moving away in massive numbers from the Democratic Party for the first time.

The failures of Barry Goldwater in 1964, Hubert Humphrey in 1968, and George McGovern in 1972 convinced those strategists that a Catholic on a presidential ticket *was not* the key to victory. It was not until 1984 that a Catholic candidate for vice president was found again: Geraldine Ferraro, who also lost heavily, along with her running mate, Walter Mondale, in yet another election in which the Catholic vote shifted massively to the Republicans. Religions were again a political factor, and Republicans and bishops understood this much better than Democrats.

THE REVERSAL OF THE MAJORITY: FROM JOHNSON TO REAGAN

A process of desecularization began to manifest itself in the world in the 1970s: in developing countries, as a result of extremely fast and chaotic industrialization; in developed countries, as a result of the deep economic crisis of the middecade.[44] It is important to underline that secularization and desecularization are *processes*, unequal in space and time, often coexisting, and still ongoing. These three characteristics make them particularly complex, and often, for convenience or laziness, they are simply ignored or gotten around through an absolutization that is much easier to sell but that has the disadvantage of not corresponding to reality.

The process of secularization in particular was long seen as absolute: as Jeffrey Haynes writes, "The belief that religion was dying became the conventional wisdom in the social sciences during most of the 20th century."[45] In fact, religion was not dying at all: that commonplace—spread not only among social scientists but also among philosophers, scientists, psychologists, writers, art directors, and more, who swung from positivist optimism to nihilist skepticism—was based primarily on what many intellectuals of the great cities of the industrialized world observed when they gathered together.

But beyond that narrow, fashionable "international intelligentsia," more or less similar everywhere, the processes of secularization occurred in the industrialized world at very different times and with very different characteristics, depending on the place, especially when it comes to European countries and the United States. Let us leave aside for now the peculiar relationship that Americans have with religion; it is sufficient to note that when, in the mid-1960s, *Time* magazine asked the question "Is God Dead?,"[46] nearly one out of two Americans claimed to participate in a religious service at least once a week, and two out of three considered religion "very important" in their lives.[47] Reproducing the "conventional wisdom" on the ineluctable decay of religion, American intellectuals reproduced nothing but their own world; yet their hegemony in newspapers, books, and movies gave their wishful thinking disproportionately exaggerated dimensions. The impact on the media was so strong that at the end of the decade the intellectual world took power within the Democratic Party.

The preconditions for what Louis Bolce and Gerald Di Maio define as the "secularist putsch" of the Democratic Convention of 1972 had already been set at the end of the previous tumultuous Convention of 1968.[48] On that occasion new rules for the election of delegates were established. Based on a quota system guaranteed to women and "minorities," they drastically reduced the weight of the representatives of the traditional core of the party: the trade unions and internal structures. Thus, the 1972 convention chose George McGovern to represent a new platform rooted in liberal issues that over time became classics (pacifism, feminism, ecology, the right to abortion, the right to alternative lifestyles). As Theodore White wrote, the convention reflected the prosperity of American capitalism (whose product went from $500 billion in 1960 to nearly twice as much in 1970), which had gradually shifted the focus from producers' to consumers' rights.[49]

That turning point had a number of consequences. One of them was immediate: the most crushing defeat ever suffered by the Democratic Party. Three were more gradual: the ultimate loss of the white working class in the North;[50] the transformation, "by default more than by overt action,"[51] of the Republican Party into the heir of American traditionalism in matters of moral values, religion, and family; and finally, the break in the preferential relationship with the Catholic Church.

With the convention of 1972 the Democratic Party had completed the metamorphosis begun in 1964 with the signing of the Civil Rights Act, when it irrevocably lost the South. Regarding this specific issue, the transition began at the end of the Second World War, when a substantial immigration block thinned the ranks of the working class in the North in an era of intense manufacturing activity, causing massive displacement of the black population from the South to the North. According to White, in the 1948 election campaign some Democratic senators from the North and the West led by Hubert Humphrey began to promote racial integration and the right to vote for blacks in the South.[52] President Truman, for his part, abolished segregation in the army (and in the South, the "third party" of Strom Thurmond—the "Dixiecrats"—won in traditional democratic strongholds of Alabama, Louisiana, Mississippi, and South Carolina).

In the 1960s the problem festered owing to the combined effect of the rate of development of industry, mainly located in the North, and the progressive social transformation of the South. Between 1910 and 1960 the black population in the South declined from 39.1 percent to 23.5 percent, and the white population increased from 60.9 percent to 72.8 percent. The relationship between the countryside and cities in the South also changed: the urbanization rate of 18.5 percent in 1910 reached 50 percent in 1960.[53] Moving north en masse, black migrants provoked among white workers a new outburst of revulsion as they had a century earlier: once again one could observe a blending of the rich owners of the South and lower classes of the North, but this time against the Democratic Party. For three-quarters of a century the ruling class of the South had kept within the Democratic

Party a veto on all hostile measures against it; between 1948 and 1964 this privilege was revoked. The South responded by moving away from the Democrats in 1964 (see map 10), then again by playing the card of the "third party" (with George Wallace, in 1968 [see map 11], who was decisive in the defeat of Hubert Humphrey), and finally by joining the Republican Party in a stable manner.

Richard Nixon and Barry Goldwater clearly distanced themselves from the campaign for civil rights of African Americans, and they cashed the electoral dividends. But it was only in 1969 that a real strategy for taking over the New Deal electoral base (landowners of the South and proletarians of the North) was sketched out, with the publication of *The Emerging*

MAPS 10–11: *Results of the presidential elections in 1964 and 1968 by state.*

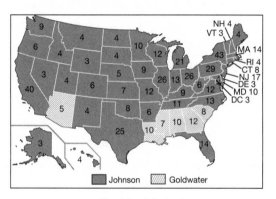

MAP 10. *Presidential election, 1964.*

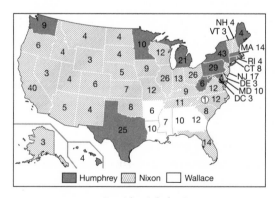

MAP 11. *Presidential election, 1968.*

Republican Majority by Kevin Phillips. According to Phillips, the intellectuals connected to public spending and to mass media could hope to win an electoral majority just by appealing to the massive base of black and Hispanic minorities; if the Republicans had invested in the "silent majority" of the country, they would have assured for themselves at least three decades in power (although, as Phillips wrote, it would probably have been marked by a democratic interregnum).[54]

Between Nixon's and Ronald Reagan's elections there were more than ten years of further intensive development in the United States, characterized among other things by the social rise of ethnic and religious groups in search of new forms of political representation. Robert Christopher gives the example of Jewish intellectuals who had moved away from liberal positions to embrace the neoconservative cause, and other individuals of Irish, Italian, Slavic, or Middle Eastern descent who joined the Republican Party, directly or through forms of demagogic dispute with the establishment.[55] In this climate there arose several formations of the "New Right," including the Heritage Foundation in 1973, the Senate Steering Committee in 1974, the Conservative Caucus and the National Conservative Political Action Committee, both in 1975; and then, in the second half of the decade, faith-based groups such as Focus on the Family in 1977, the Christian Voice in 1978, the Moral Majority and the Religious Roundtable in 1979, and the Family Research Council in 1981.

It was before an assembly of the Religious Roundtable that Ronald Reagan made his famous declaration: "I know you can't endorse me . . . but I want you to know that I endorse you and what you are doing," asserting that America had to go back to "that old-time religion" to become "that shining city upon a hill" promised by the Pilgrim Fathers. Ronald Reagan channeled the social needs of new emerging social strata, as well as the religious revival of those years, into the strategy of the Republican majority, conceived at the time of the Nixon administration, thus repeating in 1984 the overwhelming success of 1972.

But it was the Democrat Jimmy Carter who first used the religious revival as a political weapon in an attempt to set things back on track in his party after the McGovern catastrophe. One can say, together with Andrew Flint and Joy Porter, that Carter woke "the sleeping giant of evangelical Christianity,"[56] but he did not go on to show that he was able to feed it. Disappointed in Carter on all fronts, religious leaders—primarily the bishops, who were almost the only ones to react to the *Roe v. Wade* decision legalizing abortion—tried other solutions. Ronald Reagan could have wanted nothing more.

CHAPTER 5

Politics and Religion in the United States

The Evangelical Meteorite

IN THE 1960S one of the few relevant episodes of contamination between religion and politics in the United States was the civil rights movement. While the rest of the society was adjusting to a wave of secularization, ethnic minorities, particularly African Americans, were gathering around their churches—and sometimes around their mosques—in order to try to obtain the end of segregation and the recognition of their civil rights. Their religious inclination was undoubtedly genuine, but it had little to do with the new religious revival that would affect the United States, as it did the rest of the world, some ten years later. In fact, it can be compared to the religious inclination of the political opposition in many countries of the old Soviet sphere of influence or in certain Muslim countries, which found in institutions and religious buildings the only available spaces appropriate for organizing. Besides, the two best-known figures of the American civil rights movement were a Christian pastor who became a political leader, Martin Luther King, and a political leader who became a Muslim preacher, Malcolm X.

What happened in the mid-1970s was a worldwide phenomenon, not a local one, caused by the new widespread social uncertainty that interrupted the untroubled march of postwar optimism and disappointed the hopes of palingenesis aroused by decolonization. The new religious fervor assumed everywhere a special feature that it still possesses today: it was "more visible and at the same time frequently in decline," with a spirituality often subordinated to the meticulous formal observance of "a system of norms and codes," as Olivier Roy notes.[1]

In short, there was a new quest for identity, which, in the face of the failed promises of modern identities, moved toward the rediscovery of "old" identities, perceived as guarantors of stability and continuity in a world dominated by increasing unpredictability. This new *Great Awakening* expressed itself more intensively than extensively: it slowed but did not reverse the drift toward disaffection with religious practices, and it manifested itself mainly through increasingly conspicuous behaviors carried out in public space (including the wearing of distinctive signs, such as a kippah, veil, jilbab, turban, and so forth), which inevitably overflowed into the political arena.

Forty years later, we can say that the outcome of that overflow into the public sphere can be evaluated, at the very least, as ambivalent: a moderate success for politicians who managed to promote themselves riding the wave of religious identities, quite a failure for religions, which themselves have reaped almost no dividends. In particular, in the case of the United States, no remarkable results were achieved even on the most substantive symbolic front—the commitment to reverse, on the national level, the 1973 Supreme Court ruling legalizing abortion—despite the usual promises of those presidents elected thanks to the votes of born-again Christians.

In the end the colossal, and sometimes undeserved, media success of the so-called Christian right has not been matched by a comparable political success. And at last, disappointment has turned into frustration and frustration, in turn, into disaffection: "In coming years we will see the old evangelicalism whimper and wane," wrote the evangelical pastor John Dickerson at the end of 2012; the reason is that "the politically muscular force" ended up distracting "from the historical vital signs of evangelicalism: to make converts and point to Jesus Christ."[2]

The Catholic Church, for its part, seems to be neither whimpering nor waning. On the contrary, its influence on American political life has definitely increased, and now it even seems capable of reaping at least part of what evangelicals have sown.[3] This outcome is attributable mainly to three factors: an organization that knows how to be local, national, and global at the same time; a political experience accumulated over the centuries; and a diversification of the Church's investment policy. None of these features is, nor could be, within the reach of evangelical groups. The net result is the nearly total exclusion of evangelicals from the main decision-making centers of American politics, the very same spaces that are heavily occupied by Catholics.

MUCH ADO ABOUT NOTHING

"By 1930, fundamentalists and many other evangelicals had withdrawn into their own religious circles and largely detached themselves from public affairs," writes John Green.[4] According to many observers, the Scopes Monkey Trial was the last step of that process, at the end of which evangelicalism went "into a state of prolonged political hibernation"[5] and remained thus until at least the second half of the 1970s. This does not mean that in those fifty years its absence from the political scene was absolute: as Sarah Miller-Davenport reminds us, the World War II victory convinced many evangelical preachers of the need to give "a religious cast to the widely circulating notion that Americans had an obligation to spread their way of life across the world."[6] In the 1950s Billy Graham made himself famous with his impressive public demonstrations of support for the presidents-in-office and their commitment to the anticommunist crusade of the Cold War.

Yet Billy Graham and various "Gospel Crusades" can be considered political actors only in part; in fact, their role was to offer religious support to political power and to American ideology and did not call for initiatives adumbrating an opposition. Conversely, the frenzied evangelicals of the 1970s distinguished themselves primarily as an element of opposition, not so much to this or that party, at least initially, but especially to the secularization of society and to all its manifestations—from the teaching of the theory of evolution to the abolition of prayer in schools, from the weakening of sexual morality to abortion. Compared to the 1950s, evangelicalism of the 1970s followed the "desire to shift the Bible from grand symbol of the nation's faith in God to the grand shaper of domestic and foreign policy."[7]

The fight against the decriminalization of abortion has become over time the political banner of evangelicalism. We should remember, however, that when the *Roe v. Wade* decision was announced in 1973, political evangelicalism was in a mere embryonic stage. The opposition to the decision of the Supreme Court was then supported only by the Catholic Church, which since 1967 had been engaged in the fight against the legalization of abortion.

In that year, according to Timothy Byrnes, the American Law Institute supported the initiative aimed at standardizing the American legal system in the matter of abortion. It was the first great opportunity for US bishops to implement the recommendations of the Second Vatican Council: to speak not in defense of this or that particular interest of the Church but on a social topic of general interest, regardless of the religious affiliation of the people involved. The bishops released a series of statements on abortion in 1968, 1969, 1970, and 1972. In 1973 they launched a proposal for a constitutional amendment against the *Roe v. Wade* ruling, defined first and foremost as "an unspeakable tragedy for our nation."[8]

Despite a lively internal debate with those who feared losing certain tax advantages and reviving traditional anti-Catholic sentiments, as well as with those who did not consider it appropriate to favor the abortion issue over other matters of general interest, the Bishops Conference in 1975 decided to make the "Pastoral Plan for Pro-Life Activities" the cornerstone of its public commitment. In 1976, writes Byrnes, "right-to-life" had already become "the name of a growing social movement supported and funded by Catholic bishops."[9]

The abortion issue inevitably erupted into the presidential campaign in a political climate characterized by high instability. The legacy of Richard Nixon's overwhelming victory in 1972, to which the Democratic Party's miscalculations contributed more than any precise Republican strategy, was devastated by the Watergate scandal. In that context of fluidity the two candidates' special attention to the relationship with the Catholic electorate expanded the episcopate's room for maneuver. Jimmy Carter, torn between the obligation to respect the explicitly pro-choice program of his party and the desire to win the favor of the bishops, organized no fewer than four meetings with them, which only resulted in his being blamed four times over (while the Republicans' decision to support the proposal for a constitutional amendment was called "timely and important"). For the media it was clear that Gerald Ford had earned the "tacit support of the nation's Roman Catholic bishops."[10]

That support (which the bishops, however, denied ever having granted) changed neither the outcome of the vote nor the choice of the Catholic electorate, which "came back home" after deserting McGovern, with a percentage similar to that of 1968 (56–44), a gap whose size has never been reached since. Furthermore, the abortion issue seems to have played an extremely marginal role in the 1976 election: according to one study, "less than one half of one percent of the variation in voting can be explained by the abortion variable."[11] That would also mean that Jimmy Carter's emphasis on his religiosity played a far more significant role, obviously including the influence on Catholic voters, who, in the mid-1970s, were far more diligent observers when compared to Protestants (54 percent of the former claimed to attend a religious service at least once a week, compared to 40 percent of the latter).[12]

Only in the second half of that decade did abortion become one of the dominant themes of the comeback of political evangelicalism. It was on that theme that the encounter with the Republican Party actually happened, with its new policy focusing on deregulation and liberalization. In the late 1970s, in fact, the strategists of the Grand Old Party understood the spirit of the time: the dismantling of protectionist barriers in order to revive global trade after the profound crisis of 1975. The political pioneer of that policy was Margaret Thatcher, and within a few years that policy was sustained by most leaders of the old industrial powers: from Ronald Reagan to Helmut Kohl, and even François Mitterrand, though the latter had won the presidential election in France two years earlier with a diametrically opposite program. The reluctance of Soviet, Japanese, and Italian leaders to face the free-market shift can be considered the main cause of the crisis that hit their countries in the 1980s and 1990s.

In the opinion of Republican strategists the abortion issue was closely related to the despised predominance of national legislation over that of the states. The auxiliary troops of the Christian right mobilized the feelings of those who went back to considering religion as a corrective, if not as an alternative, to political deficiencies (represented, in the United States, by the defeat in Vietnam, the end of the gold standard,[13] the Watergate scandal, the crisis of 1975, and, of course, "moral decay"). The Moral Majority brought to the Republican Party the dowry of the established Catholic antiabortion network but also other demands, such as opposition to cutting tax advantages for Christian schools that still practiced racial segregation.

Thus, the Moral Majority was the instrument for conveying new religious energy to a coalition united around the free-market flag waved by Ronald Reagan. To succeed, the evangelical militants were compelled to abandon one of their traditional principles: anti-Catholicism. Deleting with a single stroke centuries of antipopery, Jerry Falwell, the southern evangelical unifier of the Moral Majority, went so far as to unashamedly state that John Paul II was the "best hope we Baptists ever had."[14] According to Susan Harding, the rhetoric of southern evangelicals then shifted from their longtime targets—blacks, Jews, and Catholics—only to set up new ones: "liberals, secular humanists, feminists, homosexuals, pornographers, abortionists,"[15] and, more generally, secularists. In attempting to get conservative Catholics (including Paul Weyrich, Terry Dolan, Richard Viguerie, and Judy and Paul Brown) and some Orthodox Jews to affiliate themselves with the Reagan coalition, the theorists of the Moral Majority were among the most zealous propagators of "Judeo-Christian" ideology—until then a marginal political tool but later promoted as the backbone of so-called Western civilization.[16]

After Jimmy Carter's failure on the religious front as on many others, Ronald Reagan positioned himself as "a God-fearing president." Speaking of the Bible, Reagan declared in 1982 that "it is an incontrovertible fact that all the complex and horrendous questions confronting us at home and worldwide have their answer in that single book."[17] But as Jacques Berlinerblau comments, "Reagan, like nearly all American presidents, did not show much desire to let the answers in that single book inform his questions about domestic and foreign policy."[18]

Berlinerblau's opinion is shared by many other observers. According to Greg Forster, "the Religious Right was already declining in power by the mid-1980s, and it withered throughout the 1990s. After the early years, it accomplished few of its legislative priorities. Politicians deftly extracted money, votes, and volunteer time from evangelicals while delivering little of substance."[19] The main topics of the political agenda of militant evangelicalism were the abolition of the right to abortion, restoration of prayer in schools, ban on teaching of those scientific disciplines conflicting with the Scriptures, defense of the traditional family, and, in foreign policy, opposition to any limitation of armaments. None of those objectives has ever been acknowledged at the federal level.

The failure is especially patent on the abortion front. *Roe v. Wade* was not changed under the presidency of Ronald Reagan or George Bush, both antiabortionists. It was not until 2003 that a very partial limitation of the right to abortion was enacted into law.[20] If to these failures one adds the fact that all attempts to elect an evangelical activist to the presidency of the United States have gone no further than the primaries stage, and that today no prominent evangelical occupies a key position in the political elite of the United States, then it can be concluded that the return on a bellicose investment in militant evangelicalism is extremely poor: much ado about nothing.

THE RESISTIBLE "EVANGELICAL GAP"

To be precise, it was not exactly "about nothing," because the Catholic Church benefited twice from the comeback of evangelicalism: through its adoption of certain practices, and by reaping a part of what it sowed.

But let us proceed in order. Let us return to the fiasco of political evangelicalism to say that its proportions are magnified by a triple overestimation of this phenomenon: by its promoters themselves, by the media, and, finally, by the Democrats, with liberals' particularly vocal ferocity.

As for the cockiness with which the architects of the religious right launched themselves into politics, it suffices to quote Tim LaHaye, one of the instigators of the Moral Majority, who said in 1985, "There are 110,000 Bible believing churches but there are only 97,000 major elective offices in America. If we launch one candidate per church, we can take over every elective office in this country within ten years."[21] When, three years later, the televangelist Pat Robertson tried to embark on his presidential campaign, he was unable to last through the primaries (in which he got less than 10 percent of the popular vote). At the end of the ten-year period forecast by LaHaye, not only had the evangelicals not conquered all elected positions, but the Republicans had lost the most important one: the White House. And today, thirty years later, there is no single evangelical in the federal government, nor in the Supreme Court, nor in the military, nor in the security leadership of the country; evangelicals make up between 18 and 25 percent of the members of Congress, according to several sources, and 14 percent of the state governors (for comparison, Catholics compose about 31 percent of both the 113th and 114th Congresses, and 38 percent of governors in January 2015, out of the total Catholic population of between 23 and 30 percent of Americans).

The media are responsible, in part, for overestimating the evangelical phenomenon from a political viewpoint. As a scholar sharing this religious sensibility wrote, "In retrospect, it now seems clear that the part these organizations [the Christian right] played in this outcome [the 'Reagan Revolution' of 1980] was not as great as either the news media or conservative evangelicals once believed."[22] No need to wonder at the media's propensity to overemphasize: besides delivering the news, they must sell it, that is, find the elements that are likely to make it more appealing to potential audiences. In this particular case newspeople were greatly helped by the uncommon sense of performance the leaders of political evangelicalism possessed and by the display of their oratorical skills, which often bordered on histrionics (many of Pat Robertson's or Jerry Falwell's remarks made the headlines).[23] But they were also helped by lurid reactions of panic, disdain, and condemnation by many of their political opponents.

According to Berlinerblau, "The Promethean evangelicals . . . strike fear in the hearts of secularists, like the Vandals descending on Rome."[24] Mark Noll writes that "a depressing proportion" of texts dedicated to political evangelicalism "has featured ideological excess instead of analytical rigor."[25] In addition to understandable polemical reasons arising from the obligations of political competition, there are two other explanations for the overestimation of the Christian right by many of its opponents: the difficulties of the latter in analyzing the phenomenon in the context of the return of religion to public life and the absolutizing of the phenomenon (which, in turn, caused an inability to notice parallel and concurrent— and perhaps even more significant—phenomena, such as the expansion of political Catholicism or the politicization of Islam). From misunderstanding to demonization there is only one step, and in politics, demonization always has the opposite of the intended effect, magnifying the enemy and contributing to its popularity. In Italy Silvio Berlusconi has for years owed a debt of gratitude to the frantic and ubiquitous activities of his most resentful enemies, whom he considered beneficial to his cause and comparable (if not superior) to the militant support of his most zealous acolytes.

The most disastrous (for the Democrats) political outcome of this blindness was "offering" their opponents the religious awakening. In fact, originally, militant evangelicalism was oriented more toward Democrats than Republicans.

Mark Noll recalls that in 1972, "white conservative Protestants . . . had organized the first postwar interest group to campaign for a presidential candidate: it was called 'Evangelicals for McGovern.' " Moreover, "the nation's best-known selfidentified [*sic*] evangelical politician was Senator Mark Hatfield of Oregon," a Republican, but in favor of civil rights, withdrawal from Vietnam, and a freeze in the nuclear arms race (which he worked on with Ted Kennedy).[26] The politician who was most hostile to abortion was Sargent Shriver, McGovern's vice presidential candidate. In the end, concludes Noll, the first major political evangelical assembly, held in November 1973 in Chicago, gave birth to a final document in support of civil rights, hostile to the war in Vietnam, and in favor of launching a campaign against poverty.

The "evangelical vote" was recorded for the first time in the 1976 elections, and its dividends were gained for the most part by Democrat Jimmy Carter. Charles Booth reports the opinion of many analysts of the time—which is also very likely exaggerated but worth mentioning—according to which "Jimmy Carter's margin of victory was probably the result of the voting of evangelicals."[27] Since then, however, evangelicals have divorced the Democrats. Pastor Rick Scarborough, author of *Liberalism Kills Kids*, a book published in 2006, says he was among those who voted for Carter in 1976 and abandoned him later because "he had betrayed everything I hold dear."[28] According to some analysts, half of white evangelicals voted for Carter in 1976; in 1980, writes Noll, their votes went to Ronald Reagan by a margin of nine points, which became sixteen points in 1984; in 2000 that margin was twenty-four points, twenty-seven in 2004, and again twenty-seven in 2008. According to the Pew Research Center,[29] which evaluates "white Protestants" and "evangelicals" separately, the margins in favor of the Republican candidate were much larger (see table 3).

TABLE 3. *White Protestant and evangelical vote, 2000–2012*

	2000		2004		2008		2012	
	Gore	Bush	Kerry	Bush	Obama	McCain	Obama	Romney
White Protestant	35	63	32	67	34	65	30	69
MARGIN		28		35		31		39
Evangelical	n/a	n/a	21	79	26	73	20	79
MARGIN	—	—		58		47		59

SOURCE: "How the Faithful Voted: 2012 Preliminary Analysis," Pew Research Center, Nov. 7, 2012.

To summarize, a real "evangelical gap" has opened up between Democrats and Republicans in consequence of three concomitant causes: the militant effort of a fierce minority of conservative and reactionary evangelicals, the mass media hunger for all clamorous and striking phenomena, and many Democrats' misunderstanding of the return of religion to the public scene and their entrenchment in liberal positions.

Nevertheless, the evangelical gap cannot in any way be identified with the "God gap." According to the aforementioned study by the Pew Center, looking at the division, on religious grounds, of the *total* number of votes (i.e., taking into account all religious sensibilities), one can see that the "God gap" does not exist, or, in the case of Catholics, it is, rather, a swing vote (see table 4).

The most important lesson that can be learned from these data is that the expansion of the evangelical gap did not penalize Obama, nor did it prevent him from winning two presidential elections. This means that the evangelical vote (as well as, more generally, that of white Protestants) has less and less influence at the electoral level. At the same time, the Catholic swing vote has more and more influence.

THE IRRESISTIBLE DECLINE OF POLITICAL EVANGELICALISM

Political evangelicalism has undoubtedly had its hours of glory. But specialists still disagree about how much it really contributed to the Republican cause and when (or if) its influence wore out.

TABLE 4. *Vote per faith, 2000–2012*

	2000		2004		2008		2012	
	Gore	Bush	Kerry	Bush	Obama	McCain	Obama	Romney
White Protestants	35	63	32	67	34	65	30	69
Black Protestants	92	7	86	13	94	4	95	5
Catholics	50	47	47	52	54	45	50	48
Jews	79	19	74	25	78	21	69	30
Other faiths	62	28	74	23	73	22	74	23

SOURCE: "How the Faithful Voted: 2012 Preliminary Analysis," Pew Research Center, Nov. 7, 2012.

According to Greg Forster, the political era of the religious right ended in 2000, with George W. Bush's election. The latter, says Forster, actually thought that everybody—believers of all faiths and nonbelievers—could and must play an irreplaceable role in public life; and "whatever you think of that, it isn't what Pat Robertson believes." As we saw, according to Forster, the decline had already been under way in the second half of the 1980s, when voters began to realize that the religious right had brought grist to the Republican mill without getting much in return.[30]

On the relationship between George W. Bush and the religious right, Michael Wear expresses a completely different opinion from Forster's. To Wear, Bush Jr. "was elected as the first president leaders of the Religious Right could claim as 'one of us.' " Nevertheless, Wear agrees with Forster's observation that "the political power to elect a candidate is different than the political power to govern," and, like Forster, he finds practical evidence: "Abortion remained legal, no federal amendment to ban gay marriage passed, and school-sanctioned prayer time remained unconstitutional."[31]

Conversely, according to Jonathan Merritt, it was the 2012 elections that marked "the end" of evangelicals' political role. Unlike Forster, Merritt claims that evangelicals had significant, perhaps "instrumental," political weight in the Republican victories from 1980 to 2004. Yet in 2012, despite their massive support for Mitt Romney, they failed to prevent the victory of his rival, Barack Obama, clearly demonstrating their "waning" influence. Among the hypotheses put forward to explain that decline—a "seismic shift in moral culture," the swelling of ranks of pro-Democratic interest groups, and the absence of a new evangelical leadership—there was also the recognition that "conservative Christian ideas are failing to shape the broader culture."[32]

For Merritt this failure is recent and owing to the "sweeping impact of globalization" and to the "digital age." Globalization and the Internet are increasingly called on to account for phenomena of the most disparate nature. Mark Noll offers a richer explanation: "In the recent United States, evangelical conservative politics has been a movement without a philosophy." Then he explains what he means: "To bring together solidly grounded conceptions of government, employment, education, capitalism, race, history, world affairs, and even Christianity into practical political action—requires political philosophy of the sort that American evangelicals have never possessed." In other words, what is needed is a capacity for analysis and synthesis that does not belong to the evangelical tradition. This capacity, adds Noll, belongs, rather, to the Catholic Church: "Theirs [evangelicals'] is not the tradition of *Rerum Novarum, Quadragesimo Anno,* or *Mater et Magistra.* It is instead the tradition of . . . Billy Sunday, who in 1919 predicted that Prohibition would empty American prisons and transform the country into a heaven on earth."[33]

In politics the key to exerting a profound influence does not lie in the ability to scream the loudest, to make the most extravagant statements, or perform the most sensational actions; it lies in the ability to organize people long-term for the purpose of achieving clear and specific objectives— where clarity and specificity of objective are essential preconditions. The failure of political evangelicals, resumes Noll, lies in the very fact that they were not capable (or, I might add, did not see the necessity) of taking the first step of any political organization aspiring to establish a profound and lasting influence: the analysis of the situation in which it operates, which is a condition of the synthesis of a political program. Their insurmountable limit was actually to believe that the Bible was the answer to *all* "the complex and horrendous questions confronting us at home and worldwide" (the same insurmountable limit—"The Koran is our constitution"—against which the political hopes of the Muslim Brotherhood in Egypt have been shattered).

Insofar as it actually existed, the success of political evangelicalism was based on the ability to grasp the new need for certainty that emerged after the profound crisis of values of the 1970s and to direct it toward the goal of a new moral recovery. It was the effect—ephemeral—of the political intuition of a group of experts in communication and flamboyant preachers, who nonetheless proved incapable of analyzing (or simply refused) and, consequently, of organizing those needs. Political evangelicalism was a loose confederation of more or less similar sensibilities, increasingly detached from reality and, therefore, more and more self-referential and marginal.

The inability to provide broader prospects to the immense demand for values did not only damage the continuity of political evangelicalism; it also helped maintain religious evangelicalism in a state of fragmentation that, in turn, continues to nourish and perpetuate its political insignificance. In 1961 Leslie Dunstan reported 6,161 Protestant denominations in the United States; in 2006, when the "nondenominational" concept had already been introduced, the *Yearbook of American and Canadian Churches* accounted for 217 Christian denominations, while the Association of Statisticians of American Religious Bodies in 2010 estimated that "over 35,000 independent or nondenominational churches" were active in the United States, where *nondenominational* almost always means "evangelical."[34] Another example of this fragmentation is the number of buildings used as places of worship, most of which house a single evangelical current or sensibility. For example, in a "secular" city such as New York, the density of Christian places of worship (one per thirty-two hundred inhabitants) is twice as high as that of a "religious" city such as Rome (one in every sixty-six hundred).

Some of those evangelical currents, while remaining independent, are officially federated; most are not. In any case, in the absence of a superior religious authority recognized by all, it is to the preacher of a single church or community that the believers (in spite of their theoretically direct and immediate contact with God) defer to in the last instance for religiously correct solutions to daily dilemmas. In political terms this fragmentation considerably weakens and dilutes the message one can send, enough to render the concept of an "evangelical stance" inappropriate. Whether it is a matter of slavery in the nineteenth century, or abortion, stem-cell research, or homosexuality today, "the Bible can always be cited *against itself*," writes Jacques Berlinerblau. "The Scriptures," he continues, "are the incubator of *multiple*, often irreconcilable, worldviews," which are therefore "*politically irrelevant*," if only because they cancel each other out.[35] Among the various evangelical currents, for example, there are churches or congregations that are violently hostile to homosexuality, others that condemn it only morally, some that do not condemn it at all, and some that direct their pastoral activity essentially toward the gay community, like the Metropolitan Community Church, with its 222 congregations scattered across 37 countries.

In short, the political decline of evangelicalism is not the result of this or that specific mistake but is intrinsic. In other words, even if political evangelicalism might enjoy another moment of glory (as it did at the time of the "Reagan Revolution"), this moment will pass quickly because it lacks an analytical basis (or, quoting Noll, a "political philosophy") and because it is doomed to end sooner or later by being sucked into the political whirlpool represented by its wish to have society conform to the dictates of the Bible. A political commentator of the Bible willing to use it as a basis on which to regulate public life will find, among his most determined opponents, other political commentators of the Bible who disagree with him. "The Bible," Berlinerblau concludes, "is to clear and coherent political deliberation as sleet, fog, hail and flash floods are to highway safety."[36]

It is quite possible that the decline of political evangelicalism and the decline of religious evangelicalism are independent; however, there is an unwritten law that says that the more a religion ventures directly onto the political field, the more it is forced to achieve tangible results. Otherwise, its credibility is compromised. We have seen that the unpopularity of theocracies—from the pope-king to Iranian ayatollahs—brings along a loss of popularity of the respective religions.

According to Michael Wear, "pastors increasingly found that a partisan politics was pushing people away from faith and causing tension among those in their churches."[37] Jonathan Merritt is even more explicit: "As American Evangelicals have become more partisan, American Christianity has suffered as more shy away from the faith."[38] This awareness, in Wear's words, is conspicuously present in the evangelical community itself. Tom Sine, leader of an evangelical think tank, observed in 2010 that "twenty-three of twenty-five major evangelical denominations, including the Southern Baptist Convention, are experiencing declining attendance patterns."[39] The aforementioned pastor John S. Dickerson published a book in 2013 entitled *The Great Evangelical Recession*, in which he describes American evangelicals as a "shrinking minority" whose weight, according to several investigations, is between 7 percent and 9 percent of the population; in absolute terms it is equivalent to the population of New York State. The reason, according to Dickerson, is that "instead of offering hope, many evangelicals have claimed the role of moral gatekeeper, judge and jury." Christians, continues Dickerson, should not of course change their beliefs to adapt to changing social currents, but they should face the world "with grace and humility instead of superior hostility." After all, concludes the author, "the core evangelical belief is that love and forgiveness are freely available to all who trust in Jesus Christ."[40]

Dickerson's reflection is remarkably similar in content but also in tone to that of Pope Francis, as expressed in the apostolic exhortation *Evangelii gaudium* of 2013, considered a sort of manifesto of his pontificate. The possibility that the thought-processes of the Catholic Church and other Christian churches dealing with the "crisis of modernity" could eventually converge was already clear. But, from this convergence, the Catholic Church has much more to gain than all the other Christian churches.

THE EVANGELICAL PATH
OF THE CATHOLIC CHURCH

The distinctive quality of the Catholic Church is its ability to secure its action on a long-term footing. Even certain defeats can contribute to its strengthening and to its becoming more entrenched. For example, according to some observers, the Italian Church engaged in the referendum against the abortion law in 1981—even knowing that it would lose—because it also knew that it could build a front of combative and militant supporters around the issue, as actually happened. According to Joseph Ratzinger, who was appointed prefect of the Congregation for the Doctrine of the Faith in that same year, the minority status that the Church holds nowadays must lead it to organize itself around "small, vital circles of really convinced believers"; in this way "it will, biblically speaking, become the salt of the earth again."[41]

The Catholic Church, as a solid and entrenched organization, is capable of accumulating energy even in defeat, and with this accumulation it can resume fighting *its* battles, which are battles of continuity and influence. This is why the failure—so far—of the movements hostile to abortion or same-sex marriage in the United States has an impact on the Catholic Church that is totally different from its impact on thousands of other churches and evangelical congregations. Religious groups that are essentially created around specific goals (whether they be abortion, prayer in schools, or the political support of the Republican right) are likely to disappear once defeated on their specific ground. In any case, as stated above, organizational evanescence and the absence of a "political philosophy" impede evangelical groups from accumulating energy, that is, from assuring the continuity of those forces that, at one given moment, they were able to put in motion.

Various surveys revealing decreasing frequency of religious practice of evangelical groups (and consequently of the collection of funds) in no way imply that those groups are disappearing or are likely to disappear any time soon. Most of their faithful continue to attend their rites and, in most cases, to follow their instructions, whether of a purely religious nature or moral or political in thrust. Some people simply attend church less frequently; others abandon their religious practice altogether; others look elsewhere for that kind of continuity or simply for that anchorage to the tradition or to a strong identity they fail to find among evangelicals. The majority of the latter come to the Catholic Church.

It is true that the number of Catholics beginning to attend evangelical groups in the two Americas today is even higher than those going the opposite way: according to another study by the Pew Research Center, "only" 69 percent of Latin Americans call themselves Catholics (i.e., fifteen points fewer than baptized Catholics), and almost half of Hispanic Protestants in the United States were raised in a Catholic environment.[42] Nevertheless, there are hundreds of thousands of Catholic converts, even though the influence of the Catholic Church—a unique case among the religions—goes far beyond the sheer size of its faithful. In the United States the reception given to Pope Francis in September 2015 has amply demonstrated it.

Although evangelicalism does not represent a theologically consistent and uniform confession, its doctrinal differences with the Catholic Church are undeniable. But the two decisive questions that keep various Christian denominations apart concern the role of the clergy as a mediator between God and believer and papal primacy. The Church of Rome, buoyed by its supremacy as the internationally recognized moral authority of the world, can afford to take a pragmatic and conciliatory approach on many of the issues that have divided the Christian community for centuries. It is equally pragmatically prepared to adopt methods of evangelization that have proven effective in experimentation by other Christian currents.

The Church of Pope Francis has come to recognize not only the valid-
ity of some of the missionary practices of evangelicalism but also to adopt
and recommend them. Since the 1960s, some groups of American Catholic
students have organized around the "charismatic" model of evangelicalism, giving life to the Catholic Charismatic Renewal, a movement that
emphasizes the role of the Holy Spirit and its "charismatic gifts."[43] The
Catholic Charismatic Movement, officially recognized by the Church in
1975, counted 120 million faithful worldwide in 2003, according to an
internal document.[44]

The key to Pentecostal, charismatic, and evangelical success lay in
the ability to meet the needs (primarily spiritual but also material) of
people, without expecting them to come looking for answers in the parishes. Luciano Mendes, the president of the Brazilian Bishops' Conference
(1987–94), outlined the difference between the evangelical and Catholic
practices in these terms: "We believe that going to Mass on Sundays is a
very generous act. But evangelicals proselytize three times a day. . . . Our
evangelical brothers have cadres who feel like an active part of the community, something we Catholics do not have."[45]

That missionary policy was made official at the Conference of Latin
American Bishops in Aparecida, Brazil, in 2006, whose tone was set by the
preceding debate. Vittorino Girardi Stellin, the Bishop of Tilarán (Costa
Rica), encouraged the flock to "rediscover the personal dimension of the
Gospel, direct contact with people starting from their particular environment"; his intention was "to establish a real visitation ministry by train-
ing people who would give time and willingness to reach the faithful in
their homes." His colleague Carlos Aguiar Retes, then bishop of Texcoco
(Mexico) and president of the Latin American Episcopal Conference between 2011 and 2015, announced a "change in underlying logic: the move
from a 'cronyist' to a decidedly missionary perspective." Filippo Santoro,
former auxiliary bishop of Rio de Janeiro and later bishop of Petrópolis
(Brazil), emphasized the "overriding" necessity of meeting the believers
"one by one" and remembering to engage all aspects of life and society,
"including culture and the media."

Cláudio Hummes, former archbishop of São Paulo, later called to
Rome to join the central government of the Church, was regarded as the

great coordinator of the Conference of Aparecida. His idea was to create an "organized continental missionary plan" that in every parish would gather two hundred to three hundred "missionaries" capable of speaking to families "weakened by the loneliness of the big cities, [who] end up learning the word of Jesus spread by sects." He accurately indicated receivers of that ambitious missionary work: the nonpracticing baptized. "The vast majority of the Catholics on our continent do not participate in the life of our church communities. They deserve to be evangelized, because with the act of baptism we committed ourselves to leading them to Jesus Christ."[46]

By implementing these recommendations, little by little, the Latin American Catholic Church began to occupy—or rather to reoccupy—the territory plowed by the evangelicals. In 2007 Hummes himself announced that "according to the latest polls, the phenomenon [of evangelical expansion] has slowed down."[47] That "Latin American" policy, strongly supported by the pope of the time, Benedict XVI, has become the official policy of Jorge Mario Bergoglio's pontificate, as he himself summarized with the phrase "Church which goes forth."[48] It is about being "permanently in a state of mission," the pope wrote in his exhortation of 2013, which should involve both the clergy and the faithful and "has a programmatic significance and important consequences" (sec. 25).

The "charismatic shift," experienced by the Latin American Church and universalized by Pope Francis, is based on what are called the "fruits of the Spirit": joy, mercy, love, peace, kindness, goodness, and gentleness—a full-scale encroachment of evangelical teachings.

CHAPTER 6

Catholicization of the United States

The Shift of Power and the Progress of Catholicism

UNDER RONALD REAGAN'S ADMINISTRATION the relations between American politics, Catholics, and the universal Catholic Church underwent two major transformations: Catholics became part of the country's political elite; and diplomatic relations with the Holy See were restored.

The Protestant Reagan managed to do what the Catholic Kennedy had not even attempted, not only because Kennedy feared awakening residual or latent antipapal sentiments in society but also because in the early 1960s the time was not yet ripe.

In the 1980s it ripened—or, at least, the first fruits were beginning to appear. Subjectively speaking, this happened as a result of the emergence of a large Catholic middle class and the social advancement of many of the faithful of the Church of Rome. Objectively speaking, it was because the politico-religious sensibility that had emerged in the previous decade had imposed itself as a permanent feature of the US political landscape. Since then, the religion has become an inescapable issue in every American election campaign.

The time also ripened for relations with the Holy See. Outside of a meager minority of eccentrics, no one in the United States thought, after John F. Kennedy's presidency, that the Roman pontiff really wanted to seize power in Washington. In this context Ronald Reagan took advantage of the apparent convergence of purpose of the United States and the Vatican against Moscow to destroy the remaining barriers to formalizing relations with the Holy See.

Following a final burst of antipapism on this very occasion, Catholics were finally in the clear, becoming a "normal" element of American political life. Now, more than twenty years later, few people have noticed the importance they assumed under George W. Bush's presidency and especially under that of Barack Obama.

Numerous hypotheses can be put forward regarding this phenomenon and its dimensions. Yet one thing is certain: beginning with George W. Bush's presidency, US administrations started to include in their political equation the variable of the relative decline of the United States. Both Bush and Obama recognized the need to reposition the country on the international chessboard at a time when—according to the terms of the US National Intelligence Council in 2008—"owing to the relative decline of its economic, and to a lesser extent, military power, the US will no longer have the same flexibility in choosing among as many policy options."[1]

To sum up, the global shifting of power and Catholicization go hand in hand in American political life. The coming years will show whether or not this is a coincidence.

RONALD REAGAN AND OVERTURES TO CATHOLICS

The first American president to open the doors wide to Catholics was Ronald Reagan. He was the first candidate to promote religion, both explicitly and instrumentally, as one of the central themes of his election campaign. Immediately before him, as we have seen, Jimmy Carter had partially managed to intercept the religious-political awakening in the second half of the 1970s because, as Berlinerblau writes, he was fluent in the same "spiritual-political dialect" spoken by this segment of the electorate.[2]

Religious fervor was a part of Carter's personality, and it did not cost him any effort to adapt and emphasize it for electoral purposes. Conversely, Ronald Reagan's religious policy was a calculation, a precise investment—if not Reagan's personally, then definitely that of his communication advisers and Moral Majority activists. In politics calculation always gains the upper hand over spontaneity, and it is for this reason that, again according to Berlinerblau, "the ambiguously evangelical Ronald Reagan trounced the incumbent liberal evangelical Jimmy Carter."[3]

The strident political statements on the importance of the Bible and of religion, rigid stands on moral issues, the repeated (but sterile) attempts to abolish *Roe v. Wade* or to reintroduce prayer in schools, the overt consonance with John Paul II, and the loud support of the "Christian right" allowed Ronald Reagan to go down in history as one of the most religious presidents of the United States. Few people remember that Reagan was also the only divorced president. Of course, his marital status does not cast any doubt on the sincerity of his faith, but it speaks volumes about the moral flexibility, bordering on relativism, of those interlocutors who exalted his religious and moral consistency for political reasons.

Although Reagan had begun to learn the ropes in politics at the time of McCarthyism, religion for him was not just an instrument of the Cold War, as it had been for Eisenhower. Owing to his personal conviction and to the fact of his being a candidate during the new Great Awakening, Reagan saw religion as a political weapon against the Soviet Union *and* a way of being in tune with the most devout fellow citizens during a time of great bewilderment.

Carter's presidency, in fact, had not even remotely contributed to re-establishing feelings of confidence and security in Americans baffled by the several crises the country underwent during the late 1960s and early 1970s. The Iranian Revolution, the hostage crisis,[4] the second oil shock, the beginning of deregulation, and, finally, the Russian invasion of Afghanistan only increased a disorientation that was aggravated further by the administration's apparent inability to cope with all of the above. Carter himself, in a famous television speech in July 1979, addressed "a crisis of confidence . . . that strikes at the very heart and soul and spirit of our national will. We can see this crisis in the growing doubt about the meaning of our own lives and in the loss of a unity of purpose for our nation."[5]

Ronald Reagan emerged as someone who would return to America and Americans their "heart and soul and spirit." His assertive economic policy, his firm attitude toward the Soviet Union, and his constant appeals to traditional values actually managed to revive American optimism for a few years, although at the expense of hiding the effects of the country's relative decline, a decline that, in spite of economic restructuring and the victories in the Cold War, continued: it was demonstrated by the rise of Japan in the 1980s, culminating with the return of the "yellow scare" in the United States[6] and with the beginning of a public debate about this relative decline. One of the highlights of this debate was Paul Kennedy's famous *The Rise and Fall of the Great Powers*: "Decision-makers in Washington," wrote Kennedy in 1987, "must face the awkward and enduring fact that the sum total of the United States' global interests and obligations is nowadays far larger than the country's power to defend them all simultaneously."[7]

In this new climate Catholics entering Washington's halls of power were more numerous than ever. Among them were one-third (eleven out of thirty-three)[8] of the ministers of various Reagan administrations; four out of six National Security advisers;[9] the leading figures of the president's speechwriting team;[10] CIA Director William Casey; and Vernon Walters, the ambassador to the United Nations (1985–89). In addition, Ronald Reagan was the first president to nominate three Catholics to the Supreme Court (Robert Bork, Antonin Scalia, and Anthony Kennedy) out of a total of six nominations; the last Catholic before them, William J. Brennan, had been appointed by Dwight Eisenhower in 1957.

Regardless of this unprecedented plethora of Catholics appointed to top institutional positions, all that is left to history from the relations between Ronald Reagan and Catholicism is the restoration of diplomatic relations with the Holy See. It was undoubtedly a breakthrough in formal terms, but as the *Washington Post* put it, it was also "a sensible and long overdue move."[11]

After the WWII experience of Roosevelt's "personal envoy," in the early 1950s, the Vatican insisted on adding a regular exchange of ambassadors. Harry Truman was in favor of this request, which, according to the Department of State, "would be of some assistance in securing the influence of the Holy See on 300,000,000 Catholics throughout the world in support of our objectives, and, to some extent, on the thirty-eight governments who now maintain diplomatic relations with the Holy See."[12] Truman went so far as to appoint an ambassador, provoking, however, a "political firestorm,"[13] partly spontaneous and partly orchestrated by the National Council of Churches, which forced him to backpedal.

The result of the new outburst of antipapal fever was that between 1951 and 1969 the United States had no official accredited representative to the Holy See. Of course, this does not mean that there were no relations between Washington and the Vatican. According to Francis Rooney, at that time, "America's primary liaison to the Vatican" was Cardinal Spellman, the archbishop of New York but also, again according to Rooney, a member of the National Committee for a Free Europe, a CIA organization that used him "to assist in its efforts to overthrow the left-leaning regime of Jacobo Arbenz in Guatemala." In that same period some of the US funds sent to Italy "to keep the Communists out of power" were "funneled through the Vatican," as had already been the case, though to a much greater extent, in support of the 1948 elections.[14]

During Kennedy's presidency the chill was palpable. The Catholic president even delayed his arrival to Rome on a planned visit in July 1963 to avoid arriving in time for Paul VI's ceremony of investiture. Besides wishing to avoid the accusation of being an instrument in the pope's hands, Kennedy was annoyed by the beginning of the so-called Vatican Ostpolitik, an opening toward Eastern European regimes, and by Pope John XXIII's intervention in the Cuban missile crisis, which was judged too favorable to the Soviets. Those who maintained contacts during Kennedy's presidency, writes Massimo Franco, were the apostolic delegate to the United States, Egidio Vagnozzi; National Security Adviser McGeorge Bundy in Washington; a political officer at the American Embassy in Italy, William C. Sherman; and the Vatican's chief of protocol, Igino Cardinale, in Rome.[15]

The State Department documents consulted by Rooney reveal that after Kennedy's death "the pope was a constant factor in the calculations of Johnson's administration. Few major foreign policy initiatives seem to have been undertaken without consideration of, or consultation with, the Vatican."[16] Finally, in 1969 Richard Nixon revived the practice of "personal envoys," later continued by his successors Gerald Ford and Jimmy Carter. This went on until the formalization of relations promoted by Reagan.

Prevailing opinion attributes the decision to reestablish diplomatic relations to the anti-Soviet convergence of the Church and the United States in the 1980s. The journalist Carl Bernstein went so far as to support the hypothesis of a "holy alliance" forged during the first face-to-face meeting of Reagan and John Paul II at the Vatican on June 7, 1982: "In that meeting," wrote Bernstein, "Reagan and the Pope agreed to undertake a clandestine campaign to hasten the dissolution of the communist empire."[17] This and other similar reconstructions reveal, according to Massimo Franco, the wish to enlist the pope "in the 'American party' of the time, without a passing thought given to the reverse, or at least complementary, possibility that it was the pope who was taking advantage of American policies for his own ends."[18] Even Rooney, in order to avoid succumbing to the same temptation, more prudently speaks of "shared goals," clarifying that the

Vatican was "extremely reluctant to abridge its neutral and independent status by entering into clandestine activity with the United States or any other country."[19] (Rooney's phrase "extremely reluctant" is, in my estimation, an additional euphemism.)

In the 1980s, Karol Wojtyła's Church and Ronald Reagan's America undoubtedly had a common will to defy Moscow; however, it remains to be seen that the objectives of this challenge were the same, as is generally asserted. It is more plausible that the theory of the coincidence of goals is a "typical way to make history in hindsight," as John Paul II himself said (calling "ridiculous" the claim that "it was the pope who brought down communism with his own hands," since these regimes "fell in the end because of the socio-economic weakness" of their system).[20] From what I have so far tried to demonstrate, it is virtually impossible that the objectives of the United States and the Church coincide; and, as a general rule, in international politics, fighting a common enemy does not mean having a common goal.

TWO DIFFERENT GEOPOLITICAL AGENDAS

In the 1980s Karol Wojtyła's Church and Ronald Reagan's America had profound disagreements about other crucial issues: Latin America and the Middle East, as well as two other pillars of Ronald Reagan's politics: economic policy and the arms race. According to Thomas Carty, Reagan accelerated the procedure of opening diplomatic relations with the Vatican to avoid any possible clash with an American episcopate, hostile on the last two points, hoping that the Polish pope would be a more open interlocutor.[21]

But the Polish pope was anything but a "natural" ally: from the very beginning of his pontificate he reconfirmed the traditional condemnation of unchecked market forces[22] and spoke against the arms race,[23] in 1982, excluding from consideration that nuclear deterrence could be considered "appropriate and safe for the preservation of international peace."[24] The Church had its own international agenda, which was not the same as that of the United States; like all popes starting with Pius XII, John Paul II was certain that "each of the two blocs harbors in its own way a tendency towards imperialism" (encyclical *Sollicitudo rei socialis*, Dec. 30, 1987, sec. 22), and maintained the traditional Church's will to immunize society from the "viruses" of the West, such as "secularism, indifference, hedonistic consumerism, practical materialism and formal atheism," against which the pope, beginning in the spring of 1990, warned countries recently freed from the Soviet yoke.[25]

The alleged coincidence of interests in Latin America—supporting the dictatorships connected to the United States and opposing leftist movements—is the second big misunderstanding that many scholars have succumbed to regarding the relationship between Karol Wojtyła and Ronald Reagan. Eric Hanson—one of the first scholars to examine the Church and international politics—wrote in 1987 that on Latin America "Vatican policy makers have taken a much more European approach which gives priority to North-South relations." Regarding this region (but also, added Hanson, regarding the Philippines, South Korea, and South Africa), "the policies of the Reagan administration have been more difficult to harmonize with national and international Catholic interests than those of the preceding administration."[26]

Throughout history the relations between Rome and Washington concerning Latin America have been confrontational: every advance of the Protestant US influence has always coincided with a decline of Catholic Latin powers (Spain, France, and Portugal). After the end of the European wars of religion, America became the chief terrain of global confrontation between waxing Protestantism and waning Catholicism. Still in 2004, Cardinal Joseph Ratzinger complained that "the United States is giving a lot of support to the Protestantization of Latin America and thus promoting the breakup of the Catholic Church by means of free church structures" expecting to produce "a moral consensus and a democratic formation of public will similar to those found in the United States."[27]

The eradication of liberation theology, carried out by John Paul II and by Ratzinger himself, was not a "favor" to Washington but one step toward the restoration of unity and coherence of purpose in a Latin American Church still disoriented by the postconciliar crisis. After all, this authoritarian intervention was not limited to liberation theology, since—as affirmed by Paul Freston and Sandro Magister, among others—this tendency represented an essentially intellectual and elitist phenomenon of European import and had little impact on the local religious and social reality.[28] The intervention of the pope and his minister of faith should be interpreted as consistent with the recognition of the "legitimate role of profit," ratified in *Centesimus annus*:[29] the distinction was not between "right" and "left" but between those who hindered economic development and those who facilitated it.

In the early 1980s José Casanova wrote that, if in Latin America the experimental model of Opus Dei in Spain had prevailed, Catholicism could have helped "to modernize Latin American societies in a technocratic-capitalist direction"; in order to succeed, "traditional Catholic anti-capitalist resistance," represented mainly by the Jesuits, would have to have been crushed.[30] This interpretation provides a better understanding of why Karol Wojtyła put Opus Dei under his personal protection while the Society of Jesus was put under temporary receivership.

Of course, the Church did not spare support to many military dictatorships responsive to the will of the United States,[31] but it later engaged in facilitating the transition of many of those regimes to democracy. That is, in reality it supported the emancipation of the American subcontinent from "Monroe Doctrine" logic, opening it up to other economic and political influences, primarily to that of the European Union. Thus, in this sense one can say that in the medium term Rome's intervention in "disciplining" the Latin American Church has contributed to the weakening of the United States in the region rather than strengthening it.

The "dress rehearsal" of the policy of democratic transition took place in the Philippines, a country geopolitically similar to Latin America. "The juxtaposition of the 1981 visits of John Paul and [Vice President] George Bush," writes Hanson, who is quoted above, "demonstrates that period's divergence of policy between the United States and the Vatican." On these visits the pope challenged the dictator Ferdinand Marcos "to improve his treatment of the people," while Bush let loose paeans to Marcos and to his "adherence to democratic principles and democratic processes."[32] In 1986 the two most important figures of the Filipino episcopate, the archbishop of Manila, Jaime Sin, and the president of the Bishops' Conference, Ricardo Vidal, called for mass mobilization through Radyo Veritas, the broadcasting station of the archbishopric, in order to force Marcos to resign. According to the former president of the University of the Philippines, Francisco Nemenzo, "without Radio Veritas [sic], it would have been difficult, if not impossible, to mobilize millions of people in a matter of hours."[33]

In the 1980s different objectives of the Church and of the United States were evident in other regions of the world as well. In the Middle East, says Hanson, Reagan brought the United States "more in line with the Vatican's orientation toward the moderate Arabs"; however, their main concerns were opposed: for Washington it was Israel's security, for the Vatican the Palestinian issue.[34] Moreover, the political leader with whom John Paul II met most often (twelve times) was Yasser Arafat: when the first face-to-face took place in 1982, the Organization for the Liberation of Palestine was still officially considered a terrorist group by the United States; and many other meetings had to follow before the PLO removed Article 12, which called for the "complete liberation of Palestine, and eradication of Zionist economic, political, military and cultural existence" from its charter.

Finally, let us return to what many regard as the litmus test of the alleged "holy alliance" between the Vatican and the United States: the policy toward Moscow and the European countries under its rule. The discussion of this matter, more than between Rome and the White House, took place within the Vatican walls, between John Paul II's faction and that of his secretary of state, Agostino Casaroli. The common goal—from the beginning of the so-called Vatican Ostpolitik, initiated by John XXIII and personified by Casaroli himself—was to relieve the episcopate of these countries of the political constraints imposed by Moscow's vassal regimes. In the 1960s, at a time when the Soviet Union was still strong, Ostpolitik had to go through a series of compromises, often greeted with coldness by the local clergy, who hoped for more determined opposition from the Vatican and sometimes even evoked the idea that "the great war . . . will free us."[35]

During the years of the Ostpolitik, Karol Wojtyła was "on the other side," the side of the local episcopate, which pushed its hostility toward the relations between Casaroli and the Warsaw regime so far as to complain directly to the pope: "The Polish Catholics regard these relations with suspicion," wrote the Primate of Poland Stefan Wyszyński to Paul VI, "fearing that rather than contributing to the consolidation of the Church, they would strengthen the communist regime."[36]

When he became pope, in an era of the Soviet Union's greater fragility, Wojtyła brought to Rome the "Polish way," which became even more confrontational when it collided with the paranoid autism of the Soviet leadership. "Casaroli," says a cardinal who was his assistant at the time, "was furious," especially when John Paul II decided to support (and finance) clandestinely the Solidarność trade union after the Polish military coup of December 1981, using all possible channels, including "the benevolent involvement of American Intelligence."[37] According to Robert Gates, then deputy director of the CIA, "there was a considerable sharing of information about developments in Poland [and] a modicum of coordination" with the Vatican.[38] As Francis Rooney says, "At the very least, the church seems to have put the agency in contact with members of Solidarity. The CIA then channelled funds and equipment to support the group during martial law."[39]

In the 1980s the United States certainly thought of using the Catholic Church for its policies, and vice versa; and, in part, both succeeded. But choosing to reestablish diplomatic relations must be considered from a strategic rather than tactical perspective: it was of course a way in which the two main competitors for the moral leadership of the world could work together better, but it was also a way to keep an eye on and hinder each other if necessary. And obviously it was a way to continue to take advantage of each other's strength in the uncertain future of international relations as well.

MOSCOW, BAGHDAD, ZAGREB, AND CAIRO

When Ronald Reagan decided to establish diplomatic relations with the Holy See, American antipapists fired their last shots. The opposition came from a multitude of religious and secular groups headed, as usual, by Protestants and evangelicals. On the front line were the National Council of Churches, "encompassing 40 million Protestants and Eastern Orthodox Christians"; the National Association of Evangelicals, "consisting of 38,000 conservative churches"; the Baptist Joint Committee on Public Affairs, "a coalition of nine Baptist groups with a combined membership of 26 million"; and the Seventh-day Adventists, "who number 3.7 million worldwide."[40] In short, according to these calculations by Kenneth

Briggs, representative organizations of dozens of millions of Protestants were mobilized—at least on paper—to which we need to add the members of the American Jewish Congress and secular militants of the Americans United for Separation of Church and State, two more organizations opposing the formalization of relations with the Holy See.

Even the official response of the American Catholic Church was marked, writes Briggs, with a "relative lack of enthusiasm." While the statement from the Bishops' Conference "guardedly welcomed the action," the director of the Jesuit magazine *America*, Joseph O'Hare, raised the first suspicion that Reagan's decision was a response to the "strong antinuclear pastoral letter" of the bishops in the spring of 1983 "that clashed with aspects of Administration defense policy." But O'Hare also clarified the deeper reasons for the bishops' lack of enthusiasm: "To upgrade the presence of the Vatican could conceivably inhibit the further development of the national identity of US bishops."[41] Let us not forget that the first function of a papal nuncio is to "Romanize" the bishops in the country where he is sent, which means precisely to prevent their sense of national identity from prevailing over their sense of Catholic identity. As we have already seen from the examples of Ireland and Poland, the stronger the local bishops are and the more strongly they are linked to national identity, the more hostile they are to the idea of having to deal with a nuncio sent from Rome to discipline them.

But the reluctance of bishops, the not-so-veiled opposition of Jesuits, the more explicit and resolute opposition of evangelicals, liberal Jews, and the groups advocating secularism were not sufficient to make Ronald Reagan back down. Those groups went so far as to denounce the president for violating the First Amendment, appealing to all court levels up to the Supreme Court. The latter, however, rejected the final appeal in 1986, stating that the opening of diplomatic relations is "one of the rare governmental decisions that the Constitution commits exclusively to the Executive Branch,"[42] and as such it cannot be modified by the Court.

From diplomatic relations with the Vatican, the United States could reap the immediate benefits, not only concerning its competition with the "evil empire" but also, as we have seen, concerning the issues on which their positions diverged more clearly and about which Washington preferred to deal directly with the interlocutor of last resort. But there were two medium- and long-term benefits as well. The first had already been identified by the State Department in 1950: "securing the influence of the Holy See on 300,000,000 Catholics throughout the world in support of our objectives, and, to some extent, on the thirty-eight governments who now maintain diplomatic relations with the Holy See";[43] since then, the number of Catholics in the world had reached about eight hundred million, and in 1983 the states with diplomatic relations with the Holy See numbered 107 (table 5).

The second benefit was pertinent to the series of countermeasures that the Reagan administration was preparing to slow down the relative decline of the United States: as during the Vietnam War, weakening its nominal rival (the Soviet Union) also meant sending a clear and strong message to its actual rivals (Japan and Europe). After the end of the 1970s, both of the latter assumed autonomous positions that were increasingly disturbing for Washington,[44] and they even invaded—with their assets—what was traditionally considered the US backyard, Latin America. In this sense the agreement with the Vatican can also be interpreted as a diplomatic corollary of the opening to Catholicism on the domestic front, with the aim of helping to restore the country's moral cohesion.

This cohesion was restored thanks to renewed economic dynamism and, of course, the rapid decomposition of the Soviet Union. Although the Reagan administration's goal in terms of the arms race and the war in

TABLE 5. *Evolution of the number of countries with which the Holy See maintains diplomatic relations*

Year	1860	1870	1880	1890	1900	1910	1920	1930	1940
Number of countries	8	8	16	19	20	23	24	30	33

Year	1950	1960	1970	1980	1983	1990	2000	2015
Number of countries	38	46	66	97	107	118	173	181

SOURCE: La Santa Sede (The Holy See), www.vatican.va.
NOTE: In the case of interrupted and subsequently resumed relations, the number refers to the resumption only. The figure for 2015 refers to 180 states plus the Organization for the Liberation of Palestine.

Afghanistan was not to cause the disappearance of the Soviet Union, the "end of communism" was retrospectively propagated as *the* great historic success of the United States, which consequently became the so-called only superpower, guarantor of the final victory of capitalism and democracy and even of the "end of History."[45]

The collapse of the bipolar order—the confrontational coleadership of the United States and the Soviet Union at the head of the world—opened the phase of "new international disorder" that is still under way. George H. W. Bush immediately tried to build a "new world order" in 1991, taking advantage of Iraq's invasion of Kuwait. It was precisely this conflict that showed to the entire world that the United States and the Vatican continued to have different, and in some cases conflicting, interests and goals.

The first sign had come a year earlier from a region with deeply rooted antagonisms: Latin America. In December of 1989 the United States invaded Panama to get rid of the former US ally Manuel Noriega, Panama's military dictator. When Noriega took refuge in the apostolic nunciature of the capital, the Vatican spokesman excluded the possibility of giving in on the front of an "occupying power." Noriega was handed over to the US military within only ten days of the nunciature siege and the attacks against the Vatican.[46]

The following year the United States put together a coalition of thirty-two countries for the "liberation" of Kuwait. All the countries of the European Community were part of it, as well as some of the (now former) Soviet bloc countries (Poland, Czechoslovakia, and Hungary), and most of the Arab countries, while the Soviet Union—on the verge of collapse—was unable to defend its traditional ally Iraq. Despite this huge coalition (probably the largest ever built in the history of wars), the Vatican strongly opposed the intervention. It activated its experienced diplomatic machinery, and it called into question "just war" theology to attack Washington's and these European capitals' viewpoint. And, above all, it launched a broad mobilization—reinforced by extremely popular slogans ("war is an adventure without return")—which found its mass base not only in Catholic movements but also in pacifists and in those with anti-American sentiments around the world. When the war broke out, writes David Willey, the pope made "no fewer than fifty-five separate calls on the combatants to end the fighting."[47]

The war was not avoided, of course, but this need not mean that all this mobilization did not have any effect. In fact, in 1991, and then again in 2003, the Catholic Church established itself as the main opposition of the United States, at a time when the Soviet Union no longer held that role, and when neither China nor the European countries could yet lay a claim to it. Nevertheless, it would be equally wrong to say that the goal was to make the Church the main antagonist of the United States. The goal was—and will always be—to defend "Catholic interests" in all circumstances, and in the Middle East the Vatican's guiding light was—and always will be—the defense of Christian minorities.

Two years after the Gulf War, the Vatican found itself on the same wavelength as the Bill Clinton administration concerning the war in the former Yugoslavia. The new American president tried to create obstacles for the newborn European Union by adopting a policy of substantial support for Croatia and Bosnia against Serbia. This policy was certainly not unpleasant for the Vatican; on the occasion of the crisis it overturned the concept of the "just war" suggested only two years earlier and replaced it with insistent evocations of active and armed "humanitarian intervention." From the very beginning of the conflict, the newspaper of the Italian bishops reprimanded Europe because it "replied to tanks with press releases," and it took a stand against "Orthodox Serbia and Muslim Bosnia," guilty of the will to "destroy the churches and memories of Catholic Croatia."[48]

The identity of views of the Yugoslav crisis did not prevent an abrupt chill in relations with the Clinton administration on the occasion of the Population Conference of the United Nations in 1994. Against the US proposal to include in the final document "access to a safe, legal and voluntary abortion [as] a fundamental right of all women," the Vatican formed an alliance with some Asian, African, and Latin American countries that permitted it to pass a resolution according to which "in no case should abortion be promoted as a method of family planning." Because of its condescending attitude, the Clinton administration failed to grasp the Church's ability to mobilize and unite forces of different origin and nature around some key themes, born of its desire to bring religions back to the center of public life.

Bill Clinton was president in a phase of expansion and renewed optimism, not only because the United States was cashing economic and political dividends of the Reagan era but also because the Japanese production machine, the main threat to the United States at the time, seemed to have gotten clogged up. No matter how efficient he was at speaking the "spiritual-political dialect" and at securing the Catholic vote (47 percent in 1992 and 54 percent in 1996), Clinton did not seem very interested in including Catholics significantly in public life or in finding in the Catholic Church support for his international policies. His successive governments included eight Catholic officials out of twenty-nine[49] (just over a quarter), just a few more than Jewish officials (five). The two judges he appointed to the Supreme Court (Ruth Bader Ginsburg and Stephen Breyer) were both Jewish.

After Bill Clinton, however, the carefree years came to a close.

A "LATENT CATHOLIC" AGAINST THE CHURCH

George W. Bush's close relationship with Catholicism revealed itself long before the 2000 election and the series of troubles the United States went through at the beginning of the new century.

According to Franklin Foer, Bush was chosen as a presidential candidate for his familiarity with concepts of Catholic origins, such as the principle of subsidiarity or compassionate conservatism.[50] At the origin of this inspiration, according to Foer, lie the works by Conservative Catholics Michael Novak and Richard John Neuhaus. The latter, a Catholic priest and former Lutheran pastor, was among Bush's mentors on the subject of social doctrine of the Church, along with John DiIulio, a political scientist and former president of the first Office of Faith-Based Initiative established in the White House in January 2001, and Deal Hudson, director of Republican Catholic Outreach in the two election campaigns of 2000 and 2004.[51]

Patricia Miller recalls that before the elections Bush met with no fewer than a dozen bishops, obtaining, among other things, the endorsement of the archbishop of New York, Edward Egan.[52] Numerous meetings continued after he was elected to office; one of his advisers, Robert George, writes that "in 1960, John Kennedy went from Washington down to Texas to assure Protestant preachers that he would not obey the pope. In 2001, George Bush came from Texas up to Washington to assure a group of Catholic bishops that he would."[53]

From the beginning of his term, the president of the Catholic League, Bill Donohue, said, "There is enough reason already to wonder whether President Bush is our second Catholic president." But he acknowledged a significant difference: "Bush is focused on matters Catholic in a way that John F. Kennedy never was."[54] During his presidency, as Daniel Burke pointed out, "some have begun to call the Bush White House the first truly Catholic presidency."[55] Among those doing so were Rick Santorum ("He's the first Catholic president of the United States, certainly much more Catholic than Kennedy");[56] Michael Gerson, the president's top speechwriter ("the key to understanding Bush's domestic policy is to see it through the lens of Rome"); John DiIulio (Bush is a "closet Catholic");[57] and Paul Weyrich, one of the founders of the "religious right" (according to whom Bush was "a secret believer").[58]

But beyond what his Catholic hagiographers think, what matters was that, according to Daniel Burke, Bush had "surrounded himself with Roman Catholic intellectuals, speechwriters, professors, priests, bishops and politicians."[59] In 2001 Patricia Miller had already mentioned that "conservative Catholics are playing a crucial role in the inner circle of the Bush administration, both formally and informally."[60] She quoted the cases of Bill Bennett, former secretary of education under Reagan; John Klink, former member of the Vatican delegation at the 1994 Cairo Conference; John Negroponte, appointed as a UN ambassador and later the ambassador in Iraq; John DiIulio; Michael Place, president of the Catholic Health Association; and Scott Evertz, openly gay, appointed as director of the White House Office of National AIDS Policy.

Two of the presidential acts of Bush Jr. are unprecedented in US history: the appointment of exclusively Catholic justices to the Supreme Court (George Roberts and Samuel Alito), and the number of meetings with popes (six in eight years). Still, Catholic members of his cabinets were relatively few (eight out of forty-six),[61] much fewer than in previous administrations and especially in the next administration of Barack Obama.

But what made some observers talk of "America's first truly Catholic presidency" more than his appointments were some of his decisions: the 2004 law defining a fetus as "a member of the species Homo sapiens, at any stage of development;"[62] the cutoff of funding to the United Nations

Population Fund, accused of supporting the policies of birth control, especially in China; the law on stem-cell research vetoed twice; the (failed) attempt to prevent selling drugs for assisted suicide, legal in some states (Oregon, Vermont, New Mexico, Montana, and Washington); and finally, the law preventing the removal of a feeding tube of a patient, Terri Schiavo, who had been in a vegetative state for fifteen years.

Simply put, the "Catholicism" of George W. Bush was much more qualitative than quantitative: "No President since Ronald Reagan," writes Rooney, "had so truly appreciated, nor been so aligned with, the values of the Holy See as President Bush."[63] But Rooney himself nuances his statement: "What upsets this idyll is the most important decision of Bush's double presidency, one which will go down in history: the Gulf War of 2003." Rooney himself admits that "the war in Iraq struck some chords of disharmony."[64] It is well known that diplomacy lives on euphemisms, but the witnesses of the time and many researchers of these events are generally inclined to believe that it was not a matter of just some chords and that it was something more than simple "disharmony."

After September 11 the pope assured the US ambassador Jim Nicholson that the United States was "justified in taking defensive action." In that meeting, says Nicholson, "the foundations were laid for the support of the Holy See for our campaign against terrorism."[65] But soon, in ecclesiastical circles, the fear arose that the green light given to attack a country where there are no Christians (Afghanistan) could be exploited for military action in Iraq, where Christians (mostly Catholic) were still numerous. This stance was almost immediately taken up by forty Italian moral theologians and published in *Avvenire*,[66] the Italian bishops' newspaper; it was followed by the critical statement of the movement Pax Christi,[67] then by the criticism of the president of the Pontifical Council for Christian Unity, Walter Kasper; of the German Bishops' Conference president, Karl Lehmann; of the US Conference of Catholic Bishops director, Joseph Fiorenza; and of French bishops. Finally, in the same November 2001 edition a letter from twenty-three Latin American bishops (mostly Brazilian) was published, denouncing the bombing of Afghanistan as "another form of terrorism practiced by governments that claim to be democratic, civil and Christian."[68]

In 2002 the US government's decision to attack Iraq was already irrevocably taken;[69] when the Church went on the counterattack, its leaders were well aware that the war would take place anyway. In February 2003 the number two of the Iraqi regime, the Catholic Tariq Aziz, headed to Rome, while Cardinal Roger Etchegaray, president of the Pontifical Councils for Justice and Peace and for Cor Unum, was sent to Baghdad, and the former nuncio Pio Laghi, a personal friend of the Bushes, to Washington. The Vatican "foreign minister," Jean-Louis Tauran, called the imminent, unilateral American attack "a war of aggression and thus a crime against peace."[70] In early March the pope announced fasting "for peace, which is put at risk by the growing threat of war."[71]

The American bishops kept a low profile on that occasion. But this attitude cannot be explained only by the "patriotic imperative" the US Church took starting from the war against Britain in 1812 but abandoned after the Vietnam War. The fact is, as some affirm, that the bishops were stymied by the eruption of the pedophilia scandal in January 2002, with a series of articles (more than 250 in four months) published in the *Boston Globe*. The charges concerned abuses that began in the 1950s: according to a survey commissioned by the American Church itself, from 1950 to 2002, 4,392 priests (4 percent of the total) were involved in 10,667 cases.[72] Already "by the end of the mid 1990s, it was estimated that six hundred priests had been named in abuse cases and more than half a billion dollars had been paid in jury awards, settlements and legal fees."[73] But the scandal broke out in full force only in 2002, at the time when the Church was going from supporting the war in Afghanistan to opposing a possible and increasingly likely war in Iraq.

Certain Catholic circles claim that the archbishop of Boston, Bernard Law, was chosen as the main scapegoat not so much for remaining silent for a long time about the abuses of which he knew but for some "political sins," specifically for opposing the sanctions against Cuba and supporting the Palestinian cause.

At any rate, the determination of the universal Catholic Church on the issue of Iraq did not slacken. When the war began, the Vatican refused to withdraw its nuncio in Baghdad, Fernando Filoni, despite the bombings, and continued to press for UN involvement. "For months after the first shots were fired," says Massimo Franco, "relations between Rome and Washington seemed to be in limbo."[74] When in January 2004, Vice President Dick Cheney met with the pope, *L'Osservatore romano*, the unofficial newspaper of the Holy See, which is usually very verbose about diplomatic issues, relegated the few lines dedicated to the event to the fifth page—without a photo. And when Bush declared his intention to visit John Paul II in June 2004, the first response of the Vatican was that the pope's schedule was already full (the president had to move up his arrival in Rome to get around this obstacle, the exact opposite of what Kennedy did in July 1963).

It took a while before a new consonance between the two sides saw the light: once Saddam was ousted, the Vatican began to demand that American troops remain in Iraq. The US intervention predictably unleashed a civil war between Shiites and Sunnis, with Christians caught in the middle: the United States, having caused the damage, had a moral, political, and military obligation to defend them. The Vatican, however, lost this game as well: Americans did remain, but the number of Christians in Iraq—about 1.5 million at the end of the 1980s—dropped to a million after the 1991 war, and declined further to 450,000, or, according to other sources, even to 200,000, after the war of 2003.[75] Like many other times in history, a United States offensive coincided with a Catholic Church retreat.

BARACK H. OBAMA:
THE PRESIDENT OF THE CRISIS

In that atmosphere of coldness and mutual resentment the Church might have been expected to take advantage of the 2004 election to "punish" George W. Bush. Instead, the Catholic hierarchy did everything it could to prevent the election of the Catholic John Kerry.

The proposal of about a dozen bishops (including the archbishop of Boston—Kerry's city—Sean O'Malley) to deny the sacrament to pro-choice politicians was supported in June 2004 by Joseph Ratzinger's official note.[76] A memorandum of the US Conference of Catholic Bishops of June 21, 2004, called "Catholics in Political Life," while renouncing the idea of making the denial compulsory, was entirely dedicated to "unequivocal commitment to the legal protection of human life from the moment of conception until natural death," without a single mention of the war in Iraq. The memorandum was obviously addressed to those faithful possibly tempted to vote for Kerry: Catholics "need to act in support of these principles and policies in public life . . . [and] should *not honor* those who act in defiance of our fundamental moral principles."[77]

In actuality, Bush was presented to American voters as the Church's candidate. At the time, many observers interpreted this preference as choosing "the less flawed of the two flawed alternatives," to use Massimo Franco's phrase,[78] an inevitable consequence of Kerry's well-known liberal positions on abortion and stem-cell research. But there is a missing element in this explanation: Barack Obama supported similar positions on so-called nonnegotiable principles of the Church, yet the hierarchies were careful not to launch at him the same virulent campaign of ostracism they had directed against Kerry. The reason for this different treatment can be understood by rereading the words of a "Vatican official, who is an American," questioned by *Time* in April 2004: "People in Rome are becoming more and more aware that there's a problem with John Kerry, and a potential scandal with his apparent profession of his Catholic faith and some of his stances, particularly [on] abortion."[79] What the Church does not want, in a nutshell, is a Catholic president who disagrees with its views; and since a president of the United States sooner or later will surely be in disagreement with the Church's positions, what the Church ultimately does not want is a Catholic president of the United States.

The 2004 elections, when almost half of the Catholic electorate voted for Kerry despite the hierarchy's instructions, relaunched the old issue of the "Catholic vote." Of the three Catholic candidates in the history of the United States, Al Smith seems to have collected almost all the votes of his coreligionists, John Kennedy about 80 percent, and John Kerry less than 50 percent. To sum up, Catholic voters became, as time passed, "more mature," less sensitive to sermons preached from the pulpit. In fact, as some affirm, considering that since 1972 Catholics have acted more or less the same way as the whole of the electorate, *including* the election of 2000,[80] the "Catholic vote" simply does not exist.[81] Others depart from similar observations—"Catholics are the bellwether voters: as go Catholics, so goes the nation"—but draw the opposite conclusion: "the contemporary

Catholic vote is now the most important swing vote in American politics,"[82] which implies an even more pressing need to intercept its fluctuations.

In fact, both parties set up their specific teams. The famous one was the "Jesus machine" created by Karl Rove in 1998 with the goal of forging a grand alliance between evangelicals and conservative Catholics in favor of George W. Bush.[83] It was flanked by a Catholic Affairs Office of the Republican National Committee directed by Deal Hudson. Democrats, on their side, after the defeat in 2004, set up their Catholic outreach (a contact group specifically for Catholics); during these elections, a vague "outreach to believers" had been improvised only six months before the vote, directed by a young woman who had not even turned thirty and, according to Dan Gilgoff, was assisted by "an unpaid intern" (while the Republican staff could count on a committee in each State, a database of thousands of churches, and "tens of thousands of evangelical volunteers").[84]

Yet Kerry's defeat—in addition to the Church's censure, Democrats' persistent failure to grasp the political weight of religion, and organizationally botched improvisation—should be attributed to yet another cause: "Americans seeking firm moral answers," writes Franco, "wanted a president with a strong religious faith." Kerry, however, in his campaign, kept an "admirable . . . silence in matters of religion," a silence, adds Franco, that was also "outdated."[85] In an article published in October 2004, even the secular *New York Times* warned: "Polls suggest that Mr Kerry may be paying a price for his privacy."[86]

It would be absurd to affirm that Barack Obama managed to impose himself in 2008 thanks only to the fluency of his "God talk" or to the clear desire to refute the image of a secular Democratic Party, leaving the Republicans a monopoly on faith. Other factors contributed to Obama's victory; these have been variously analyzed, including that (of not least importance) of the $745 million raised during the campaign, more than double the $368 million raised by his rival, John McCain.[87] The main factor, however, was the sudden acceleration, in September 2008, of what Ben Bernanke, then the chairman of the Fed, called the "worst financial crisis in global history, including the Great Depression."[88]

Obama, in a certain sense, is a product of that crisis. The "American Century" had closed on the triumphant note (slightly boastful) of the "sole superpower," but the beginning of the new century turned this enthusiasm to doubt, fear, and bewilderment. After the dot-com bubble burst in early 2000, there came the 9/11 attacks, the disastrous outcome of the Gulf War of 2003, and finally, the global crisis of 2008. In 2008 the United States was in the same situation of a "crisis of confidence" described by Carter in 1979 but with more than thirty years in relative loss of heft. In 1980 American industrial production accounted for 31.5 percent of the world's total; in 2009 that percentage was only 17.6 percent. The document of the National Intelligence Council mentioning the reduction of US margins of maneuver "owing to the relative decline of its economic, and to a lesser extent, military power," was published on the eve of the 2008 election.

Obama also won because he knew how to simultaneously embody the need for the downsizing of the United States and the will to undertake a fresh start marked by traditional American voluntarist optimism, the "audacity of hope." In his version the impossibility of continuing to act as an arrogant and untouchable power was turned into a free and voluntary choice to transform the United States into a "benign" force, more influential because of its soft power than its hard power.

Such a considerable step forward required a substantial dose of that "supplement of soul" Henri Bergson once spoke of, that religious rescue that Ronald Reagan had already availed himself of thirty years earlier. After all, it is no coincidence that Douglas Kmiec—a Catholic "Reagan Democrat" in 1980 and later a collaborator of Mitt Romney—wrote an article for *Slate* in February 2008 entitled "Reaganites for Obama?" in which he explained: "An audaciously hope-filled Democrat like Obama is a Catholic natural."[89]

As early as June 2006, Obama did not hesitate to attack Kennedy's thesis of an absolute separation of church and state, affirming that "secularists are wrong when they ask believers to leave their religion at the door before entering into the public square."[90] Obviously he was addressing not only Catholics. On the contrary, the religious experience, as he added on the same occasion, "has been shared by millions upon millions of Americans—evangelicals, Catholics, Protestants, Jews and Muslims alike." But in that religious galaxy Catholics represent a world apart because of their number, long experience, and unity but also because of their social services. All religious groups provide services, but what Catholics offer is by far superior: the Catholic Church is the second-largest supplier of social services in the country after the federal government, something even more valuable in times of excessive debt and budgetary constraints.

It is no coincidence that, welcoming Pope Francis at the White House, Obama opened his speech acknowledging the debt: "All Americans, from every background and of every faith, value the role that the Catholic Church plays in strengthening America. . . . I've seen first-hand how, every day, Catholic communities, priests, nuns, and laity feed the hungry, heal the sick, shelter the homeless, educate our children. . . . Catholic organizations serve the poor, minister to prisoners, build schools and homes, and operate orphanages and hospitals."[91]

During his two terms in office, Obama was not always on good terms with the Catholic Church. In particular, during the health care reform he was accused of trying to impose on Catholic institutions the obligation to provide birth control services for their employees.[92] Nevertheless, he filled key political, judicial, and military positions of the country with Catholics. Dario Fabbri noted that out of thirteen people pictured in the photograph of the National Security officials present during the live coverage of Osama bin Laden's killing on May 1, 2011, "nine are Catholic or received Jesuit education."[93]

Under the Obama administration Catholics included Vice President Joe Biden; more than a third (twelve out of thirty-two) of the ministers who alternated in the government; two of the four White House chiefs of staff, Bill Daley and Denis R. McDonough; the Speaker of the House of Representatives from 2008 to 2012, Nancy Pelosi (replaced in 2013 by the Catholic John Boehner, replaced in 2015 by the Catholic Paul Ryan), who later became the Democratic leader of the House; the three directors of the CIA (Leon Panetta, John Brennan, and David Petraeus); FBI director James Comey and three of the four vice directors; Chairman of the Joint Chiefs of Staff Martin Dempsey; both chiefs of staff of the army, Dempsey, already mentioned, and Raymond Odierno; the commandant of the Marine Corps, Joseph Dunford; the chief of staff of the US Air Force, Mark Welsh; Chief of Naval Operations Jonathan Greenert (that is, five of the seven members of the joint chiefs of staff); and, finally, the former national security adviser Thomas Donilon (2010–13). Last but not least, the first judge Obama appointed to the Supreme Court was the Catholic Sonia Sotomayor, an appointment that (after Elena Kagan's appointment in 2010) led to a completely new configuration of the Court, on which until February 2016, were sitting six Catholics and three Jews.

Numerous explanations can be given to account for the fact that out of the thirteen Catholic justices throughout American history, six were sitting together in the first Supreme Court without a single representative of white Anglo-Saxon Protestantism.[94] Equally numerous explanations can be given to account for the plethora of Catholics appointed by Barack Obama to positions of highest responsibility. But what stands out in the history of the last thirty years is that the relative decline of the United States has been constantly accompanied by a relative rise of Catholics in the political life of the country, in a movement that is curiously complementary to the relative rise of Americans in the life of the universal Catholic Church.

CHAPTER 7

The Americanization of the Catholic Church

In America We Trust

THE INFLUENCE OF THE AMERICAN Catholic Church on the universal Catholic Church dates to the late nineteenth century. It was back then that American prelates brought to Rome the solicitations of Catholic labor unions, thus providing Leo XIII with a practical example of the benefits of the social doctrine of the Church founded on the principle of subsidiarity. "American gold" constituted the next stage in what was to be a five-stage process: between the late nineteenth century and early twentieth, Catholics from across the Atlantic Ocean supplanted the French and German faithful as the main financiers of the Church. The third stage was the American bishops' condemnation, as early as 1942, of the massacre of Jews. While Rome kept an opaque silence on the issue, the message of the American bishops suggested that, after such a tragedy, the two-millennia-old condemnation of the "deicidal people" was no longer sustainable. The fourth stage was the increasingly massive participation of the faithful in parish-life activities, which was acknowledged by the Second Vatican Council with the phrase "people of God."

It is precisely that Council that, to a certain extent, made American influence official, albeit while taking a great many precautions and, amid some open resistance, adopting the principles of freedom of conscience and religious freedom—that is, the principles of the "free market of faith."

Free competition between different confessions to gain the favors—and offerings—of the faithful developed the entrepreneurial mind-set that is quite commonly regarded as the main cause of American religious vitality. In the American free market of faith, Catholics found themselves favored because they were backed by the most experienced institution in the world and because their Church had been founded by Irish and German immigrants who came from frontier conditions in which Catholicism was engaged in a constant struggle for survival.

The acceptance of the principle of freedom of conscience was unavoidable because religious pluralism was no longer an option but a reality. And this happened not only in the countries where Catholics' relative weight was eroding in favor of other religions but also in traditionally Catholic countries, where the disaffection of many of the faithful as a result of secularization was supplemented by the growing presence of immigrants raised in different religious traditions. The "American model" broke a deadlock, and it did so with reasonable expectations of success, not only because it proved empirically effective but also because free competition would, in the long run, necessarily reward those competitors who were better equipped.

The last stage—chronologically speaking—of the Church's "Americanization" was the election of the first American pope. The bishop of Rome who hailed "almost from the end of the world," as he himself remarked on the evening of his appointment, Jorge Mario Bergoglio brought from Buenos Aires the theory—and especially the practice—of a Church that "goes forth," "in a permanent state of mission," that de facto rejects the Eurocentric pillar and its advantageous monopolizing position without, however, renouncing centralization, which is to say, without renouncing the very existence of the Catholic Church.

The Church of Pope Francis is thus much more a North American than a South American church, because in the United States—not only by virtue of the First Amendment but also by virtue of a traditional anti-Catholic hostility—the Church has always been disconnected from state institutions and forced to "go forth," whereas in Latin America, and particularly in South America, it has long walked hand in hand with political power. And often, that power assumed the macabre facet of military dictatorships.

As Charles Morris observes in *American Catholic*, the United States Catholic Church "is arguably still the most successful national Catholic Church in the world."[1] This is why, in the eyes of the Catholic hierarchy, its example deserves to be followed and universalized.

A CHURCH IN CRISIS?

In Morris's statement the adverb *still* betrays a certain pessimism about the Church's future. It is a pessimism that he shares with the declinist tendency, very popular among Catholics, according to which the American Church is in crisis. There are supporting data for this assumption: a sharp decline in the number of priests, nuns, and seminarians; a decrease in the number of Catholic schools and students; a drop in attendance at religious services; and a reduction in the number of baptisms and religious marriages. Moreover, according to some surveys, only about 70 percent of the baptized consider themselves Catholics, and a good number of them, following the "American way of life," represent the quintessence of "cafeteria Catholicism" or "DIY Catholicism," against which the Church has spent a lot of energy during the past forty years.[2]

Table 6 shows a summary by decades (1965–2014) of the quantitative presence of the Catholic Church in the United States with regard to its cadres, major ceremonies and sacraments, and some social services.

If we look at the data, the decline seems indisputable. In reality, though, a more discerning evaluation is in order. Here are some reasons why: (1) the

TABLE 6. *Cadres of the American Church, religious life, and Catholic social services in the United States, 1965–2014*

	1965	1975	1985	1995	2005	2014
Cadres						
Priests	58,632	58,909	57,317	49,054	41,399	38,275
Ordinations	994	771	533	511	454	494
Graduate seminarians	8,325	5,279	4,063	3,172	3,308	3,631
Permanent deacons	n/a	898	7,204	10,932	14,574	17,464
Religious sisters	179,954	135,225	115,386	90,809	68,634	49,883
Religious life						
Mass attendance (%)[a]	n/a	44	39	31	23	24
Baptisms	1,310,000	894,992	953,323	981,444	929,545	713,302
Marriages	352,458	369,133	348,300	294,144	207,112	154,450
Social services						
Elementary schools	10,667	8,414	7,764	6,964	6,122	5,368
Secondary schools	1,527	1,624	1,425	1,280	1,325	1,200
Colleges/Universities	305	245	243	231	229	225
Hospitals	800	657	631	600	571	549

SOURCE: Center for Applied Research in the Apostolate (CARA), Washington, DC, 2015; and General Social Survey, NORC at the University of Chicago.
[a] Percentage of Catholics attending Mass regularly on a weekly basis (General Social Survey, NORC at the University of Chicago).

figures alone are not enough to account for any social reality, even less so for a reality as complex as the Catholic Church; (2) raw data are not always significant, especially when it comes to the influence of the Church on society and political life; (3) at times, comparisons with the past are likely to be misleading; and (4) raw data sometimes hide a more complex reality that invalidates their alleged "irrefutable" meaning.

As a general rule, we should bear in mind what Joseph Ratzinger wrote in 1997: "Statistics is not one of God's measurements. . . . After all, we're not a business operation that can look at the numbers to measure whether our policy has been successful and whether we are selling more and more."[3] Obviously, Ratzinger was uttering only a half-truth, because it is hardly true that the Church is not interested in figures. If it were true, the Church wouldn't bother to publish its *Statistical Yearbook*, which takes timely account of even the most minimal quantitative changes in its life. But the meaning of Ratzinger's statement is that the successes (or failures) of the Church should be measured not *only* in terms of quantity but, rather, *primarily* in terms of quality.

Let us cast a glance at the case of the declining number of priests. Two preliminary remarks on this issue are necessary. The first is that the number of priests is significant only when compared to the number of faithful that they must organize; the second is that, in any case, their number is *not* proportional to the political influence of the Church. In India, the country with the highest recruitment rate of priests in the world (in relation to the Catholic population), in 2005 there was one priest for every 854 faithful, while in Italy there is one for every 1,151, but no one would think of affirming that the Catholic Church is more influential in India than in Italy.[4]

To stick to the same statistical basis, in the early twenty-first century there was one priest for every 1,439 faithful in the United States. According to two other facts established by CARA, the proportion in 2014 was 1 to 1,744, or 1 to 2,081, depending on the method used to count Catholics in the United States. And if we take as the basis the number of the baptized, the proportion rises even further, to approximately one priest for every twenty-five hundred laypersons. As we can see, the reliability of these figures is weakened by the multiplicity of statistical bases available and by the ways they can be considered.

In fact, there are at least *three* different methods of evaluating the number of Catholics in the United States. The first is based on the number of the baptized: in the Church's eyes this is the only universally valid means because, according to its internal rules, whoever is baptized remains a Catholic forever.[5] If we take this criterion into account, in 2014 American Catholics amounted to ninety-six million persons, one-third of the country's population. The second method is based on self-declared Catholics, figures taken from the American Religious Identification Survey (ARIS), which is used by the US Census Bureau to determine the religious composition of the population.[6] According to this survey, Catholics amounted to 25 percent of Americans, that is, approximately seventy-six million people in 2008 (whereas CARA estimates the percentage of the self-declared as 24.1 percent of the population in 2014). The third method is that used by the American Church itself, reported by the Official Catholic Directory (OCD), which takes into account only those faithful who have been registered in parishes and attend religious services regularly. According to this evaluation, in 2014 American Catholics amounted to 66.6 million, or 20.8 percent of the population, which leads one researcher at CARA, Mark Gray, to say that "the Church systematically *undercounts* its population."[7]

Table 7 summarizes a rather elusive reality: the number ranges from 66.6 million, estimated by the Official Catholic Directory, to 96 million, estimated on the basis of the baptized—a difference of nearly thirty million people. This can only complicate the task of anyone wanting to assess the health of the American Church by numbers alone.

There is another issue to consider in the recurring question of the decrease in the number of priests—the pertinence of historical comparisons.

TABLE 7. *Number of Catholics in the United States*

	Baptized	Self-Declared		OCD
		ARIS	CARA	
Number (in millions)	96	76	79.7	66.6
% of the population	30	25	24.1	20.8
Year	2014	2008	2014	2014

SOURCES: US Census Bureau; American Religious Identification Survey (ARIS); Center for Applied Research in the Apostolate (CARA), Washington, DC; and Official Catholic Directory (OCD).

It is true that between 1965 and 2014 the number of priests dropped by almost 35 percent. But does it make sense to compare the 2014 figures with those of 1965? In the mid-1960s the shattering effects of the Second Vatican Council were already becoming apparent, which led, among other things, to the exodus of about one hundred thousand priests worldwide between 1970 and 2000, according to Sandro Magister,[8] and probably to an even greater number of nuns. As early as 1966, two American Catholic liberal organizations claimed that "several thousand US Roman Catholic priests and nuns have asked Church officials to 'laicize' them."[9]

But we need to consider another fact that makes the comparison questionable: as another CARA document states, "the number of ordinations in the mid-20th century was extraordinary."[10] According to the data published by Mary L. Gautier, Paul M. Perl, and Stephen J. Fichter, the number of priests in the United States almost doubled (from about seventeen thousand to about thirty thousand) between 1908 and 1938, and then again (from thirty thousand to sixty thousand) between 1938 and 1958.[11] This nearly exponential growth justifies the use of the adjective *extraordinary* and invalidates comparisons with any other more "ordinary" period.

This growth explains the drop in the number of priests much better than any speculation about a crisis of the Church. In fact, as the CARA report goes on to state, "many of the surviving priests ordained in that period are now in their 70s or even older. Replacing them all is a big challenge." The average age rose from thirty-five years old in 1970 to sixty-three in 2009, and this is a problem that only another—though unlikely—"extraordinary" period could resolve. Therefore, the problem is not a presumed crisis of attractiveness of the American Church but the fact that "the number of diocesan priests dying or departing the priesthood annually is larger than the number of new priests ordained."[12]

As we know, new ordinations are preceded by many years of studies in seminary. The number of seminarians has also dropped incontrovertibly since the end of the Second Vatican Council: at that time, in addition to tens of thousands of priests and nuns who decided to leave the Church, many of those who had considered entering it gave up on the idea. With the rapid acceleration of secularization in the 1960s and with the crisis triggered by the Council, the social prestige enjoyed previously by the clergy disappeared almost completely. The decline continued until the 1990s, but "since the mid-1990s the number of seminarians has remained about as stable as the number of new ordinations." To be precise, ordinations had actually already stabilized in the previous decade: "one of the most stable trends in U.S. Church data since the mid-1980s has been the annual numbers of diocesan ordinations."[13]

As far as the recruitment of priests is concerned, one can therefore say that the twentieth century had two distinct and opposing phases: the first—from the beginning of the century through the end of the 1950s—was characterized by an "extraordinary" explosion, when the number of American priests multiplied four times (while the American population grew by "only" half that rate); the second—from the 1960s to the late 1980s—was characterized by a mass exodus of male and female clergy and a sharp depletion of seminaries, the sources of generational turnover. After that, the situation stabilized around generally growing, although slowly, trends. In short, the years from 1986 to 2016 have been essentially characterized by a negative demographic balance, not a crisis.

Furthermore, this phenomenon is intertwined with spectacular growth in the number of permanent deacons, whose recruitment saw a steady increase even in the years when the sexual abuse scandal broke (between 1995 and 2005, the recruitment increased by about 50 percent). In 2014 American permanent deacons made up almost 42 percent of all permanent deacons in the world. Moreover, they represent a socially well-defined model: according to a 2009 CARA survey, deacons belong to the most educated segments of the population (54 percent have a high school diploma or a college degree, 28 percent a master's or a doctoral degree), as well as the most rooted in American history (81 percent are registered as "white, non-Hispanic," much higher than the 69 percent of "white, non-Hispanic" present in the new generation of priests).[14] In the United States the diaconate is no longer a second-best choice, and neither is the decision to take vows. Catholic Church personnel are certainly less numerous today than they were in the "extraordinary" 1950s, but they are definitely more determined, more educated, and more informed (see table 8).

TABLE 8. *Overview of the processes of cadre recruitment in the American Catholic Church, 1985–2014*

	1985	1990	1995	2000	2005	2010	2014
Ordinations	533	595	511	442	454	549	494
Seminarians	4,063	3,658	3,172	3,474	3,308	3,483	3,631
Permanent deacons	7,204	9,356	10,932	12,378	14,574	16,649	17,464

SOURCE: Center for Applied Research in the Apostolate (CARA), Washington, DC, 2015.

A CREATIVE MINORITY

Before and during his pontificate, Joseph Ratzinger insisted on the need to compensate for the undeniable quantitative weakening of the Church through qualitative reinforcement: "Here we must agree with [the British historian Arnold] Toynbee that the fate of a society always depends on its creative minorities. Christian believers should look upon themselves as just such a creative minority."[15]

In economic terms, to produce more with less people means to increase productivity, so we can say that the universal Catholic Church, and the American Catholic Church in particular, has, in recent decades, increased its productivity. I do not mean in economic terms—although the Church is also a big economic actor on the global level—but in terms of social and therefore political influence, beginning precisely with the United States. Sometimes, the effects of this increased productivity can be measured quantitatively and sometimes only indirectly—by inference.

Let us take the example of two services recorded by the above-mentioned CARA survey: universities[16] and hospitals. The number of Catholic universities dropped from 305 in 1965 to 235 at the end of the 1970s and to 225 in 2014; but in 1965 the number of students was 409,471, whereas it was 536,799 in the late 1970s and 787,574 in 2014. There were 800 Catholic hospitals in 1965, 642 in 1980, and 549 in 2014; but they attended to 16.9 million patients in 1965, to 36.5 million in 1980, and to 88.8 million in 2014. In these two cases, increased productivity of provided services and increased reliability went hand in hand, resulting in the fact that the number of people turning to these social and cultural Catholic structures is significantly higher today than it was in 1965 (see table 9).

There are cases of elementary and secondary schools in which the decrease in the number of facilities actually implies a decrease in their users. This is a phenomenon that, as we have seen, had already begun to manifest itself after the war, following the move of many Catholic families toward suburban environs and the progressive abandonment of ethnic and religious self-segregation. Yet the interesting thing is that the higher up we move in those levels of education crucial for a future career, the more we observe a certain stability in the number of students (the number of Catholic high school students has not changed significantly from the beginning of the 1990s) or, as is the case with universities, a steady increase.

What's more, the importance of universities cannot be measured only quantitatively. Catholic universities mold the Catholic political leadership that is imposing itself in some key positions in the country. According to Dario Fabbri, "The universities that make up the so-called Catholic Ivy League—Notre Dame, Georgetown, Boston College, Fordham, Villanova, Holy Cross—are among the most prestigious in the United States."[17] And it is the Catholic universities that mold part of American political leadership, which is not always and not necessarily Catholic.

This is nothing new. As early as 1960, the Italian liberal journalist and politician Ernesto Rossi recalled that approximately ten years earlier (c. 1950), the historian Gaetano Salvemini had spoken to him about the only American university offering a course for diplomats at that time, Georgetown University's School of Foreign Service. "American Protestants," commented Salvemini, "have their heart in the right place and their head

TABLE 9. *Evolution of the number of services (hospitals and universities) and users, 1965–2015*

	1965	1975	1985	1995	2005	2015
Hospitals	800	657	631	600	571	549
Patients	16.9m	29.9m	36.6m	56.4m	84.7m	88.8m
Ratio	1:21,125	1:45,510	1:58,003	1:94,000	1:148,336	1:161,749
Colleges/ Universities	305	245	243	231	229	225
Students	409,471	432,597	545,461	653,927	752,718	787,574
Ratio	1:1,343	1:1,766	1:2,245	1:2,831	1:3,287	1:3,500

SOURCE: Center for Applied Research in the Apostolate (CARA), Washington, DC, 2015.

nowhere: they do not even realize the importance of the fact that half of their diplomatic staff has passed through a school run by the Jesuits."[18] Today, seventy-five years later, they still do not seem to realize it.

Yet, in addition to a number of politicians from all over the world,[19] this school has been attended by hundreds of ambassadors (and not only Americans), judges, MPs, and ministers but also by prominent non-Catholic policy makers such as Bill Clinton. The same applies to other prestigious Catholic universities, from which other important non-Catholic protagonists of American political life have graduated, like, for example, Condoleezza Rice, from Notre Dame.

The Catholic influence spreads through big institutions, but it would be a mistake to consider these alone. Its influence spreads via various social ramifications that have a direct impact on the life of Main Street. Indeed, one could say that, if the Church were not able to impose itself socially, that is, to appear as credible and reliable, then it would not be able to establish itself politically, either. As the sociologist Enzo Pace states, one of the conditions for the success of a religion is "to succeed in producing socially useful effects in both collective and individual terms."[20]

Therefore its influence extends through the dense network of its 17,483 parishes, spread across 195 dioceses, through 38,275 priests, 49,883 nuns, 4,318 monks, and 17,464 permanent deacons;[21] through hundreds of publications and newsletters with a combined circulation estimated to be in the tens of millions; and, of course, through the network of social services, which we explored in the previous chapter. Last, but not least, the power of this arsenal is multiplied by the Catholic presence in the United States, which is concentrated in California and the Northeast (see map 12).

According to the statistics of the network Catholic Charities USA, in 2010 there were about 240,000 people involved in Catholic charity work in the United States. It seems, however, that the number of the faithful involved in volunteer activities within the parish or grassroots—from extracurricular activities for children to food centers for the poor—is much higher than what is officially recorded.

In the 1990s Charles Morris completed his substantial investigation of American Catholics, visiting a number of parishes in the United States that differed in their sensibility, attachment to traditions, openness, and

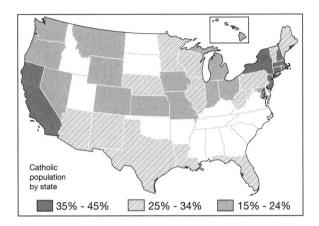

MAP 12. *Catholic presence in the United States. Various shades of gray mark the states where Catholicism is the first religious denomination by the number of faithful. In North Dakota and South Dakota the most widespread denomination is Lutheran, although the percentage of Catholics (30 percent and 25 percent respectively) is higher than in most states with a Catholic majority.*

so forth. He observed that between a fifth and a third of the faithful were actively engaged in one or more parish activities. "Like no other generation in the history of the Church," notes Morris, "active American Catholics are educated, literate, informed, and interested in their religion." In short, "none of the so-called Catholic countries of Europe and Latin America can match the activism, wealth, and dynamism of the American Church."[22]

Since then, American Catholics have become even more educated, wealthy, and informed and, in all likelihood, more interested in their religion and the activities taking place around their parishes. Between 1987 and 2011 the percentage of Catholics without high school degrees fell from 21 to 14 percent; and the percentage of university graduates rose from 20 to 27 percent. In 1987 only 20 percent of Catholic families had an annual income of more than $40,000. In 2011 the figure reached 60 percent.[23] Let us suppose that the parishes Morris visited in the 1990s represented special cases and that the average percentage of believers actively engaged in one or more activities linked to the parish is—despite their better education and greater wealth compared to what it was at that time—around 10 percent. Even in this case, taking as the reference-point the lowest figure of the Official Catholic Directory, the result would still be 6.5 million people.

We do not know whether the historian Paul Kennedy is among the 240,000 officially recorded volunteers. It is equally unlikely that this number includes all the parishioners and the Yale students who, like him, "work in the lunchtime soup kitchen of the St. Thomas More Catholic chaplaincy at Yale University" (a food center created in the early 1980s "to meet the needs of the poor and hungry"), all of them volunteers who "would never expect to be remunerated." Kennedy's vivid description of the charitable activities of his parish ends on an observation that echoes the one Morris made twenty years before, especially in its enthusiasm: "This is not a dead or decaying church. It is vibrant and pulsing. . . . It is *our* Catholic Church. Nobody is leaving it."[24]

A final consideration of the political potential of the Catholic Church concerns precisely the mass of its faithful. It is true that American Catholics "have grown up" and make their decisions more and more often without regard for what their pastors say. One can see this from the way they vote, how massively they ignore dictated sexual morality, and how often they attend services and sacraments. From a political point of view, however, it would be a serious mistake to underestimate the Church's capacity for mobilization. As René Rémond pointed out, among others, "Even in the most secularized societies, the religious fact appreciated statistically . . . is by far the most massive social fact of voluntary nature."[25] According to the data on attendance at religious services in 2014 advanced by CARA, every week nearly 24 percent of all Catholic Americans (approximately twenty million) traveled voluntarily, without being solicited, to hear what the Church had to tell them. If we consider further that, according to CARA again, 40 percent of Catholics attend church at least once a month,[26] the number of people who regularly and directly listen to the voice of the Church becomes almost thirty-two million, whereas, if we take into account the data proposed by the *National Catholic Reporter* for 2011, we must conclude that 31 percent of American Catholics go to church at least once a week (approximately twenty-five million) (see table 10).

No political party, no union, no cultural organization, no TV preacher, in the United States or elsewhere, has such an ability to mobilize people—not only people willing to listen but people willing to leave their homes, whatever the distance and the weather, to go listen. One could object that these people

TABLE 10. *Percentages of Catholics attending religious services weekly,*
1985–2014

Mass Attendance (weekly)							
CARA				NCR			
1985	1995	2005	2014	1987	1993	1999	2011
39%	31%	23%	24%	44%[a]	37%	34%	31%

SOURCES: Center for Applied Research in the Apostolate (CARA), Washington, DC; and
Mary L. Gautier, "How Parish Life Has Changed," National Catholic Reporter, Oct. 24, 2011.

a General Social Survey, NORC at the University of Chicago.

go to church not for political reasons but for purely spiritual reasons. This
is indisputably true, but from a political point of view, once the experience,
the means, and the ability to mobilize a certain number of people are gained,
for whatever reason, it will be possible to mobilize them—or at least a part
of them—for other reasons. As the demonstrations in France against the
bill on same-sex marriage showed, the Church managed to involve several
hundred thousand people, drawing primarily from among the millions of
faithful who regularly attend its functions and various activities.[27]

The Church has built this potential everywhere in the world. But it is
in the United States that it has transformed itself more massively into realities that have a direct impact on the country's leadership. This is why
the American Church has become a model for the universal Church.

THE FREE MARKET OF FAITH

"While European prelates languished in the tawdry palaces of a deraci-
nated nobility and extracted money and spirit from ignorant peasants,
the American blend of patriotism, unionism, social moderation, and religiosity produced one of the most vibrant popular churches."[28] This is
how Charles Morris describes the reasons for the advantage the Catholic
Church of the United States gained over the parasitic European (and we
could add, Latin American) Churches.

The principal merit of John Carroll and his successors was their ability
to adapt Catholicism to a hostile environment, with perspicacity and sense
of balance. Throughout its history the Catholic Church had always fought
other religions, but in the thirteen colonies, and later across the United
States, it had to learn to cohabit with them at the risk of disappearing. Yet

the Church's ability to adapt would not have been sufficient if it had not been for the two beneficial and mutually dependent environmental conditions: a deeply religious climate and the First Amendment.

Regarding the first condition, little can be added to what has already been said and written, so I will just illustrate it briefly with the following example. If we compare the "rate of religiosity"[29] in ten countries with the highest per capita product in the world (excluding "atypical" cases like Monaco, Liechtenstein, Qatar, etc.) and eight countries with the lowest per capita product, we will see that as a general rule, the higher the per capita product, the less religious the population, and—what is more important—vice versa. The United States, second among the powers when it comes to per capita product, is a striking exception, with a rate of religiosity of 65 percent. Among the remaining top nine positions, all countries, with the exception of Austria, have a rate of religiosity below 50 percent, with the minimum reached by Norway (first in per capita product, with 20.5 percent of religiosity) and Sweden (eighth, with 16.5 percent). At the other extreme, a partial exception is Zimbabwe, which is third to last in pro capita product but has the lowest rate of religiosity (87.5 percent) in the group of the poorest countries (fig. 1).

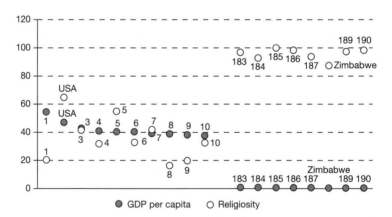

FIGURE 1. *Per capita product and religiosity.*
LEGEND: Norway (1), United States (2), Switzerland (3), Australia (4), Austria (5), Netherlands (6), Canada (7), Sweden (8), Iceland (9), and Belgium (10); the poorest, Afghanistan (183), Madagascar (184), Niger (185), Somalia (186), Liberia (187), Zimbabwe, Burundi (189), and the Democratic Republic of Congo (190). On the ordinate--the "rate of religiosity"; on the abscissa--the per capita product (descending). Source: CIA World Factbook regarding the per capita product (1993–2010); and Gallup Institute survey (2006–8) regarding the "rate of religiosity."

Among the explanations given for Americans' extraordinary religious vitality, the thesis of the "free market of faith" currently seems to be prevailing. According to Jon Meacham, for example, "The American culture of religious liberty helped create a busy free market of faith: by disestablishing churches, the nation made religion more popular, not less."[30] John Micklethwait and Adrian Wooldridge go so far as to overturn the cliché about "innate godliness" of Americans: "Pre-Revolutionary America," they write, "was not that religious. . . . America became religious after the Constitution separated church from state, thus ensuring that religious denominations could only survive if they got souls into pews."[31] Free competition among various confessions to gain the favor—and offerings—of the faithful developed the entrepreneurial mind-set that was strenuously opposed by the chronic parasitic dirigisme of European churches, which, according to Grace Davie and to Peter Berger,[32] is at the origin of the decline of religiosity in the Old Continent.

The thesis of the "free market of faith" is the most popular explanation, but it is also the oldest. In fact, in the early nineteenth century Tocqueville already compared Europe, where "the spirit of religion and the spirit of liberty march almost always in opposite directions," to the United States, where they are "intimately joined the one to the other." Conversing with "the faithful of all communions [and] the company of priests," Tocqueville noticed that "all attributed the peaceful dominion that religion exercises in their country principally to the complete separation of Church and State."[33]

Another observation made by Tocqueville allows us to leap forward to the present day and to get an idea of the extent to which the American model has been an example for the universal Church. Researching the differences between Europe and the United States on the matter of religious devotion, Tocqueville discovered "with surprise" that American Catholic priests "fill no public position." Moreover, "most of its members seemed to remove themselves voluntarily from power, and to take a kind of professional pride in remaining apart from it."[34] It took the universal Church almost two centuries to acknowledge the political benefits of religious freedom and of separation from the state and almost two and a half centuries to affirm, as Pope Francis did in September 2013, that "the people of God want pastors, not clergy acting like bureaucrats or government officials."[35]

This statement was not only a figure of speech. It was meant to have programmatic value and was a kind of recommended task for a Church called "to step outside itself and go to those who do not attend Mass, to those who have quit or are indifferent."[36] And it is in this sense—in the sense of trying to "get souls into pews" by stepping outside to go looking for them—that the appointment of Jorge Mario Bergoglio to the papacy can be said to represent the culmination of the process of the Catholic Church's "Americanization."

THE AMERICANIZATION
OF THE CATHOLIC CHURCH

The beginning of the process can be dated to 1888. That year, Leo XIII authorized the Church's official patronage of the Knights of Labor, the Catholic proto-union whose cause had been defended in Rome by Cardinal James Gibbons on behalf of the majority of US bishops. The ideas Gibbons put forward, writes Morris, "contribute[d] to a sharp reorientation of Rome's social teachings,"[37] and this reorientation was reflected in the *Rerum novarum* in 1891.

It is worth recalling that this encyclical acknowledged not only the need to create, wherever possible, associations "consisting either of workmen alone, or of workmen and employers together" but also the principle of subsidiarity, which is probably the most genuinely *American* theoretical contribution of the Catholic Church.[38] In fact, whereas in Europe, as a general rule, social initiative comes from the state, in the United States it is society that organizes itself from below, and the state—the endlessly castigated "Big Government"—is asked to abstain from intervening as much as possible. In American culture the terms *grassroots democracy* and *subsidiarity* are often interchangeable. This phenomenon was described by Tocqueville as well: "Wherever, at the head of some new undertaking, you see the government in France, or a man of rank in England, in the United States you will be sure to find an association."[39]

To continue this chapter on the growing importance of the US Church over the universal Church, it is impossible not to mention again the influence that is the most objective and measurable of all: St. Peter's Pence. But there is another field in which the American Church may have contributed to a very important turning point: the abandonment of the traditional hostility of Catholics toward Jews. As early as November 1938, the US bishops publicly condemned the pogroms of *Kristallnacht*;[40] and, in the already quoted letter of November 14, 1942, they expressed their "revulsion against the cruel indignities heaped upon the Jews in conquered countries."[41] The prelates believed they had to dissociate themselves not so much from the virulent anti-Semitism of the pro-Nazi priest Charles Coughlin as from their own past (and present). In fact, as Leonard Dinnerstein writes, the US entry into the war "brought smouldering Catholic-Jewish animosities into the open, as both Catholic periodicals and priests forcefully expressed anti-Semitism."[42] Nevertheless, whether it was out of opportunistic patriotism or personal conviction, American bishops condemned the persecution of Jews at the time when no other national episcopate did, let alone the universal Catholic Church.

Speaking of relations with the Jewish world, few people remember that some of the US delegates to the Second Vatican Council—along with some of the Germans—threatened to leave if the Council yielded to the demand from their Middle Eastern and traditionalist colleagues ("mostly from some Latin American, Italian and Spanish bishops")[43] to withdraw the document that officially repealed the curse on the Jewish people.[44] Daniel Goldhagen, the author of a book highly critical of "the role of the Catholic Church in the Holocaust and its unfilled duty of repair," writes in his afterword that "the American Catholic Church has shown itself to be the most progressive and innovative in giving guidance to its faithful about the Church's past regarding Jews."[45]

According to John Tracy Ellis, it is precisely at the time of the Second Vatican Council that the American hierarchies "involved themselves more resolutely in the affairs of the universal Church."[46] Sixty-one "experts" from the United States were invited to participate in the preparatory work (with 126 not Italian and 201 total), and 246 American bishops attended various sessions. Their contribution was decisive to the debate on religious freedom, to which they brought, says Ellis, their "175-year experience of separation between Church and State."[47]

A leading role was played by the Jesuit theologian John Courtney Murray, the author of a joint declaration written with Protestant and Jewish leaders on postwar reconstruction, published in 1943. For his interfaith activities and his ideas on the relationship between the Church and the state, in 1954 the Holy Office (the old name of the department for the Doctrine of the Faith) suspended him from teaching and prohibited him from expressing himself publicly. It was not until just before the end of the first working session of the Council that Murray was invited to participate as "expert," following the insistence of Archbishop of New York Spellman. Subsequently, the Jesuit theologian worked on the third and fourth draft of the document on religious freedom, which was approved with 2,308 votes "for" and 70 "against" on December 7, 1965, the day before the closing of the Council.

As the Canadian theologian Gregory Baum, another "expert" of the Council, recalls, the approval of the document "came after 'vehement debate' with strong opposition from many Vatican officials and bishops from strongly Catholic countries such as Spain and Italy, where Catholicism was the state religion."[48] For Charles Morris, "Murray and Spellman had the signal satisfaction, in 1965, of seeing the fathers, for all practical purposes, jettison two millennia of pronouncements on Church and state and more or less officially declare in favor of the American system."[49]

The 1965 choice was more an act of realpolitik than a conversion. The possibility of Catholic expansion—on the basis of the military conquest of new territories by Catholic powers and of the forced conversion of conquered peoples—was precluded forever after the end of colonialism. In addition, it is precisely decolonization and universalization of the capitalist system of development that were putting in motion the processes of rural exodus, urbanization, and industrialization, which necessarily led to the massive and dramatic population movements that we are witnessing today. The new conditions of this phenomenon, which with time took the name of globalization, made the religious melting pot a planetary reality for which the Catholic Church had to gear up. And the most successful example of a religious melting pot was still that of the United States.

Throughout its history the Church has been forced to change its position in response to unwelcome external circumstances that it often resisted with all the available instruments. But its ability to adapt, although sometimes obstructed by a long, costly, and futile resistance, is one of the keys to its historical continuity, if not *the* key, and one of the keys to its social success. This is true for its social doctrine, for reconciliation with Judaism and the principle of freedom of religion, but it is also true for the scandals of pedophilia: another case in which the American experience may be regarded as the basis of a major moral reorientation.

Olivier Roy has pointed out that "a religion's normativeness is always subject to revision, depending on the social and cultural understanding of these norms." Among other examples, Roy mentions "paedophilia in the Catholic Church: it has always been condemned by Church leaders, who used to treat it as a minor issue, but within the space of a few years it became unacceptable in public opinion."[50] And the United States is the first place in which it became unacceptable. As a consequence of the campaign launched by the *Boston Globe* in January 2002, eight dioceses (Portland, Tucson, Spokane, Davenport, San Diego, Fairbanks, Wilmington, and Milwaukee) were forced to declare bankruptcy, and three more (Gallup, Helena, and Minneapolis-Saint Paul) had to file for bankruptcy after payment of compensation for moral and material damages to the victims. According to the website BishopAccountability.org, which provides a detailed list of the cases resolved legally, the sums paid in settlements, damages, and legal fees by several American dioceses between 1994 and 2012 exceed $3 billion, of which almost $750 million were paid by the Diocese of Los Angeles alone.

It is unlikely that child abuse was more widespread among the clergy in the United States than anywhere else in the world, but the conditions existed in the States for the scandal to break and to force the universal Church to face it no longer locally, on a case by case basis, but globally, to the extent of creating a pontifical ad hoc commission that has been active since September 2014.[51]

The first senior Church official who advocated for an institutional intervention aimed at limiting this phenomenon was Joseph Ratzinger, even before he became pope. Benedict XVI, as well as his predecessor on the throne of St. Peter, "had a genuine and abiding fondness for America," writes Francis Rooney: "In a sense," continues the former ambassador to the Holy See, "Benedict's model for the proper relationship between religion and civil society was the United States of America."[52] The scandal, besides being excessively costly in financial terms, also risked being exorbitant in terms of the presentation and credibility of this model.

All the pontiffs who reigned after the Second Vatican Council showed, in word or in deed, admiration for the American model. Jorge Mario Bergoglio is less inclined to sing public praises of the North American "Big Brother," since he comes from a subcontinent that, for a century and a half, has suffered under its stranglehold.[53] Nevertheless, Bergoglio represents the culmination of the Americanization of the Catholic Church, not only because he is the first American pope in its history but especially because he brought to Rome a "Pan-American" method for "get[ting] souls into pews."

A PAN-AMERICAN POPE

The Italian historian Andrea Riccardi called Bergoglio "an almost Pan-American Pope." Riccardi was referring mainly to the "major political role" played by the US cardinals in funneling the votes of the conclave to the Argentinian candidate.[54] According to the "Vaticanist" Marco Politi, the eleven US cardinal-voters arrived in Rome with a "shared agenda" but did not seek votes for themselves. They preferred "to be kingmakers, rather than eligible candidates." The archbishop of Washington, DC, Donald Wuerl, explained why: "A pope from the American superpower would face many obstacles in presenting a spiritual message to the world."[55] Let me just note briefly that if, for the reasons that I have provided, the election of a Catholic president of the United States is unlikely, the election of a leader for the Catholic Church coming from the United States seems even more unlikely.

Of course, the choice of "an almost Pan-American Pope" cannot only be the result of an extemporaneous convergence among cardinals of the New World. Even with the margins of randomness that always exist behind the election of a pope, one cannot, with regard to the conclave of 2013, ignore the role played by two major geopolitical developments.

The first is the reduction in the weight of Europe between 2005—when a German pope was elected who chose the name of the patron saint of the Old Continent—and 2013. Many connected this reduction to the relative decrease in the number of European faithful compared with the rest of the world: in 1950 half the Catholics in the world lived in Europe, whereas today less than a quarter do so, and in 2050 less than one-sixth will (see table 11). But this decrease had already been in progress for several decades before 2005; it was mostly connected with well-known demographic trends and, therefore, greatly predictable.

The Church has begun to acknowledge its relative decline in Europe since the 1950s, when Pius XII opened the College of Cardinals to prelates from former colonies or colonies in the process of decolonization. As demonstrated in table 12, the weight of the so-called Third World cardi-

TABLE 11. *Where Catholics live: Evolution, 1950–2050*
(data as a percentage of total number of Catholics in the world)

	Europe	Americas	Asia	Africa	Oceania
1950	49	41	6	3	1
2000	27	49	10	12	1
2014	23	48	11	17	0.8
2025	20	49	13	16	1
2050	16	48	13	22	1

SOURCE: Various sources; the figure for 2014 is taken from the 2016 Pontifical Yearbook.

TABLE 12. *Cardinals appointed since the beginning of the twentieth century*
(by continent of birth)

	Europe		America		Africa	Asia	Oceania	Total	Europe	A+A+LA
	Total	Italy	US-Can	Lat. Am.					%	%
Pius X (1903–1914)	47	18	3	0	0	0	0	50	94.0	0.0
Benedict XV (1914–1922)	31	18	1	0	0	0	0	32	96.9	0.0
Pius XI (1922–1939)	69	44	4	2	0	1	0	76	90.8	3.9
Pius XII (1939–1958)	36	13	6	9	1	3	1	56	64.3	23.2
John XXIII (1958–1963)	37	21	5	6	1	3	0	52	71.2	19.2
Paul VI (1963–1978)	83	39	14	16	12	13	5	143	58.0	28.7
John Paul I (1978)	0	0	0	0	0	0	0	0	0.0	0.0
John Paul II (1978–2005)	128	48	22	36	18	23	4	231	55.4	33.3
Benedict XVI (2005–2013)	52	26	10	9	8	11	0	90	57.7	31.1
Francis (2013–)[a]	15	8	1	11	5	5	2	39	38.4	53.8

NOTE: A+A+LA = Africa, Asia, Latin America.
[a] Up to the conclave on Feb. 14, 2015.

nals has accentuated over time, with a relative slowdown under Benedict XVI and a new, decisive acceleration under Pope Francis.

But the first non-European cardinal was appointed by Pope Pius IX in 1875: the archbishop of New York, John McCloskey. Since then, the number of US cardinals has grown at a fairly regular pace, becoming the second largest national group after the Italians, as can be seen in tables 13 and 14. In table 15 I compare the evolution, within the College of Cardinals, of four particularly significant national groups (excluding Italy): the French one, which had been the second national group for centuries; the German (Austria and Germany), which the Church leaned on in the late nineteenth and early twentieth centuries; that of the United States; and that of Brazil, the country with the largest number of Catholics in the world.

Of course, drawing a geopolitical conclusion based solely on the College of Cardinals would be reductive. Even so, it cannot be denied that some of the changes the college has undergone are geopolitically significant. The "Pan-American" statement of 2013 can also be seen in the light of the setback that the process of European integration experienced following the defeat of the French referendum of 2005. Joseph Ratzinger was elected after a series of successes in the project of European unification, culminating in the birth of the single currency; the conclave of 2013 came

TABLE 13. *Cardinals present at the conclaves (1878–2013),*
by country and regional area

	Europe		America			Africa	Asia	Oceania	Total	% USA
Conclave	Total	Italy	USA	Canada	Lat. Am.					
1878	62	40	1	1	0	0	0	0	64	1.56
1903	63	39	1	0	0	0	0	0	64	1.56
1914	60	33	3	1	1	0	0	0	65	4.62
1922	56	31	2	1	1	0	0	0	60	3.33
1939	56	36	3	1	2	0	1	0	63	4.76
1958	36	17	2	2	9	0	3	1	53	3.77
1963	55	29	5	2	12	1	6	1	82	6.10
1978	57	26	9	3	19	13	9	4	114	7.89
2005[a]	58	20	11	3	21	11	10	2	116	9.48
2013[a]	60	28	11	3	19	11	10	1	115	9.57

[a] Only cardinal-electors.

TABLE 14. *Major national groups within the College of Cardinals (voters + nonvoters), by May 5, 2015*

Italy	USA	Spain	Germany	Brazil	France	Poland	India
49	16	11	10	10	9	6	5

TABLE 15. *Evolution of four national groups in the College of Cardinals, when voting in conclave, 1878–2013*

Conclave	1878	1903	1914	1922	1939	1958	1963	1978[a]	2005[a]	2013[a]
France	7	7	7	5	6	6	7	7	4	3
Germany	6	8	8	5	4	2	4	8	7	7
USA	1	1	3	2	3	2	5	9	11	11
Brazil	0	0	1	1	1	3	3	6	5	4

[a] Only cardinal-electors.

after years of political setbacks of the same project, aggravated by the 2008 economic crisis and turmoil around the euro, particularly in connection with the situation in Greece.

The second development to be taken into account concerns the Catholic integration of the American continent (Anglo-Saxon north and Latin south), which is far more advanced than its economic or political integration.

According to Samuel Huntington, who wrote in the first half of the 1990s, Latin America was external to so-called Western Christianity (although "culturally close to the West") insofar as it was still a land of exclusively Catholic Christianity, indolent because it benefited from an advantageous monopolistic position and from overintimate relations with political power. One of the characteristics of "Western civilization," according to Huntington, was precisely the Protestant contribution to the indispensable Roman Catholic foundation; the Reform, in fact, reacts "to the stagnation and corruption of existing institutions . . . preach[es] work, order and discipline; and appeal[s] to emerging dynamic middle-class people."[56] In Latin America things had not yet reached this point, but, added the author, "that is changing rapidly."[57] Things have changed, indeed, since the time that Huntington was writing but not the way he imagined. At that time the apparently unstoppable progress of evangelicalism seemed to be able to make Latin America "more like the mixed Catholic-Protestant societies of the West." In fact, more than a result of the spread of "Protestant ethics," the change resulted from the new attitude of the Catholic Church, at the same time less and less institutional and less focused on pauperism, which was made official at the Fifth Conference of the Bishops of the region in 2007 and became universally known in 2013 after the election of Jorge Mario Bergoglio.

But the Catholic integration on the American continent is also a consequence of massive migrations. It is true that the Latin American *campesinos* who immigrate to the North encounter a very different social reality from that of their original countries, but the same happens when they migrate from the countryside to cities within their own countries. Once a migratory odyssey has been completed, the language and the religion are the same in North and South, as are, very often, the new social conditions of the urbanized former peasants, who remain on the lower rungs of the social ladder. It is therefore no coincidence that even the religious experiences in these destinations are quite similar: the percentage of Latino immigrants in the United States who abandon Catholicism is almost the same as that of migrant Latinos within their own countries or of those who move from one Latin American country to another. Thus the solution of the Church that "goes forth" and is "in a permanent state of mission" is, first and foremost, a "Pan-American" one.

If this solution works in both Americas, whose conditions were originally very different, there is no reason whatsoever why it should not work in the rest of the world. This seems all the more probable as it works especially well in the North, where the Church does not have the handicap of having been institutional, that is to say, weighed down by centuries of privilege and an advantageous position. And if the "Pan-American" Church is setting the pace for the universal Church, it is more than natural that a "Pan-American Pope" be placed at its head.

Conclusion

"AS AMERICA BECAME MORE CATHOLIC in the twentieth century, the Catholic Church became more American," wrote the former US ambassador to the Vatican, Francis Rooney.[1] Yet this trend did not end with the twentieth century. On the contrary, it accelerated at the beginning of the twenty-first.

There is a widespread temptation to attribute the increased weight of Catholics in American political life to demographic factors. Some even think that the combined effect of fertility, immigration, and conversion rates could help American Catholics reach and exceed the Protestant population in the second half of this century.[2] Whether this is true is not the point. Over the course of this book I have tried to demonstrate how the "Catholicization" of the United States is much more significant in terms of quality than in quantity, much more so in substance than in form, and much more so in the medium and long terms than in the present.

The question of the benefits that the Church might draw from the Catholicization of American politics can only be answered in perspective. Every Catholic who occupies an important position at the forefront of the United States political stage comes with a network of relationships of which other Catholics are inevitably a part, and very often this network is linked to a university or some other Catholic institution, a parish, or even a single priest. As a Catholic ascends to the upper levels of power, his or her entire network ascends accordingly.

There is not, and there cannot be, immediate implementation of the principles defended by the Church in the legislative arsenal of the United States. This is true for several reasons: first, the normative priorities of the Church change, as demonstrated by the pontificate of Pope Francis; second, it is not at all certain that the Church really takes advantage of any (however target-worthy) solutions to the problems raised by its stances; and third, an American Catholic politician is first of all an American, and only then a Catholic: his or her connection to the Church—whatever it might be—is primarily intended to reinforce the United States. At the same time, for Washington's ruling class—"of every background and of every faith"—an increased role for the Catholic Church means a reduction in federal social spending, contribution to the consolidation of the moral cohesion of the country, and a widening of its range of action on the international stage.

From the 1950s on, the State Department recommended a close relationship with the Vatican to try to orient the sentiments of Catholics all over the world in a manner favorable to the United States and to secure an important channel of communication—and, if possible, influence—with the countries with which the Holy See has diplomatic relations. In terms of international politics it is certain that these two reasons continue to lie at the root of the American desire to maintain the best possible relationship with the Catholic world, even though it is clear that the Catholic Church and the United States each has its own agenda and that, over the course of history, the two agendas have coincided only incidentally.

But many things have changed since the 1950s. The days of the "great euphoria" are far behind us: although the country is still, by far, the leading world power, it is a declining power, gradually losing some of the benefits and privileges produced in the twentieth century by its undisputed world economic, political, and military hegemony. The Church, in contrast, has sacrificed much of its history to the necessity of reconnecting with a rapidly changing world, managing, after a long and difficult ordeal, to take the lead in the world's religious revival that began in the 1970s. This is ever more evident today.

Rather than measured by numbers—whose meaning has been analyzed in detail in this book—the new vitality of the Church can be measured by the attention, respect, admiration, and sometimes even flattery with which its voice is heard and its representatives are received. Wherever the pope goes, he is greeted simultaneously as a head of state, a prophet, a tutelary deity, and a rock star, with a distinction and regard that no other religious leader—and no other political leader—can seriously hope to match. "We unquestionably exercise an influence on the world stage whenever the opportunity arises," confessed an anonymous cardinal in 2007. He continued, "We are the only religious power to have such ability. . . . We are so accustomed to it that we fail to remember to what degree our position is exceptional."[3]

The solemnity with which Pope Francis was received in the United States in September 2015 attests to the growth of this influence. With each visit of the last three popes the attention of American society, media, and politicians has grown in size and intensity. The speech before Congress in a plenary meeting marked a new, important step, a recognition that until recently would have been inconceivable. The United States is "the land of the free and the home of the brave," as Bergoglio said, with a wink, at the beginning of his speech to American lawmakers; but it has also been, for most of its history, the land and home of those who regarded the pope as an enemy of religion and of America. As recently as 1987, when Ronald Reagan undertook to establish diplomatic relations with the Holy See, a wide range of religious and secular organizations, representing on paper tens of millions of Americans, appealed to the Supreme Court to block the president's plan to "appoint an ambassador to a church," as one of the leading Southern Baptists, James Dunn, said.[4] Even John Paul II, despite his alleged role in the fall of the Soviet "evil empire," was not granted the congressional podium to speak to three hundred million Americans through their representatives.

Furthermore, the role of American Catholics in US politics has also completely changed since the 1950s: a Catholic political leadership has been gradually formed, coming to occupy, under the Obama administration, an unprecedented number of key political, judicial, military, and defense positions at the highest levels of the country's institutions of power. Dario Fabbri has pointed out that during Barack Obama's second term, the "second, third, fourth and fifth positions in the Federal state are Catholic,"[5] that is, respectively, the vice president, Joe Biden; the former Speaker of the House, John Boehner; the president pro tempore of the Senate, Patrick Leahy; and Secretary of State John Kerry.[6] To this we can add, as we have seen, more than one-third of the members of the government, all the most important military positions, two-thirds of the Supreme Court, and 38 percent of US governors.

Contributing to this result has been the spectacular social—and therefore economic and cultural—growth, starting in the very same decade, of the Catholic population of the United States (as well as the fact that this population is concentrated in the richest and most dynamic states). But its growth might not have been sufficient without a deep, and certainly still unsatisfied, need for a moral reorientation of the country.

In a 2002 document on the commitment of Catholics in politics, the Congregation for the Doctrine of the Faith wrote, "Civil society today is undergoing a complex cultural process as the end of an era brings with it a time of uncertainty in the face of something new."[7] From 2002 until today, the progression of the "end of an era" has been accelerated by the disaster in Iraq, the weakening in 2005 of the rising momentum of the European project, and, of course, the global economic crisis that followed the 2008 crash. The great international disorder has spread to Syria, Libya, Mali, Nigeria, Ukraine, Burma, the islands off the coast of China, and elsewhere, in direct proportion to the now clearly obvious inability of the United States to manage all fronts simultaneously and to the doubts, also more and more obvious, about the existence of a strategy for trying to manage at least some.

In such a situation Catholics can present themselves as the champions of moral certainties of which "civil society" is in such desperate need. Uncertainty, wrote Peter Berger, "is a condition that many people find very hard to bear; therefore, any movement (not only a religious one) that promises to provide or to renew certainty has a ready market."[8]

This climate of unrest is universal, as is the chase after old and new identities with which to entrench one's anxiety about the future. But the uncertainty about the future of the United States is—politically—the most relevant, and the most disturbing, no matter how it is viewed. In fact, Americans have the most to lose from the ongoing shift of power.

It would be absurd to claim that the United States has no moral compass: the cohesion of the country, which it has proved in times when its future has been at stake, is still important geopolitical capital that the US government can count on in this new phase of international disorder. But this cohesion has hitherto been built on the certainty—and then proven by facts—that such a future will be better, on the certainty that being part of the big family gathered around the star-spangled banner is the best guarantee that Americans will have, on average, a better life than that of all other peoples on Earth. Today that certainty is gone, and there is no assurance that there exists a new moral compass to provide cohesion for the American people in times of ineluctable decline.

In 1997 Charles Morris concluded his *American Catholic* by writing that "if America does not need the Catholic Church, it may need something very much like it, a confident and constant source for norms of responsibility and mutual respect."[9] The thing is, though, that there is nothing "very much" like the Catholic Church.

January–October 2015

Notes

NOTES TO INTRODUCTION

1. This analysis has been conducted in my *Il secolo cattolico: La strategia geopolitica della Chiesa* (Rome: Laterza, 2010).

2. These data are collected in "Annuarium Statisticum Ecclesiae 2013," in *Bollettino Sala stampa della Santa Sede*, April 16, 2015.

3. Nicholas J. Spykman, "Geography and Foreign Policy," *American Political Science Review* 32, no. 1 (1938): 28–50.

4. Henry Kissinger, *Diplomacy* (New York: Simon and Schuster, 1995), 703.

5. See John Allen Jr., "Opus Dei Prestige on Display at Centenary Event," *National Catholic Reporter*, Jan. 18, 2002.

6. Paul Kennedy, *The Rise and Fall of the Great Powers: Economic Change and Military Conflict from 1500 to 2000* (New York: Random House, 1987), xxii.

7. Ibid., 436–37.

8. Robert J. Samuelson, "The Shutdown Heralds a New Economic Norm," *Washington Post*, Oct. 14, 2013.

9. Or, rather, too rich. My point here is that within Obama's administration there were perhaps too many different ideas, too many different motivations, and too many different projects to enable the president to give a definite and coherent line to his presidency, thus contributing to an increase in the sense of distress among Americans (and among America's allies).

10. Kennedy, *The Rise and Fall of the Great Powers*, 515.

11. US National Intelligence Council, *Global Trends 2025: A Transformed World* (Washington, DC: US National Intelligence Council, 2008), 93.

12. The numbers of Catholics in the United States change considerably depending on the sources and on the method used to count them. We will see in chapter 7 that their numbers increase from the lowest estimate of 66.6 million people to the highest, of 96 million.

13. Robert C. Christopher, *Crashing the Gates: The De-WASPing of America's Power Elite* (New York: Simon and Schuster, 1989).

14. Quoted in Joseph Ratzinger and Marcello Pera, *Without Roots: The West, Relativism, Christianity, Islam* (San Francisco: Basic Books, 2006), 80.

15. Seth Masket, "Minority Rule: How Labor Unions and Civil Rights Activists Beat the Big Guys," *Pacific Standard*, Jan. 9, 2014.

16. *Both Sides with Jesse Jackson*, CNN, Jan. 30, 2000.

17. Paul VI, "Udienza generale: La 'città sul monte'?" (General audience: The "city on a hill"), May 25, 1966.

18. Center for Applied Research in the Apostolate (CARA), "Frequently Requested Church Statistics," Washington, DC, Oct. 21, 2014.

19. René Rémond, *Religion et société en Europe: Essai sur la sécularisation des sociétés européennes aux XIXe et XXe siècles, 1789–2000* (Paris: Seuil, 1998), 46.

20. Joseph Ratzinger, *Salt of the Earth: The Church at the End of the Millennium: An Interview with Peter Seewald* (San Francisco: Ignatius Press, 1997)—translated here from the Italian text, *Il sale della terra: Cristianesimo e Chiesa cattolica nel XXI secolo* (Cinisello Balsamo: San Paolo Edizioni, 1997), 299, because the English translation ("we can no longer take for granted a universal Christian atmosphere" [265]) is formally slightly different but, substantively, considerably different. More recently, Pope Francis repeated the same concept: "We are no longer in the era of Christianity. Today we are not the only ones that produce culture, we are not the first nor the most listened to" (message to participants of the International Pastoral Congress on the World's Big Cities, Nov. 27, 2014).

21. Charles Morris, *American Catholic: The Saints and Sinners Who Built America's Most Powerful Church* (New York: Times Books, 1997), 380.

22. Quoted in Peter J. Boyer, "Party Faithful: Can the Democrats Get a Foothold on the Religious Vote?" *New Yorker*, Sept. 8, 2008, www.newyorker.com/magazine/2008/09/08/party-faithful.

23. Pope Francis, "Apostolic Exhortation: *Evangelii gaudium*" (Città del Vaticano: Vatican Press, 2013), sec. 24, 25, 30.

24. Carl Schmitt, *Roman Catholicism and Political Form* (Westport, CT: Greenwood Press, 1996), 5, 7. Originally published as *Römischer Katholizismus und politische Form* (Hellerau, Dresden: Jakob Hegner, 1923).

25. Ibid., 4.

26. The Congregation de Propaganda Fide (for the Propagation of the Faith) was established in 1622 by Pope Gregory XV to preside over the conversion activities of the natives in the colonies.

27. See Massimo Franco, "Dietro il sacrificio estremo di un intellettuale le ombre di un 'rapporto segreto' choc," *Corriere della Sera*, Feb. 12, 2013.

28. For a list of these and other cardinals see www.gcatholic.org/hierarchy/cardinals-alive-country.htm.

29. Schmitt, *Roman Catholicism and Political Form*, 12.

30. Encyclical *Pacem in Terris*, April 11, 1963, sec. 51. The same quotation appears in Pope Francis's encyclical *Laudato si'*, May 24, 2015, sec. 175. Unless stated otherwise, all quotations from encyclicals and other major documents can be found on the official Vatican website, www.vatican.va.

NOTES TO CHAPTER I

1. Commissione per la pubblicazione dei documenti diplomatici, *I Documenti diplomatici italiani*, vol. 11, Dec. 31, 1861–July 31,1862 (Rome: Libreria dello Stato, 1986), 331.

2. See Office of the Press Secretary, "Readout of the President's Audience with His

Holiness Pope Francis," press release, www.whitehouse.gov/the-press-office/2014/03/27/readout-president-s-audience-his-holiness-pope-francis.

3. Two Jews settled in the English colonies, in 1621 and in 1649 respectively. Three others arrived separately in New Amsterdam in 1654, the same year as the arrival of a first group of twenty-three refugees from Brazil, fleeing Catholic persecutions. In 1776 approximately two thousand Jews were living in the thirteen colonies.

4. See Kenneth C. Davis, "America's True History of Religious Tolerance," *Smithsonian Magazine*, Oct. 2010.

5. The reference is to the Sermon on the Mount (Matt. 5:14), where Jesus compares his disciples to a "city on a hill," which cannot go unnoticed.

6. Charles O'Connor and William Lucey, "Massachusetts, Catholic Church In," *New Catholic Encyclopedia*, 2003, www.highbeam.com/doc/1G2-3407707255.html.

7. Albert West, "Rhode Island," *The Catholic Encyclopedia*, vol. 13 (New York: Robert Appleton, 1912), 22, www.newadvent.org/cathen/13020a.htm.

8. James H. O'Donnell, "Diocese of Hartford," in *History of the Catholic Church in the New England States*, ed. William Byrne and William A. Leahy (Boston: Hurd and Everts, 1899), 16.

9. See Edward McGuire, "State of New York," *The Catholic Encyclopedia*, vol. 11 (New York: Robert Appleton, 1911), 35.

10. Jay P. Dolan, *The American Catholic Experience: A History from Colonial Times to the Present* (New York: Doubleday, 1985), 84.

11. See Frank Lambert, *The Founding Fathers and the Place of Religion in America* (Princeton, NJ: Princeton University Press, 2003), 150.

12. According to some historians, the number of Americans of Catholic ascendency could have been far greater, but many settlers of Irish, French, German, or Dutch origin converted to the prevailing Protestantism.

13. John K. Wilson, "Religion Under the State Constitutions, 1776–1800," *Journal of Church and State* 32, no. 4 (1990): 761.

14. Walter Stahr, *John Jay: Founding Father* (New York: Hambledon and London, 2005), 78.

15. Frank Whelan, "French-Indian War Fueled Anti-Catholic Fears," *Morning Call*, April 28, 1985. McCarthyism (named after Catholic Senator Joseph McCarthy) was a period characterized by the hunt for alleged communist influence in US institutions (1950–54).

16. See Jason K. Duncan, *Citizens or Papists? The Politics of Anti-Catholicism in New York, 1685–1821* (New York: Fordham University Press, 2005), 25. Seceders were followers of a minor Presbyterian group.

17. George Washington, "General Orders," Nov. 5, 1775, George Washington Papers, 1741–99, Library of Congress, Washington, DC.

18. Duncan, *Citizens or Papists?* 35.

19. Charles Morris, *American Catholic: The Saints and Sinners Who Built America's Most Powerful Church* (New York: Times Books, 1997), viii.

20. The cotton gin, invented in 1793, is a machine that quickly separates cotton fibers from their seeds, allowing a twenty-five-fold increase in productivity per slave. One of the consequences of this increase in production was the growth in numbers of slaves (from around seven hundred thousand in 1790 to around 3.2 million in 1850) and of slave states (from six in 1790 to fifteen in 1860). By 1860 the Southern states were providing two-thirds of the world's supply of cotton and up to 80 percent of the British market.

21. See Friedrich Adolph Sorge, *Il movimento operaio negli Stati Uniti d'America: Corrispondenze dal Nord America* (Milan: Pantarei, 2002), 18.

22. At that time the term *Native* applied to those born in the United States or descended from the first settlers. The movement that defended Natives' supremacy and opposed the arrival of immigrants from Europe was called Nativism. From the 1970s the term began to denote the descendants of the natives who inhabited the current territory of the United States before the arrival of colonizing powers.

23. See William P. Dillingham et al., *Senate Documents, 61st Congress, 3rd Session: Statistical Review of Immigration 1820–1910* (Washington, DC: Government Printing Office, 1911). According to this document, between 1820 and 1910, 28 million immigrants entered the United States, more than a half of whom were Catholics. 30 percent of the total came from Germany, Austria and Hungary; 15 percent from Ireland, and 11 percent from Italy. Poles, officially recorded among Russians and Austrians, made up about 5 percent (this estimate took into account the number of people who spoke Polish in 1910 and the number of immigrants registered as "Russian" but who were most likely Polish). See: "Mother Tongue of the Foreign-Born Population: 1910 to 1940, 1960, and 1970," United States Census Bureau, March 9, 1999.

24. According to the most frequently quoted figure, nine thousand workers were employed on the construction of the Erie Canal, a third of whom were Irish. According to Carol Sheriff, "by the 1830s, the majority of canal diggers in North America would be Irish." See Carol Sheriff, *The Artificial River: The Erie Canal and the Paradox of Progress, 1817–1862* (New York: Hill and Wang, 1996), 36.

25. On these incidents see Jack Tager, *Boston Riots: Three Centuries of Social Violence* (Boston: Northeastern University Press, 2000); and Jeanne Hamilton, "The Nunnery as Menace: The Burning of the Charlestown Convent, 1834," *U.S. Catholic Historian* 14 (Winter 1996): 35–65.

26. See Kathryn Wilson and Jennifer Coval, "City of Unbrotherly Love: Violence in Nineteenth-Century Philadelphia," in *Exploring Diversity in Pennsylvania History* (Philadelphia: Historical Society of Pennsylvania, n.d.), http://hsp.org/sites/default/files/legacy_files/migrated/thephiladelphiariotsof1844.pdf.

27. Quoted in Thomas J. Shelley, *The History of the Archdiocese of New York: New York Catholicism in the Twentieth Century*, vol. 2 (Strasbourg: Éditions du Signe, 1998), 1859.

28. See Massimo Franco, *Parallel Empires: The Vatican and the United States—Two Centuries of Alliance and Conflict* (New York: Doubleday, 2008), 9.

29. The origin of the name lies in the semisecret organization of the party, which had different actual names—for example, American Party, American Republican Party, and Native American Party.

30. Charles Morris cites a then popular joke: " 'God bless the two greatest organizations in the world,' proclaimed the tippling Irishman of legend, 'the Catholic Church and Tammany Hall!' 'What's the second one?' asked his drinking companion" (Morris, *American Catholic*, 11). Tammany Hall controlled New York City and New York state politics from the 1840s to the New Deal.

31. Morris, *American Catholic*, 6.

32. In many cities certain Protestant foundations were charged with the supervision of the programs and the compliance of textbooks with the teachings of the Bible.

33. Lyman Beecher, *A Plea for the West* (Cincinnati, OH: Truman and Smith, 1835), 111, 56.

34. Morris, *American Catholic*, 74.

35. Ibid., 76.

36. Ibid., 78.

37. According to Albon P. Man, the number of casualties was at least ten times higher, between twelve hundred and fifteen hundred. The Colored Orphan Asylum, considered a temple of the rich Protestant abolitionists, was attacked with cries of "Kill the nigger children!" The 233 children were evacuated by the police a few moments before the orphanage was set on fire. See Albon P. Man Jr., "The Church and the New York Draft Riots of 1863," *Records of the American Catholic Historical Society of Philadelphia* 62, no. 1 (1951): 33–50.

38. John T. McGreevy, *Catholicism and American Freedom: A History* (New York: Norton, 2003), 91.

39. Roger Aubert, "L'Église catholique de la crise de 1848 à la Première Guerre mondiale," in *Nouvelle histoire de l'Église*, vol. 5, ed. Jean Daniélou, Ludovicus Jacobus Rogier, Roger Aubert, and David Knowles (Paris: Seuil, 1975), 588.

40. Quoted in *John Tracy* Ellis, *American Catholicism* (Chicago: University of Chicago Press, 1956), 139.

41. The first quotation is a statement by Cardinal James Gibbons, bishop of Baltimore and dean of the American bishops, the day before the declaration of war; see Ellis, *American Catholicism*, 138. The second is from a letter sent by the bishops to Woodrow Wilson two weeks after the United States entered the war; see James J. Hennesey, *American Catholics: A History of the Roman Catholic Community in the United States* (New York: Oxford University Press, 1981), 225. The presidency of the NCWC was entrusted to Cardinal George Mundelein, bishop of Chicago, who was of German origin.

42. See Ellis, *American Catholicism*, 139.

43. Morris, *American Catholic*, 114. According to Mary L. Gautier, Paul M. Perl, and Stephen J. Fichter, in the early twentieth century the number of American priests was seventeen thousand; see Mary L. Gautier, Paul M. Perl, and Ste-

phen J. Fichter, *Same Call, Different Men: The Evolution of the Priesthood since Vatican II* (Collegeville, MN: Liturgical Press, 2012), 2.

44. This growth of salaries, though, must be compared to the increase of the output of coal by 800 percent, of miles of railway track by 567 percent, and of crude petroleum by 1,833 percent, more or less in the same period (1865–98); see Paul Kennedy, *The Rise and Fall of the Great Powers: Economic Change and Military Conflict from 1500 to 2000* (New York: Random House, 1987), 242. The American relative share of world manufacturing output went from 7.2 percent in 1860 to 23.6 percent in 1900 (ibid., 149).

45. See the case of Edward McGlynn, pastor of St. Stephen's in New York, who supported the candidacy of the Labor Party member Henry George for mayor of the city in 1886. The hierarchy branded George's theories "unsound and unsafe, and contrary to the teachings of the Church," and endorsed Abram Hewitt, a candidate of Tammany Hall (then run by Richard Croker, whom Morris describes as "a thug who had once been tried for murder" and whose deputies "lived off prostitution, white slavery and gambling"). In the poll Hewitt won 90,552 votes, George 68,110, and the Republican candidate, Theodore Roosevelt, 60,435. Edward McGlynn was accused by his bishop of embezzlement and "sexual misconduct" and eventually excommunicated (Morris, *American Catholic*, 94).

46. Almost every Polish parish had its school (as compared with one out of ten Italian parishes); see Thomas I. Monzell, "The Catholic Church and the Americanization of the Polish Immigrant," *Polish American Studies* 26, no. 1 (1969): 3.

47. David P. Baker, "Schooling All the Masses: Reconsidering the Origins of American Schooling in the Postbellum Era," *Sociology of Education* 72, no. 4 (1999): 197–215.

48. In 1852 there were not yet any Irish among the thirty-two bishops (nine were born in the United States, eight in France, two in Belgium, two in Canada, and one each in Austria, Spain, and Switzerland). In 1866 the number of bishops born in Ireland was already eleven out of forty-five (of others, fourteen were born in the United States, ten in France, three each in Canada and Spain, and one each in Austria, Belgium, Germany, and Switzerland). In 1884, finally, out of seventy-two bishops, forty were of Irish origin and sixteen of German origin. The priests continued to be largely of Irish origin, although the proportion of the Irish in the total of American Catholics dropped below half in 1900 and was scarcely one-third in the 1920s.

49. John Tracy Ellis, "Les États-Unis depuis 1850," in *Nouvelle histoire de l'Église*, vol. 5, ed. Jean Daniélou, Ludovicus Jacobus Rogier, Roger Aubert, and David Knowles (Paris: Seuil, 1975), 294.

50. According to data provided by John T. Ellis, the Polish National Catholic Church (which was merged at the time with the Lithuanian Church) had more than 280,000 faithful in 1960, the American Carpatho-Ruthenian Orthodox little more than one hundred thousand in 1972 (Ellis, "Les États-Unis depuis 1850," 295). Today their membership has dropped, respectively, to around twenty-five thousand (2011) and fourteen thousand (2006).

51. Quoted in Philip Martin and Peter Duignan, *Making and Remaking America: Immigration into the United States* (Stanford, CA: Hoover Institution on War, Revolution, and Peace, Stanford University, 2003), 5.

52. McGreevy, *Catholicism and American Freedom*, 163.

53. Morris, *American Catholic*, 276.

54. Robert C. Christopher, *Crashing the Gates: The De-WASPing of America's Power Elite* (New York: Simon and Schuster, 1989).

55. Thomas D. Snyder, ed., *120 Years of American Education: A Statistical Portrait* (Washington, DC: National Center for Education Statistics, 1993), 83.

56. Morris, *American Catholic*, 277.

NOTES TO CHAPTER 2

1. I will examine the Congregation de Propaganda Fide in greater detail below.

2. Peter McDonough, *The Catholic Labyrinth: Power, Apathy, and a Passion for Reform in the American Church* (New York: Oxford University Press, 2013), xv.

3. Carl Schmitt, *Roman Catholicism and Political Form* (Westport, CT: Greenwood Press, 1996), 7; originally published as *Römischer Katholizismus und politische Form* (Hellerau, Dresden: Jakob Hegner, 1923).

4. The members of the Society of Jesus, created in 1540, who actually arrived in the colonies after the Dominicans and Franciscans, eventually took them over. The Jesuit Francisco Javier arrived in India in 1542 and Japan in 1549; that same year, the Jesuits landed in Brazil and in 1557 in Ethiopia; in 1563 they arrived in Angola; Matteo Ricci arrived in China in 1601, where some members of the Society had already been since 1582. In 1567 Santa Elena became the base of operations for Jesuits in Florida; in Canada the first Jesuit schools were opened in 1615.

5. Massimo Franco, *Imperi paralleli: Vaticano e Stati Uniti: due secoli di alleanza e conflitto, 1788–2005* (Milan: Mondadori, 2005), 2. Because the English is incomplete, we had to translate directly from the Italian version of the book.

6. Massimo Franco, *Parallel Empires: The Vatican and the United States—Two Centuries of Alliance and Conflict* (New York: Doubleday, 2008), 23.

7. Quoted in Helen A. Heinz, " 'We Are All as One Fish in the Sea . . .' Catholicism in Protestant Pennsylvania: 1730–1790 (PhD diss., Temple University, 2008), 437.

8. Charles Francis Adams, ed., *The Works of John Adams, Second President of the United States*, vol. 7 (Boston: Little, Brown, 1856), 110.

9. Francis Rooney, *The Global Vatican: An Inside Look at the Catholic Church, World Politics, and the Extraordinary Relationship Between the United States and the Holy See* (Lanham, MD: Rowman and Littlefield, 2013), 27.

10. John Carroll became an advocate of using English in religious ceremonies: "Can there be anything more preposterous than an unknown tongue?" he asked in 1787. The direct reference was to Latin, the indirect to French, the language of the Archdiocese of Quebec. See Peter Guilday, *The Life and Times of John Carroll, Archbishop of Baltimore, 1735–1815* (New York: Encyclopedia Press, 1922), 130.

11. John Carroll to Lord Petre, Jan. 17, 1790, quoted in William Thomas Russell, *Maryland, the Land of Sanctuary: A History of Religious Toleration in Maryland from the First Settlement Until the American Revolution* (Baltimore: J. H. Furst, 1907), 509.

12. At the beginning of the eighteenth century two subsequent popes' decrees condemned the "Chinese rites," that is, the attempt of Jesuits to convert the Chinese to Christianity by adopting sinological customs and some of those rites. This decision, taken when in China, according to François Hominal, the Catholic community numbered two hundred thousand faithful, marks the end of the expansion of Catholicism in China for almost two centuries. See François Hominal, "L'évangélisation de la Chine et la querelle des rites," Ricci Institute of Paris, Seminar in Nantes, Dec. 1, 2014, slide 57.

13. With the law of July 1790 the French Constituent Assembly imposed the oath of loyalty on the clergy, rendering their status equivalent to that of civil servants. In the letter *Quod aliquantum* (March 1791), Pius VI condemned the decision: "The necessary effect of the constitution decreed by the Assembly is to annihilate the Catholic Religion and, with her, the obedience owed to Kings. With this purpose it establishes as a right of man in society this absolute liberty that not only insures the right to be indifferent to religious opinions, but also grants full license to freely think, speak, write and even print whatever one wishes on religious matters." See Pope Pius VI, "Religious Liberty, a 'Monstrous Right,'" http://traditioninaction.org/religious/no51rp_ReligiousLiberty.htm. In 1792, about seventy thousand "refractory priests" were forced to leave France.

14. J. Robert Moskin, *American Statecraft: The Story of the U.S. Foreign Service* (New York: St. Martin's, 2013), 54.

15. See Peter C. Kent and John F. Pollard, "A Diplomacy Unlike Any Other: Papal Diplomacy in the Nineteenth and Twentieth Centuries," in *Papal Diplomacy in the Modern Age*, ed. Peter C. Kent and John F. Pollard (Westport, CT: Praeger, 1994), 12.

16. See Gerald P. Fogarty, *The Vatican and the American Hierarchy from 1870 to 1965* (Collegeville, MN: Liturgical Press, 1985), 117.

17. In 1830 there were the July Revolution in France, the separation of Belgium from the Netherlands, and the anti-Russian uprising in Poland; in 1831 there was an anti-Austrian insurrection in Modena and the uprising of the Legations of Bologna, Ferrara, Forlì, and Ravenna against the Papal States. Gregory XVI, just elected, sought and obtained the intervention of the Austrian army to quell the revolt.

18. Pope Gregory XVI, *Mirari vos* (1832), secs. 14, 15. See www.papalen cyclicals.net/Greg16/g16mirar.htm for the English version.

19. Pope Gregory XVI, *In supremo apostolatus*, www.papalencyclicals.net/ Greg16/g16sup.htm.

20. Quoted in Franco, *Parallel Empires*, 30.

21. See Thomas Brynmor Morgan, *The Listening Post: Eighteen Years on Vatican Hill* (New York: G. P. Putnam, 1944), 73.

22. See James F. Connelly, *The Visit of Archbishop Gaetano Bedini to the United States of America* (Rome: Libreria editrice dell'Università gregoriana, 1960), 78n12.

23. Pius IX, *Iamdum cernimus*, www.totustuustools.net/magistero/p9iamdum .htm. I was not able to find an English version of this encyclical; this is my translation from the Italian version.

24. Timothy A. Byrnes, *Catholic Bishops in American Politics* (Princeton, NJ: Princeton University Press, 1991), 13.

25. Blanche Marie McEniry, *American Catholics in the War with Mexico* (Washington, DC: Catholic University of America Press, 1937), 13.

26. He had met with the bishops, appointed two Jesuit chaplains, and ordered the troops to respect Mexicans' places of worship. For these two decisions the Nativists demanded his resignation. See Ted C. Hinckley, "American Anti-Catholicism During the Mexican War," *Pacific Historical Review* 31, no. 2 (1962): 121–37.

27. Fredrick B. Pike, "Le catholicisme en Amérique Latine," in *Nouvelle histoire de l'Église*, vol. 5, ed. Jean Daniélou, Ludovicus Jacobus Rogier, Roger Aubert, and David Knowles (Paris: Seuil, 1975), 364.

28. On this subject see John C. Pinheiro, *Missionaries of Republicanism: A Religious History of the Mexican-American War* (New York: Oxford University Press, 2014); Robert R. Miller, *Shamrock and Sword: The Saint Patrick's Battalion in the US-Mexican War* (Norman: University of Oklahoma Press, 1989); James Callaghan, "The San Patricios," in *American Heritage*, Nov. 1995; and Michael Hogan, *The Irish Soldiers of Mexico* (Trafford, UK: Intercambio Press, 1997).

29. See Giacomo Martina, *Pio IX: 1851–1866* (Rome: Editrice Pontificia Università Gregoriana, 1985), 536.

30. *La civiltà cattolica*, year 46, ser. 16, vol. 2 (Rome: La civiltà cattolica, 1895), 375.

31. Actually, the French emperor was forced to abdicate three years later, dragging down with him what was left of the Papal States.

32. Luca Castagna, *Un ponte oltre l'oceano: Assetti politici e strategie diplomatiche tra Stati Uniti e Santa Sede nella prima metà del Novecento, 1914–1940* (Bologna: Il Mulino, 2011), 72n. Henceforth, I will quote from the English translation—*A Bridge Across the Ocean: The United States and the Holy See Between the Two World Wars* (Washington, DC: Catholic University of America Press, 2014)—except when the translation is incorrect or omits something. In this case (page 18) the English translation ignores this entire note.

33. The historian Arturo Carlo Jemolo writes that the Church authorities realized little by little that "the temporal power had been a burden to the Holy See, and that . . . the possibility of working more and better in spreading Catholicism in the world, and of governing by the firm hand of the Church, only increased with the loss of that power." See Arturo Carlo Jemolo, *Chiesa e stato in Italia negli ultimi cento anni* (Turin: Einaudi, 1948), 42.

34. Orestes A. Brownson, "Are Catholics Pro-slavery and Disloyal?" *Brownson's Quarterly Review*, 3rd New York series, vol. 4 (July 1863): 367–79, 372.

35. Albon P. Man Jr., "The Church and the New York Draft Riots of 1863," *Records of the American Catholic Historical Society of Philadelphia* 62, no. 1 (1951): 35.

36. Charles Morris, *American Catholic: The Saints and Sinners Who Built America's Most Powerful Church* (New York: Times Books, 1997), 79.

37. Quoted in Charles E. Curran, *Catholic Moral Theology in the United States: A History* (Washington, DC: Georgetown University Press, 2008), 15.

38. James J. Hennesey, *American Catholics: A History of the Roman Catholic Community in the United States* (New York: Oxford University Press, 1981), 145.

39. All quotations used in this and the following two paragraphs are from Man, "The Church and the New York Draft Riots of 1863," 39–48.

40. James M. McPherson, *Battle Cry of Freedom: The Civil War Era* (New York: Oxford University Press, 1988), 431.

41. Martina, *Pio IX*, 486, 487.

42. "La schiavitù, considerata di per sé e in assoluto, non ripugna il diritto naturale e divino," Instruction 1293, *Collectanea Sacrae Congregationis de Propaganda Fide: Seu decreta, instructiones, rescripta pro apostolicis missionibus*, vol. 1 (Rome: Typographia polyglotta, 1907), 715–20.

43. Quoted in Hudson Strode, ed., *Jefferson Davis: Private Letters, 1823–1899* (New York: Harcourt, Brace and World, 1966), 473.

44. Martina, *Pio IX*, 494.

45. Quoted in Rooney, *The Global Vatican*, 55.

46. John F. Pollard, *Money and the Rise of the Modern Papacy* (Cambridge: Cambridge University Press, 2005), 73.

47. David I. Kertzer, *Prisoner of the Vatican: The Popes, the Kings, and Garibaldi's Rebels in the Struggle to Rule Modern Italy* (Boston: Houghton Mifflin, 2006).

48. Castagna, *A Bridge Across the Ocean*, 11–58. The "Roman Question" began when Rome was declared the future capital of Italy, in March 1861. It ended in 1929, when the Holy See and Italy agreed on the creation of the Vatican City State and the payment, by Italy, of 750 million lira, plus consolidated bearer bonds with a coupon rate of 5 percent and a nominal value of 1 billion lira, as definitive settlement of the claims concerning territories and property lost by the Papal States between 1860 and 1871.

49. Morris, *American Catholic*, 102.

50. Roger Aubert, "L'Église catholique de la crise de 1848 à la Première Guerre mondiale," in *Nouvelle histoire de l'Église*, vol. 5, ed. Jean Daniélou, Ludovicus Jacobus Rogier, Roger Aubert, and David Knowles (Paris: Seuil, 1975), 85. The artillery officer Alfred Dreyfus, of Alsatian descent and accused of spying for Germany, was degraded and sentenced. The accusations, entirely fabricated, unleashed a wave of anti-Semitism ridden by broad sectors of Catholicism. In a book of 1933 the priest Joseph Brugerette, a "Dreyfusard," recalled the climate of the time: "The majority of priests and bishops remain convinced that Dreyfus is guilty." See Joseph Brugerette, *Le prêtre français et la société contemporaine*,

tome 2, *Vers la Séparation (1871–1901)* (Paris: J. de Gigord, 1935), 440–41. The law of separation of church and state, passed in 1905, preceded by one year the rehabilitation of Dreyfus.

51. Aubert, "L'Église catholique de la crise de 1848 à la Première Guerre mondiale," 85. In a conversation with the Baron of Montagnac, hostile to the policy of rallying, Leo XIII made his intentions explicit: "Once the Catholics have entered the republic, they will go everywhere, to places and polling stations; henceforth they will be the masters and overthrow the republic, which they will replace with a monarchy, if they want. Believe me, no one more than I want the fall of the republic." See Emmanuel Barbier, *Rome et l'action libérale populaire: Histoire et documents* (Poitiers: Blais and Roy Imprimeurs, 1906), 60.

52. See Morris, *American Catholic*, 102.

53. Pope Leo XIII, *Concerning New Opinions, Virtue, Nature and Grace, with Regard to Americanism*, www.papalencyclicals.net/Leo13/l13teste.htm.

54. John Tracy Ellis, "Les États-Unis depuis 1850," in *Nouvelle histoire de l'Église*, vol. 5, ed. Jean Daniélou, Ludovicus Jacobus Rogier, Roger Aubert, and David Knowles (Paris: Seuil, 1975), 303. Gallicanism is the attempt to separate the French Catholic hierarchy from Rome, subduing it to the authority of the state. Its roots are lost in the fourteenth century, when the making of modern France begins.

55. Ibid., 302.

56. Sophie Ramond, "La crise de l'origine: La science catholique des Évangiles et l'histoire au XXᵉ siècle," *Esprit et vie*, no. 171 (May 2007).

57. Ellis, "Les États-Unis depuis 1850," 304.

58. Pope Leo XIII, *In amplissimo*, secs. 3, 5, w2.vatican.va/content/leo-xiii/en/encyclicals/documents/hf_l-xiii_enc_15041902_in-amplissimo.html.

59. Pollard, *Money and the Rise of the Modern Papacy*, 32. This is what the Vatican website provides regarding St. Peter's Pence: "Peter's Pence is the name given to the financial support offered by the faithful to the Holy Father as a sign of their sharing in the concern of the Successor of Peter for the many different needs of the Universal Church and for the relief of those most in need" (www.vatican.va/roman_curia/secretariat_state/obolo_spietro/documents/index_en.htm).

60. Edoardo Soderini, *Il pontificato di Leone XIII* (Milan: Mondadori, 1932), 402–3.

61. Morris, *Catholic American*, 187.

62. As reported in the journal of the Baron Carlo Monti, a personal friend of the pope and intermediary with the Italian Government, on January 3, 1917. See *La conciliazione ufficiosa: Diario del barone Carlo Monti incaricato d'affari del governo italiano presso la Santa Sede: 1914–1922*, vol. 2 (Rome: Libreria editrice vaticana, 1997), 4.

63. Thomas E. Hachey, ed., *Anglo-Vatican Relations, 1914–1939: Confidential Annual Reports of the British Ministers to the Holy See* (Boston: G. K. Hall, 1972), 71.

64. Pollard, *Money and the Rise of the Modern Papacy*, 137.

1. Quoted in Paolo Mieli, "Chiesa e diritti umani: Una lunga diffidenza," *Corriere della Sera*, April 17, 2012.

2. Ibid.

3. See Luca Castagna, *A Bridge Across the Ocean: The United States and the Holy See Between the Two World Wars* (Washington, DC: Catholic University of America Press, 2014), 32.

4. Massimo Franco, *Imperi paralleli: Vaticano e Stati Uniti—Due secoli di alleanza e conflitto, 1788–2005* (Milan: Mondadori, 2005), 3. Here again I use the Italian version because there are some essential words lost in translation; here is the sentence in the English version: "They are the only institutions with a truly global reach." Massimo Franco, *Parallel Empires: The Vatican and the United States—Two Centuries of Alliance and Conflict* (New York: Doubleday, 2008), xi.

5. Castagna, *A Bridge Across the Ocean*, 11.

6. Benedict XV, *Ad beatissimi apostolorum principis*, sec. 5, w2.vatican.va/content/benedict-xv/en/encyclicals/documents/hf_ben-xv_enc_01111914_ad-beatissimi-apostolorum.html.

7. Stewart A. Stehlin, "The Emergence of a New Vatican Diplomacy During the Great War and Its Aftermath, 1914–1929," in *Papal Diplomacy in the Modern Age*, ed. Peter C. Kent and John F. Pollard (Westport, CT: Praeger, 1994), 75.

8. In the encyclical of November 1914, among other things, the pope wrote that "he who contumaciously resists the legitimate exercise of human authority, resists God and is preparing for himself eternal punishment," an admonition whose corollary was "the obligation of obeying the commands of those in authority, not in any kind of way, but religiously, that is conscientiously" (*Ad beatissimi apostolorum principis*, sec. 10).

9. Castagna, *A Bridge Across the Ocean*, 38. James Gibbons, the archbishop of Baltimore, served as the unofficial representative of the American bishops in government circles.

10. Pope Benedict XV, *Pacem, Dei munus pulcherrimum*, sec. 17, w2.vatican.va/content/benedict-xv/en/encyclicals/documents/hf_ben-xv_enc_23051920_pacem-dei-munus-pulcherrimum.html.

11. Pius XI, *Ubi arcano Dei consilio*, sec. 45, w2.vatican.va/content/pius-xi/en/encyclicals/documents/hf_p-xi_enc_23121922_ubi-arcano-dei-consilio.html.

12. Richard Nikolaus von Coudenhove-Kalergi, *Pan-Europa* (Zurich: Paneuropa, 1923).

13. On this subject see my two articles "La Chiesa e l'Europa, cinquant'anni di vantaggio," *Limes*, no. 1 (Feb. 2008): 269–83; and "Europa magistra mundi: La grande strategia della Chiesa di Roma," *Limes*, no. 5 (Oct. 2009): 91–106.

14. Stehlin, "Emergence of a New Vatican Diplomacy," 79.

15. For a long time the Vatican kept an open mind about Soviet Russia. Kent and Pollard write that after 1917 "the Holy See sought to exploit the chaos in Russia by sending in missionaries," and, to this effect, made "persistent attempts

to seek good relations with the Bolsheviks between 1917 and 1929." Peter C. Kent and John F. Pollard, "A Diplomacy Unlike Any Other: Papal Diplomacy in the Nineteenth and Twentieth Centuries," in *Papal Diplomacy in the Modern Age*, ed. Peter C. Kent and John F. Pollard (Westport, CT: Praeger, 1994), 17. Jonathan Luxmoore and Jolanta Babiuch report that, a few months after the revolution of October 1917, "some Vatican sources" referred to a "positive evolution" in Russia. The same authors note that a Catholic vicariate was created in Siberia in 1921 and was transformed in 1923 into the diocese of Vladivostok. See Jonathan Luxmoore and Jolanta Babiuch, *The Vatican and the Red Flag: The Struggle for the Soul of Eastern Europe* (London: Geoffrey Chapman, 1999), 9, 10. Stewart Stehlin adds that "Moscow initially showed interest, but was not willing to negotiate on matters considered vital to [the] Vatican, such as the founding of [a] religious school in Russia" (Stehlin, "Emergence of a New Vatican," 81). The rupture between Moscow and the Vatican can be dated to the end of the 1920s, when the tone of the Church's anticommunist campaign grew more and more vehement.

16. Charles Morris, *American Catholic: The Saints and Sinners Who Built America's Most Powerful Church* (New York: Times Books, 1997), 229.

17. See Luca Castagna, *Un ponte oltre l'oceano: Assetti politici e strategie diplomatiche tra Stati Uniti e Santa Sede nella prima metà del Novecento, 1914–1940* (Bologna: Il Mulino, 2011), 264. In the English version (page 129) the second part of the sentence has been omitted.

18. Dominic Tierney, *FDR and the Spanish Civil War: Neutrality and Commitment in the Struggle That Divided America* (Durham, NC: Duke University Press, 2007), 122.

19. Michael Barone, "Franklin D. Roosevelt: A Protestant Patrician in a Catholic Party," in *FDR, the Vatican, and the Roman Catholic Church in America, 1933–1945*, ed. David B. Woolner and Richard G. Kurial (New York: Palgrave Macmillan, 2003), 9.

20. Morris, *American Catholic*, 238.

21. Charles R. Gallagher, *Vatican Secret Diplomacy: Joseph P. Hurley and Pope Pius XII* (New Haven, CT: Yale University Press, 2008), 135–36.

22. See Domenico Tardini, *Pio XII* (Città del Vaticano: Tipografia poliglotta vaticana, 1960), 163.

23. See Philippe Chenaux, *Une Europe vaticane? Entre le plan Marshall et les Traités de Rome* (Bruxelles: Éditions Ciaco, 1990), 27.

24. Agostino Casaroli, Pope Paul VI's "foreign minister," remembers that for years one could read in the Pontifical Yearbook "a note, although partial and a little awkward" concerning "Breslavia, Breslau, Wrocław," even defined an "Eastern German" city in a caption that appeared in *L'Osservatore romano* on April 5, 1967. See Agostino Casaroli, *Il martirio della pazienza: La Santa Sede e i paesi comunisti (1963–1989)* (Torino: Einaudi, 2000), 260.

25. Italo Garzia, "La diplomazia vaticana e il problema dell'assetto postbellico," in *Pio XII*, ed. Andrea Riccardi (Rome: Laterza, 1984), 217.

26. Joseph S. Rossi, *Uncharted Territory: The American Catholic Church at the United Nations, 1946–1972* (Washington, DC: Catholic University of America Press, 2006), xii.

27. *Antequam ordinem*, address to the cardinals during the secret consistory on March 10, 1919 (quoted in Henri Laurens, "Le Vatican et la question de la Palestine," in *Nations et Saint-Siège au XXe siècle*, ed. Hélène Carrère d'Encausse and Philippe Levillain [Paris: Fayard, 2000], 311).

28. See Esther Webman, "Adoption of the Protocols in the Arab Discourse on the Arab-Israeli Conflict, Zionism, and the Jews," in *The Global Impact of the Protocols of the Elders of Zion: A Century-Old Myth*, ed. Esther Webman (London: Routledge, 2011), 176. Unlike many other historians, Webman affirms on this same page that the very first translation from French into Arabic was made by an Egyptian priest, al-Khuri Anton Yamin, who published the book "in the mid-1920s" under the title *Mu'marat al yahudiyya 'ala al-shu'ub* (The Jewish plot against the nations). The Protocols of the Elders of Zion is a text forged in the early twentieth century by the Russian secret police and disseminated as an authentic document composed by a sort of council of Jewish elders, containing plans to take over the world. In many Middle Eastern countries today the *Protocols* are officially presented as genuine. On this subject see Sergio Romano, *I falsi protocolli: Il "complotto ebraico" dalla Russia di Nicola II a oggi* (Milan: Corbaccio, 1992).

29. Cardinal Maglione to the apostolic delegate in London, William Godfrey, May 4, 1943, in *Actes et documents du Saint Siège relatifs à la Seconde Guerre mondiale*, ed. Pierre Blet, Robert A. Graham, Angelo Martini, and Burkhart Schneider, vol. 9, *Le Saint Siège et les victimes de la guerre janvier–décembre 1943* (Rome: Libreria editrice vaticana, 1975), 272.

30. *Auspicia quaedam*, May 1948; *In multiplicibus curis*, October 1948; and *Redemptoris nostri*, April 1949.

31. "La cristianità di fronte al dramma della Terra Santa," *Agenzia Internazionale Fides*, May 7, 1949. The article was reproduced in its entirety in *La Civiltà cattolica*, 1949, 2:584–87.

32. Robert Michael, *A Concise History of American Antisemitism* (Lanham, MD: Rowman and Littlefield, 2005), 150.

33. Quoted in Paul Charles Merkley, *Christian Attitudes Towards the State of Israel* (Montreal: McGill-Queen's University Press, 2001), 142, 143.

34. Morris, *American Catholic*, 230.

35. There is significant literature regarding the debate in the Vatican on postwar political arrangements. Pius XII would have preferred a "Spanish" solution; while the cardinals Alfredo Ottaviani and Domenico Tardini would have favored a plurality of Christian parties, without excluding, as writes Sandro Magister, a "Christian Communist" party; see Sandro Magister, *La politica vaticana e l'Italia, 1943–1978* (Rome: Editori Riuniti, 1979), 39. According to Giulio Andreotti, Pius XII feared the inevitable compromises that a nominally Christian party would have to accept; see Giulio Andreotti, *Intervista su De Gasperi* (Rome: Laterza, 1977),

22. It was the Americans, writes Paul Ginsborg, who settled the issue by choosing to support the DC (Paul Ginsborg, *Storia d'Italia dal dopoguerra ad oggi: Società e politica, 1943–1988* (Turin: Einaudi, 1988), 62.

36. Pio XII, Address to the Sacred College on June 2, 1948. See also Chenaux, *Une Europe vaticane?* 35.

37. Francesco Traniello, "Pio XII," in *Enciclopedia dei Papi* (Rome: Treccani, 2000), www.treccani.it/enciclopedia/pio-xii_(Enciclopedia-dei-Papi)/.

38. Peter Hebblethwaite, "Pope Pius XII: Chaplain of the Atlantic Alliance?" in *Italy in the Cold War: Politics, Culture and Society*, ed. Christopher Duggan and Christopher Wagstaff (Oxford: Berg, 1995), 68.

39. Dorothy Day, "Where Are the Poor?" *Catholic Worker*, no. 1 (Jan. 1955): 6.

40. See, e.g., John Cooney, *The American Pope: The Life and Times of Francis Cardinal Spellman* (New York: Times Books, 1984), 306.

41. Ennio di Nolfo, *Vaticano e Stati Uniti, 1939–1952: Dalle carte di Myron C. Taylor* (Milan: Franco Angeli, 1978), 674.

42. See Chenaux, *Une Europe vaticane?* 233.

43. Of the cardinals appointed by Pope Pius XII, 23.2 percent came from Asia, Africa, and Latin America (compared to only 3.9 percent of those appointed by his predecessor). See Chapter 7.

44. See Roger Aubert, "Le demi-siècle qui a préparé Vatican II," in *Nouvelle histoire de l'Église*, vol. 5, ed. Jean Daniélou, Ludovicus Jacobus Rogier, Roger Aubert, and David Knowles (Paris: Seuil, 1975), 633.

45. Pope Paul VI, *Populorum progressio*, March 26, 1967, sec. 3, w2.vatican.va/content/paul-vi/en/encyclicals/documents/hf_p-vi_enc_26031967_populorum.html.

46. Henry Kissinger, *Diplomacy* (New York: Simon and Schuster, 1995), 703.

NOTES TO CHAPTER 4

1. Mark Feldstein, "JFK's Own Dirty Trick," *Washington Post*, Jan. 14, 2011.

2. Charles Morris, *American Catholic: The Saints and Sinners Who Built America's Most Powerful Church* (New York: Times Books, 1997), 151.

3. It is worth mentioning that the birth of the "social doctrine" of the Church corresponded to its transformation into a leading figure of financial capitalism. On this subject see John F. Pollard, *Money and the Rise of the Modern Papacy* (Cambridge: Cambridge University Press, 2005); Alberto Caracciolo, *Roma capitale: Dal Risorgimento alla crisi dello Stato liberale* (Rome: Riuniti, 1956), chaps. 5 and 6; and my *Il secolo cattolico: La strategia geopolitica della Chiesa* (Rome: Laterza, 2012), chap. 2.

4. In his encyclical *Laudato si'* of May 2015 Pope Francis reiterates: "The absolute power of a financial system . . . will only give rise to new crises after a slow, costly and only apparent recovery." Pope Francis, *Laudato si'*, sec. 189, w2.vatican.va/content/francesco/en/encyclicals/documents/papa-francesco_20150524_enciclica-laudato-si.html.

5. Quoted in Eugenio Pacelli, ed., "Circa la situazione della Santa Sede in

Italia," minutes of the internal meeting of the Congregation, March 29, 1917, in "Le città di Dio," *Limes*, no. 3 (1993): 115.

6. Francis J. Lally, *The Catholic Church in a Changing America* (Boston: Little, Brown, 1962), 49.

7. See, e.g., John T. McGreevy, "Catholics in America: Antipathy and Assimilation," in *American Catholics, American Culture: Tradition and Resistance*, vol. 2 of *American Catholics in the Public Square*, ed. Margaret O'Brien Steinfels (Lanham, MD: Rowman and Littlefield, 2004), 15.

8. Pope Pius XI, *Quadregesimo anno*, sec. 107, w2.vatican.va/content/pius -xi/en/encyclicals/documents/hf_p-xi_enc_19310515_quadragesimo-anno.html.

9. After all, Roosevelt did not hide that he was "deeply impressed by what he [Mussolini] has accomplished," announcing to the American ambassador in Rome (June 1933) that he wanted to stay "in fairly close touch with that admirable Italian gentleman"; see, e.g., John Patrick Diggins, *Mussolini and Fascism: The View from America* (Princeton, NJ: Princeton University Press, 1972), 279.

10. Michael Barone, "A Protestant Patrician in a Catholic Party," in *FDR, the Vatican, and the Catholic Church in America, 1933–1945*, ed. David B. Woolner and Richard G. Kurial (New York: Palgrave Macmillan, 2003), 3.

11. See Luca Castagna, *Un ponte oltre l'oceano: Assetti politici e strategie diplomatiche tra Stati Uniti e Santa Sede nella prima metà del Novecento, 1914–1940* (Bologna: Il Mulino, 2011), 204–5. Here again I have translated from the Italian original because the entire citation was expurgated from the English edition (see Luca Castagna, *A Bridge Across the Ocean: The United States and the Holy See Between the Two World Wars* [Washington, DC: Catholic University of America Press, 2014], 104–5).

12. Castagna, *A Bridge Across the Ocean*, 120 (my emphasis).

13. Ibid., 123.

14. Quoted in George Q. Flynn, *American Catholics and the Roosevelt Presidency, 1932–1936* (Lexington: University Press of Kentucky, 1968), 54.

15. Walsh never got to serve, however; he died on his way to Washington, where he was going to attend Roosevelt's inauguration.

16. Leonard Dinnerstein, *Anti-Semitism in America* (New York: Oxford University Press, 1994), 133. Also according to Elena Fallo, "one of the most hostile ethnic groups to the Jews was certainly that of the Irish"; Elena Fallo, *Antisemitismo in America* (Boves: Araba Fenice, 2008), 70.

17. Morris, *American Catholic*, 253.

18. Timothy A. Byrnes, *Catholic Bishops in American Politics* (Princeton, NJ: Princeton University Press, 1991), 5.

19. Charles Morris draws up a long list: various Catholic bar associations and Catholic medical societies (which includes the Catholic Physicians' Guild, "the largest organization of Catholic doctors in the world"); the National Council of Catholic Nurses; the American Catholic Sociological Society; the National Catholic Education Association; the Catholic Press Association; the American Catho-

lic Philosophical Association; the American Catholic Historical Association; the Catholic Anthropological Association; the Catholic Writers' Guild of America; the Catholic Poetry Society of America; the Catholic Economic Association; the American Psychological Association; the Association of Catholic Trade Unionists; the Catholic Summer Resort Movement; the Catholic Legion of Decency; the National Catholic Youth Organization; as well as the National Council of Catholic Men and National Council of Catholic Women, Catholic Action Department, and the Knights of Columbus, which in time became the main reference point for Catholic businessmen (see Morris, *American Catholic*, 160–61).

20. Byrnes, *Catholic Bishops in American Politics*, 4–5.

21. Jacques Berlinerblau, *Thumpin' It: The Use and Abuse of the Bible in Today's Presidential Politics* (Louisville, KY: Westminster John Knox Press, 2008), 9.

22. Ibid., 10. A legal case took place between July 10 and 21, 1925, in Dayton, Tennessee, against John Thomas Scopes, who was accused of teaching the theory of evolution in contravention of the state law that prohibited denying "the Story of the Divine Creation of man as taught in the Bible." Scopes was convicted, but his defense attorney, Clarence Darrow, illustrated so brilliantly the contradictions in the Bible that, thereafter, the case was considered a great victory for the evolutionists.

23. Berlinerblau refers to the decisions of the Supreme Court in the cases of *McCollum v. Board of Education* (which forbade religious education in public schools, 1948), *Engel v. Vitale* (which forbade prayers in public schools, 1962), and of *Abington School District v. Schempp* (which forbade the reading of the Bible in public schools, 1963). To these rulings need to be added some legislative measures, including those taken between 1958 and 1967 abolishing all laws that restricted the teaching of biology to what is written in the Bible, thus excluding, among other things, the theory of evolution (the bone of contention in the Scopes Monkey Trial of 1925).

24. Lydia Saad, "Churchgoing Among U.S. Catholics Slides to Tie Protestants," Gallup Institute, April 9, 2009, www.gallup.com/poll/117382/church-going -among-catholics-slides-tie-protestants.aspx.

25. There is also a link between the improving of material conditions of existence and the *increase* in religious practice when—to outline it briefly—an increase of income is accompanied by a persistent social uncertainty. On this subject see my *Guerra santa e santa alleanza: Religioni e disordine internazionale nel XXI secolo* (Bologna: Il Mulino, 2014), 55–61.

26. Liston Pope, "Religion and Class Structure," *Annals of the American Academy of Political and Social Science* 256 (March 1948): 84–91.

27. Morris, *American Catholic*, 256.

28. Andrew Greely, *The Catholic Myth: The Behavior and Beliefs of American Catholics* (New York: Touchstone, 1990), 73. Byrnes describes a 1974 investigation by the National Opinion Research Center that confirmed the superiority of the average income of Catholics but at the same time explains that "in terms of occupational prestige, . . . Catholics continued to fall well below the national average" (Byrnes, *Catholic Bishops in American Politics*, 36).

29. Lewis Perry, *Intellectual Life in America: A History*, (Chicago: University of Chicago Press, 1989), 435.

30. Patrick J. Reardon, "JFK and the Cafeteria Bishops: 50 Years After Kennedy Asserted Independence from the Pope, the Tide Has Turned," *National Catholic Reporter*, August 10, 2010.

31. Mark Tooley, "Eisenhower's Religion," *American Spectator*, Feb. 14, 2011. On the concept of "Judeo-Christianity" see Graziano, *Guerra santa e Santa alleanza*, 141–43.

32. Quoted in Kevin M. Kruse, *One Nation Under God: How Corporate America Invented Christian America* (New York: Basic Books, 2015), 109.

33. Dwight D. Eisenhower, "Statement by the President upon Signing Bill to Include the Words 'Under God' in the Pledge to the Flag," June 14, 1954, *The American Presidency Project*, by John T. Woolley and Gerhard Peters, www.presidency.ucsb.edu/ws/?pid=9920.

34. Between April 1958 and December 1959 the percentages of those who were hostile to a Catholic president had many ups and downs, reaching a minimum of 21 percent and a maximum of 27 percent; and among those who saw no problem in a Catholic candidate, the peak was 72 percent and the dip 67 percent. See David W. Moore, "Little Prejudice Against a Woman, Jewish, Black or Catholic Presidential Candidate," Gallup Institute, June 10, 2003, www.gallup.com/poll/8611/little-prejudice-against-woman-jewish-black-catholic-presidenti.aspx. According to the same institute, the historical series covering the period from 1937 to 2003 shows less reluctance among American voters about a Jewish candidate than about a Catholic candidate (although, against three Catholic candidates for the presidency and five for the vice presidency, in the entire history of the United States, there has been only one Jewish candidate for the vice presidency: Joe Lieberman, in 2000).

35. Richard M. Nixon, *Memoirs* (New York: Touchstone, 1978), 215. This explains why, when the Methodist minister Norman Vincent Peale ("possibly the nation's most prominent Protestant minister of the time") publicly stated that the Catholic hierarchy would force Kennedy "to bring American foreign policy into line with Vatican objectives," Nixon reacted angrily: "I knew we were in for real trouble"; see Gary A. Donaldson, *The First Modern Campaign: Kennedy, Nixon, and the Election of 1960* (Lanham, MD: Rowman and Littlefield, 2007), 107. Note that Peale's statements provoked, according to Donaldson, an "overwhelming outcry," with a public condemnation of a hundred religious leaders, Protestants and Jews, to the point of forcing him to suspend his cooperation in numerous newspapers.

36. John Tracy Ellis, "American Catholics and the Intellectual Life," *Thought* 30 (Autumn 1955): 351–88, 386.

37. According to Byrnes, those positions were encouraged by two other factors: the outcome of the Second Vatican Council, which "rejected a defensive posture and called for the Church to move out into the world . . . and [to] bring the gospel

to bear on the world's problems"; and "the nationalization of the policy power" in the 1960s, which "greatly increased the federal government's authority and obligations." See Byrnes, *Catholic Bishops in American Politics*, 39–40, 45–46.

38. John Neuhaus, *The Naked Public Square: Religion and Democracy in America*, 2nd ed. (Grand Rapids, MI: William B. Eerdmans, 1986), xi.

39. The famous speech delivered before the (Protestant) Greater Houston Ministerial Association on September 12, 1960, from which this declaration is taken, had a distinct defensive note: "I believe in an America," said Kennedy, "where no Catholic prelate would tell the President—should he be Catholic—how to act . . . where no church or church school is granted any public funds or political preference . . . where no public official either requests or accept[s] instructions on public policy from the Pope, the National Council of Churches or any other ecclesiastical source; where no religious body seeks to impose its will directly or indirectly upon the general populace or the public acts of its officials." See Robert V. Friedenberg, *Notable Speeches in Contemporary Presidential Campaigns* (Westport, CT: Praeger, 2002), 56.

40. Massimo Franco, *Parallel Empires: The Vatican and the United States—Two Centuries of Alliance and Conflict* (New York: Doubleday, 2008), 77.

41. Theodor H. White, *The Making of the President 1960* (New York: Atheneum House, 1961), 240.

42. Eric O. Hanson, *The Catholic Church in the World Politics* (Princeton, NJ: Princeton University Press, 1987), 11.

43. Jonathan Beale, "Pope May Find US on His Wavelength," *BBC News*, April 15, 2008, http://news.bbc.co.uk/2/hi/europe/7348087.stm.

44. I refer the reader again to my *Guerra santa e Santa alleanza*, dedicated specifically to the return of religion to the public stage. Regarding the 1970s, see chapters 2 through 7.

45. Jeffrey Haynes, *An Introduction to International Relations and Religion* (Harlow, UK: Pearson Education, 2007), 9.

46. In this issue (April 8, 1966) some articles replied negatively to this question, and only three and a half years later (Dec. 26, 1969), the same magazine published another cover story entitled "Is God Coming Back to Life?"

47. Frank Newport, "In U.S., Four in 10 Report Attending Church in Last Week," Gallup Institute, Dec. 24, 2013, www.gallup.com/poll/166613/four-report -attending-church-last-week.aspx.

48. Louis Bolce and Gerald De Maio, "Our Secularist Democratic Party," *Public Interest* 149 (Fall 2002): 9.

49. Theodor H. White, *The Making of the President 1972* (New York: Atheneum House, 1973), 35.

50. According to various analyses, it appears that Kennedy and Johnson obtained 60 percent of the white working-class votes, while McGovern obtained 32 percent, Clinton (1992) 39 percent, and Barack Obama 47 percent in 2008 and 36 percent in 2012. Thus the strategy of the recovery of the white working class,

described by Ruy Teixeira and Joel Rogers in 2000 in their book *America's Forgotten Majority: Why the White Working Class Still Matters* (New York: Basic Books, 2000), does not seem to have been successful. According to Charlie Cox, the reason is that the Democrats "subordinated their traditional focus on helping lower and working class Americans to move up the economic ladder in favor of other noble priorities" (Charlie Cox, "Democrats Paved the Way for Their Own Decline," *National Journal*, Dec. 1, 2014). On this subject see also Andrew Levison, *The White Working Class Today: Who They Are, How They Think and How Progressives Can Regain Their Support* (Lexington, KY: Democratic Strategist Press, 2013).

51. Bolce and Di Maio, "Our Secularist Democratic Party," 8.

52. Theodor H. White, *The Making of the President 1968* (New York: Atheneum House, 1969), 422–23.

53. See Franco Palumberi, "Bipartitismo e strategia a Sud," *Lotta comunista*, Sept. 2008. In 2005 the urbanization rate had risen to 64.2 percent (the states considered being Alabama, Arkansas, Georgia, Louisiana, Mississippi, the Carolinas, Tennessee, and Virginia).

54. Phillips considers four cycles starting from 1828 (1828–60, 1860–96, 1896–1932, and 1932–68) of the duration between thirty-two and thirty-six years of a party supremacy, all with an interregnum of eight years of the second party; see Kevin Phillips, *The Emerging Republican Majority* (New Rochelle, NY: Arlington House, 1969). The same periodization (with the addition of the period from 1800 to 1828) has been proposed by Walter D. Burnham in his *Critical Elections and the Mainsprings of American Politics* (New York: Norton, 1970), 8. Navy Vet Terp says that the Republican era 1968–2008 was marked by two interregna; but both Carter and Clinton, elected under exceptional circumstances (the first, after the Watergate scandal, and the second thanks to the "third party" candidacy of Ross Perot), "were arguably Republican Lite"; see Navy Vet Terp, "The Emerging Republican Majority—44 Years Later," *Daily Kos*, August 19, 2013.

55. Robert Christopher, *Crashing the Gates: The De-WASPing of America's Power Elite* (New York: Simon and Schuster, 1989), 80, 81.

56. Andrew R. Flint and Joy Porter, "Jimmy Carter: The Re-emergence of Faith-Based Politics and the Abortion Rights Issue," *Presidential Studies Quarterly* 35, no. 1 (2005): 28–51.

NOTES TO CHAPTER 5

1. Olivier Roy, *Holy Ignorance: When Religion and Culture Part Ways* (Oxford: Oxford University Press, 2013), 5, 194.

2. John S. Dickerson, "The Decline of Evangelical America," *New York Times*, Dec. 15, 2012, www.nytimes.com/2012/12/16/opinion/sunday/the-decline-of-evangelical-america.html?_r=0.

3. On the occasion of Pope Francis's visit to the United States in September 2015, many surveys demonstrated the growing popularity of the Catho-

lic Church and the pope. The Barna Group compared the pope's popularity in 2014 and in 2015, noting a ten-point increase (from 48 percent to 58 percent) among interviewed Protestants. See "What Americans Think of Pope Francis and His Policies," Barna Group, Sept. 16, 2015, www.barna.com/research/what -americans-think-of-pope-francis-and-his-policies.

4. John C. Green, "Seeking a Place: Evangelical Protestants and Public Engagement in the Twentieth Century," in *Toward an Evangelical Public Policy: Political Strategies for the Health of the Nation*, ed. Ronald J. Sider and Diane Knippers (Grand Rapids, MI: Baker Books, 2005), 19.

5. Jacques Berlinerblau, *Thumpin' It: The Use and Abuse of the Bible in Today's Presidential Politics* (Louisville, KY: Westminster John Knox Press, 2008), 9. In this chapter I will use the term *evangelicalism* to indicate a larger concept including Christian Fundamentalists, Pentecostals, and Charismatic Christians. These currents do not always overlap, but going into detail would require a separate study, which would be immediately challenged because, even among experts in the field there is no agreement on these definitions.

6. Sarah Miller-Davenport, " 'Their Blood Shall Not Be Shed in Vain': American Evangelical Missionaries and the Search for God and Country in Post–World War II Asia," *Journal of American History* 99, no. 4 (March 2013): 1109–32, 1109.

7. Berlinerblau, *Thumpin' It*, 14.

8. Timothy A. Byrnes, *Catholic Bishops in American Politics* (Princeton, NJ: Princeton University Press, 1991), 56–57.

9. Ibid., 60.

10. Edward Walsh, "Bishops Like Ford's Stand on Abortion," *Washington Post*, Sept. 11, 1976.

11. Maris A. Vinovskis, "Abortion and the Presidential Election of 1976: A Multivariate Analysis of Voting Behavior," *Michigan Law Review* 77, no. 7 (1979): 1750–71.

12. Lydia Saad, "Churchgoing Among U.S. Catholics Slides to Tie Protestants," Gallup poll, April 9, 2009, www.gallup.com/poll/117382/church-going -among-catholics-slides-tie-protestants.aspx.

13. The "gold standard" (also called "dollar standard") adopted at the Bretton Woods Conference in 1944 established a fixed parity ($35 per ounce) between the dollar and gold, thus making the dollar the pivot of international trade. The revival of the economies of the defeated countries (resulting in the growing deficit of the balance of payments) and the costs of the war in Vietnam forced Richard Nixon to put an end to the by-then-fictitious parity in August of 1971.

14. See Richard J. Neuhaus, "Mechanic of the New Right—With No Apologies," *Commonweal*, Oct. 9, 1981, 555–57. Neuhaus also cites Weyrich, stating that "if we didn't know that the Pope agrees with us . . . we Catholics of the New Right would have serious conscience problems."

15. Susan F. Harding, *The Book of Jerry Falwell: Fundamentalist Language and Politics* (Princeton, NJ: Princeton University Press, 2000), 63.

16. For an in-depth analysis of the "invention of the West" see my *Guerra santa e santa alleanza: Religioni e disordine internazionale nel XXI secolo* (Bologna: Il Mulino, 2014), 138–43.

17. Ronald Reagan, "The King James Bible," *Newsweek*, Dec. 27, 1982.

18. Berlinerblau, *Thumpin' It*, 140.

19. Greg Forster, "Evangelicals and Politics: The Religious Right (Born 1979, Died 2000)," *Public Discourse*, May 2, 2012, www.thepublicdiscourse.com /2012/05/5216/.

20. The law passed in 2003 provides that the state is involved in the decision from the third month of pregnancy. Since 1992, however, a Supreme Court ruling has allowed the states to bring restrictions on the freedom of abortion. Some states have also tried to ban abortion. It is significant, however, that, in all cases (except one) in which the matter was submitted to a popular referendum, the proposed ban was rejected (in Massachusetts in 1986, with 58.2 percent against 41.8; in Arizona in 1992 with 68.6 percent against 31.5; in South Dakota in 2006, with 55.6 percent against 44.4, and then again in 2008, with 55.2 percent against 44.8; in Colorado three times—in 2008, with 73.2 percent against 26.8, in 2010 with 70.5 percent against 29.5, and in 2014 with 64.9 percent against 35.1; in Mississippi in 2011, with 57.9 percent against 42.1; in North Dakota in 2014, with 64.1 percent against 35.9). The exception is Tennessee, where a proposal authorizing the legislature to prohibit abortion passed in 2014, with 52.6 percent against 47.4. Also note that two referenda were held to extend the right to abortion, in Nevada in 1990 (63.5 percent for and 36.5 against) and in Washington State in 1991 (50.1 percent for and 49.9 against). These results may explain the reason why all pro-life presidents have been reticent about keeping their campaign promises on the issue.

21. Quoted in Katherine Yurica, "Excerpts from the New Messiahs," www .yuricareport.com/Art Essays/The New Messiahs Excerpts.htm.

22. Larry Eskridge, "Evangelicals and Politics," Wheaton College, Institute for the Study of American Evangelicals, 1996–2012, www.wheaton.edu/ISAE/ Defining-Evangelicalism/Politics.

23. Take, for example, Jerry Falwell's statements on Pat Robertson's *700 Club* on September 13, 2001: "The abortionists have got to bear some burden for this [9/11 attacks] because God will not be mocked. And when we destroy 40 million little innocent babies, we make God mad. I really believe that the pagans, and the abortionists, and the feminists, and the gays and the lesbians . . . all of them who have tried to secularize America—I point the finger in their face and say 'you helped this happen.'" Robertson, for his part, explained in the same terms the earthquake in January 2010 in Haiti, which caused the deaths of one hundred thousand people: "They [Haitians] were under the heel of the French. You know, Napoleon the Third or whatever, and they got together and swore a pact to the Devil. They said, 'We will serve you if you get us free from the French.' True story. And so, the Devil said, Ok, it's a deal. And they kicked

the French out. You know, the Haitians revolted and got themselves free. But ever since they have been cursed by one thing after another—desperately poor" (*The 700 Club*, Jan. 13, 2010).

24. Berlinerblau, *Thumpin' It*, 12.

25. Mark A. Noll, "Jesus and Jefferson," *New Republic*, June 9, 2011. Noll cites as examples Randall Balmer, *Thy Kingdom Come: How the Religious Right Distorts the Faith and Threatens America* (New York: Basic Books, 2006); Michelle Goldberg, *Kingdom Coming: The Rise of Christian Nationalism* (New York: Norton, 2007); Kevin Phillips, *American Theocracy: The Peril and Politics of Radical Religion, Oil, and Borrowed Money in the 21st Century* (New York: Penguin, 2006); Jim Wallis, *God's Politics: Why the Right Gets It Wrong and the Left Doesn't Get It* (New York: HarperCollins, 2005); and Mel White, *Religion Gone Bad: The Hidden Dangers of the Christian Right* (New York: Penguin, 2006).

26. Noll, "Jesus and Jefferson."

27. Charles E. Booth, *Bridging the Breach: Evangelical Thought and Liberation in the African-American Preaching Tradition* (Chicago: Urban Ministries, 2000), 96.

28. Quoted in David D. Kirkpatrick, "The Evangelical Crackup," *New York Times*, Oct. 28, 2007.

29. "How the Faithful Voted: 2012 Preliminary Analysis," Pew Research Center, Nov. 7, 2012, www.pewforum.org/2012/11/07/how-the-faithful-voted-2012-preliminary-exit-poll-analysis/.

30. Forster, "Evangelicals and Politics."

31. Michael Wear, "The Changing Face of Christian Politics," *Atlantic*, Feb. 17, 2014, www.theatlantic.com/politics/archive/2014/02/the-changing-face-of-christian-politics/283859/.

32. Jonathan Merritt, "Election 2012 Marks the End of Evangelical Dominance in Politics," *Atlantic*, Nov. 13, 2012, www.theatlantic.com/politics/archive/2012/11/election-2012-marks-the-end-of-evangelical-dominance-in-politics/265139/.

33. Noll, "Jesus and Jefferson."

34. Leslie Dunstan, *Protestantism* (New York: George Braziller, 1961); National Council of Churches, *Yearbook of American and Canadian Churches* (Nashville, TN: NCC, 2006); Association of Statisticians of American Religious Bodies, *Religion Census: Religious Congregations & Membership Study* (Lenexa, KS: ASARB, 2010).

35. Berlinerblau, *Thumpin' It*, 23, 32.

36. Ibid., 134.

37. Wear, "The Changing Face of Christian Politics"

38. Jonathan Merritt, "The Religious Right Turns 33: What Have We Learned?" *Atlantic*, Jan. 8, 2012, www.theatlantic.com/politics/archive/2012/06/the-religious-right-turns-33-what-have-we-learned/258204/.

39. Tom Sine, "A Wakeup Call for Evangelicals," *Patheos*, August 13, 2010.

40. Dickerson, "The Decline of Evangelical America."

41. Joseph Ratzinger, *Salt of the Earth: The Church at the End of the Mil-*

lennium: An Interview with Peter Seewald, trans. Adrian Walker (San Francisco: Ignatius Press, 1997), 193. Note that, in an interview with *La Repubblica*, Pope Francis expressed the same idea: "Personally I think that being a minority is actually a strength. We have to be a leavening of life and love and the leavening is infinitely smaller than the mass of fruits, flowers and trees that are born out of it" (Eugenio Scalfari, "Il Papa a Scalfari: 'Così cambierò la Chiesa,'" *La Repubblica*, Oct. 1, 2013).

42. Pew Research Center, "Religion in Latin America," Nov. 13, 2014, www .pewforum.org/2014/11/13/religion-in-latin-america/.

43. The "charismatic gifts" are those received by the Apostles from the Holy Spirit at Pentecost: the ability to speak unlearned languages, to heal the sick, and to work miracles. The same notions are supported by Pentecostalism, an evangelical current with a much more distinct personality.

44. See Anna Maria Peselli, "Invito alla crescita spirituale," www.diovive .com/letteratura/invito_crescita1.htm. According to the author, the charismatic faithful of other Christian denominations are six hundred million.

45. Dom Luciano Mendes de Almeida, "Brasile: Le sette ci interrogano," *Nuovo Progetto*, April 2009, www.sermig.org/it/dom-luciano-mendes-de-almeida/141-nuovoprogetto/ speciali/foresta-che-cresce/1215-brasile-le-sette-ci-interrogano.

46. All quotations cited in this and the preceding paragraph are from Gerolamo Fazzini, "Oltre i confini," *Avvenire*, June 1, 2007.

47. Gianni Cardinale, "Il cardinale Hummes: 'Sette, aborto e laicismo i nodi del Continente ma il cattolicesimo è forte,'" *Avvenire*, May 6, 2007.

48. Pope Francis, *Evangelii gaudium*, chap. 1.1.

NOTES TO CHAPTER 6

1. USNIC, *Global Trends 2025: A Transformed World* (Washington, DC: US Government Printing Office, 2008), 93.

2. Jacques Berlinerblau, *Thumpin' It: The Use and Abuse of the Bible in Today's Presidential Politics* (Louisville, KY: Westminster John Knox Press, 2008), 35. Later in his book Berlinerblau affirms that "God-talk in the United States is articulated either in Southern, Midwestern, or mountain region drawl" (93).

3. Ibid., 11.

4. In November of 1979 fifty-two employees of the US Embassy in Tehran were taken hostage and held captive for 444 days. They were released on the day of Ronald Reagan's oath of office, in January 1981.

5. Jimmy Carter, "Energy and National Goals: Address to the Nation," in *Public Papers of the Presidents of the United States: Jimmy Carter, 1979* (Washington, DC: United States Government Printing Office, 1980), 1237.

6. In the 1980s the Japanese built up strong trade surpluses, became the world's leading manufacturer in some industries previously dominated by Americans (particularly the automotive industry), and launched a series of spectacular acquisitions on US territory, such as Columbia Pictures, CBS Records, the Rockefeller Center

and Radio City Music Hall in New York, as well as the most famous golf course in the country, the Pebble Beach Golf Links in California. All this gave rise to an intense countercampaign, characterized by some violent actions against Japanese interests (and the beating death of a young Chinese man, Vincent Jen Chin, in Michigan, who was mistakenly perceived as Japanese).

7. Paul Kennedy, *The Rise and Fall of the Great Powers: Economic Change and Military Conflict from 1500 to 2000* (New York: Random House, 1987), 515.

8. Secretary of State Alexander Haig, Secretaries of the Treasury Donald Regan and Nicholas Brady, Secretary of Defense Frank Carlucci, Secretary of the Interior William Clark Jr., Secretary of Agriculture Richard Lyng, Secretaries of Labor Raymond Donovan and Ann McLaughlin, Secretary of Health and Human Services Margaret Heckler, and Secretaries of Education William Bennett and Lauro Cavazos.

9. Richard Allen, William Clark, Robert McFarlane, and Frank Carlucci.

10. Peggy Noonan, Pat Buchanan, Bob Reilly, Car Anderson, and Tony Dolan.

11. Editorial, "An Ambassador to the Vatican," *Washington Post*, Jan. 13, 1984.

12. Quoted in Everett Gleason and Frederick Aandahl, eds., *Foreign Relations of the United States, 1950*, vol. 3, *Western Europe* (Washington, DC: Department of State, 1950), 1791.

13. Francis Rooney, *The Global Vatican: An Inside Look at the Catholic Church, World Politics, and the Extraordinary Relationship Between the United States and the Holy See* (Lanham, MD: Rowman and Littlefield, 2013), 110.

14. Ibid., 114–15. At the approach of the 1948 elections, Rooney writes, "the CIA descended on Rome and went to work. With the help of the Vatican's network of priests and other religious [personnel], and filtering resources through Catholic Action, the agency used propaganda and millions of lira to influence the outcome of the election" (108).

15. Massimo Franco, *Parallel Empires: The Vatican and the United States—Two Centuries of Alliance and Conflict* (New York: Doubleday, 2008), 79.

16. Rooney, *The Global Vatican*, 126.

17. Carl Bernstein, "The Holy Alliance," *Time*, Feb. 24, 1992.

18. Franco, *Parallel Empires*, 91.

19. Rooney, *The Global Vatican*, 142–43.

20. The first quote is from Luigi Geninazzi, *Avvenire*, June 8, 2004. The second and third are from Karol Wojtyła [John Paul II], *Mémoire et identité: Conversations au passage entre deux millénaires* (Paris: Flammarion, 2005), 65 and 198.

21. Thomas Carty, "White House Outreach to Catholics," in *Catholics and Politics: The Dynamic Tension Between Faith and Power*, ed. Kristin E. Heyer, Mark J. Rozell, and Michael A. Genovese (Washington, DC: Georgetown University Press, 2008), 186.

22. In his first encyclical, dated March 1979, *Redemptor hominis*, John Paul II condemned "the propensity to exploit the whole of material progress and technology of production for the exclusive purpose of dominating others or of favor-

ing this or that imperialism" (sec. 15); and in *Laborem exercens*, dated 1981, he affirmed further that "in consideration of human labor and of common access to the goods meant for man, one cannot exclude the *socialization*, in suitable conditions, of certain means of production" (sec. 14).

23. "We are troubled also by reports of the development of weaponry exceeding in quality and size the means of war and destruction ever known before. . . . We applaud the decisions and agreements aimed at reducing the arms race" (Address to the 34th General Assembly of the United Nations, Oct. 2, 1979).

24. Letter to the scientists of the Ettore Majorana Foundation and Centre for Scientific Culture, August 20, 1982. In 1983 the US Bishops' Conference called deterrence "morally inacceptable" but was forced to remove this judgment following intervention by John Paul and replace it with a direct quotation of this same pope: "In current conditions 'deterrence' based on balance, certainly not as an end in itself but as a step on the way toward a progressive disarmament, may still be judged morally acceptable." See United States Conference of Catholic Bishops, *The Challenge of Peace: God's Promise and Our Response*, May 3, 1983, www .usccb.org/upload/challenge-peace-gods-promise-our-response-1983.pdf.

25. Message to the members of the Czechoslovakian Bishops' Conference, April 21, 1990, w2.vatican.va/content/john-paul-ii/it/speeches/1990/april/docu ments/hf-jp-ii_spe_19900421_conf-episc-praga.html.

26. Eric O. Hanson, *The Catholic Church in the World Politics* (Princeton, NJ: Princeton University Press, 1987), 273.

27. Joseph Ratzinger, "Europa: I suoi fondamenti spirituali ieri, oggi e domani," Lectio magistralis to the Library of the Italian Senate, May 13, 2004, http://leg16 .senato.it/notizie/21359/21361/21363/27861/41958/genpagina.htm. Note that, in the English translation of the text, instead of "the United States" we find "certain circles in the United States"; see Joseph Ratzinger, *Europe: Today and Tomorrow* (San Francisco: Ignatius Press, 2007), 27. For this reason I have used the Italian version of this quote.

28. Paul Freston, "Christianity and Conflict in Latin America," panel held at the National Defense University's School for National Security, Washington, DC, April 6, 2006; Sandro Magister, "Con Hummes arriva in curia un Brasile campione del mondo," *L'Espresso*, Nov. 3, 2006, http://chiesa.espresso.repub blica.it/ articolo/94562.

29. "The Church acknowledges the legitimate *role of profit* as an indication that a business is functioning well. When a firm makes a profit, this means that productive factors have been properly employed and corresponding human needs have been duly satisfied" (John Paul II, *Centesimus annus*, 1991, sec. 35).

30. José Casanova, "Religion and Conflict in Latin America: Conversation with Otto Maduro," in *Telos* 58 (Jan. 1983): 194–95. Casanova's thesis was picked up by Samuel Huntington and, more than fifteen years later, by Peter Berger in almost identical terms. See Samuel Huntington, *The Clash of Civilizations and the Remaking of World Order* (New York: Simon and Schuster, 1996), 99; and

Peter L. Berger, "The Desecularization of the World: A Global Overview," in *The Desecularization of the World: Resurgent Religion and World Politics*, ed. Peter L. Berger (Grand Rapids, MI: Wm. B. Eerdmans, 1999), 16, 17.

31. It was particularly the case in Argentina, whose bishops, in a document dated September 10, 2000, publicly begged forgiveness for having been "indulgent with totalitarian positions, hurting democratic freedoms which spring from human dignity," and for having "discriminated against many of our brothers without committing ourselves sufficiently to the defense of their rights." In another document, published in 2006, the Bishops' Conference apologized for "huge mistakes against life," although not as Christians or men of the Church but as "Argentineans."

32. Hanson, *The Catholic Church in the World Politics*, 273.

33. Francisco Nemenzo, "A Nation in Ferment: Analysis of the February Revolution," in *The Aquino Alternative*, ed. Murugaiah Rajaretnam (Singapore: Institute of Southeast Asian Studies, 1986), 28–53.

34. Hanson, *The Catholic Church in the World Politics*, 273.

35. These are the words used by the Czechoslovak bishop Stanislav Zela, whom Casaroli met in October 1964 and who had been freed just a short time earlier after thirteen years in prison. See Agostino Casaroli, *Il martirio della pazienza: La Santa Sede e i paesi comunisti, 1963–1989* (Torino: Einaudi, 2000), 131.

36. Ibid., 309. We need to remember that, in the Polish case, the opposition of the local clergy was aggravated by the continuing refusal of the Vatican to recognize the new borders of the postwar period, when Danzig, Silesia, and Pomerania were transferred from Germany to Poland.

37. The cardinal in question, anonymous, gave a long interview to the French journalist Olivier Le Gendre, which became a book; see Olivier Le Gendre, *Confession d'un cardinal* (Paris: JC Lattès, 2007), 11, 22. Among other sources of financing, the cardinal names Opus Dei and the IOR, the "Vatican Bank."

38. Robert Gates, *From the Shadows: The Ultimate Insider's Story of Five Presidents and How They Won the Cold War* (New York: Simon and Schuster, 2006), 237.

39. Rooney, *The Global Vatican*, 142.

40. Kenneth A. Briggs, "Church Groups Denounce Reagan Move," *New York Times*, Jan. 11, 1984.

41. Quoted in ibid.

42. D.D.C., *Menachem Binyamin Zivotofsky v. Secretary of State*, no. 03-1921, and *Dan Odenheimer and Jocelyn Odenhdimer [sic] v. US Department of State and Colin L. Powell*, no. 03-2048, Op. Gladys Kessler, D.J. (n.d.), 11, http://www.state.gov/documents/organization/78199.pdf.

43. See note 11 above.

44. In 1975 the "solitary" power of the United States was supported by a "directorate" of industrial powers (the Group of Five), comprising, in addition to the United States, France, Britain, and the two powers defeated in WWII, Japan and Germany; in 1978 Japan signed a peace treaty with China, and Europe created

the Monetary System, a fixed exchange rate system based on the German mark, from which later the euro would be born.

45. The theory that the collapse of the Soviet Union was an unintended consequence of Reagan policies deserves a separate work. I will limit myself by referring readers to my *Guerra santa e santa alleanza: Religioni e disordine internazionale nel XXI secolo* (Bologna: Il Mulino, 2014), 133–36; and my *Essential Geopolitics: A Handbook—Manuel essentiel de géopolitique* (Amazon e-book, 2011), chap. 6. The theory of the final victory of democracy was developed by Francis Fukuyama in his famous book *The End of History and the Last Man* (New York: Avon, 1992).

46. Kevin Bucley, *Panama* (New York: Touchstone, 1991), 247. In a statement released to the *New York Times* (Dec. 30, 1989), the archbishop of New York, John O'Connor, said he was "appalled by the attacks against the Church and Holy See." Quoted in Rooney, *The Global Vatican*, 169.

47. David Willey, *God's Politician: Pope John Paul II, the Catholic Church, and the New World Order* (New York: St. Martin's, 1992), 94.

48. See *Avvenire*, August 10, 1991.

49. Bruce Babbitt (Interior), William Daley (Commerce, who became White House chief of staff to President Barack Obama 2011–12), Alexis Herman (Labor), Donna Shalala (Health and Human Services), Henry Cisneros and Andrew Cuomo (Housing and Urban Development), Federico Peña (Transportation, then Energy), and William Richardson (Energy), without counting Secretary of State Madeleine Albright, who was born into a Jewish family and converted to Catholicism but later became Episcopalian. Two of the four chiefs of staff, Leon Panetta and John David Podesta, were also Catholic; both returned to the political stage under the Obama administration.

50. According to the principle of subsidiarity, if a lower social order (e.g., the family) can perform its task, the higher social order (e.g., the state) should not interfere but at most support it. The concept was expressed for the first time by Leo XIII in *Rerum novarum*: "We have said that the state must not absorb the individual or the family; both should be allowed free and untrammelled action so far as is consistent with the common good and the interest of others" (sec. 28). Compassionate conservatism is a political theory according to which conservatism must not tend toward the defense of privileges but toward the improvement of society. The concept is generally attributed to the Catholic historian Doug Wead.

51. Franklin Foer, "Spin Doctrine," *New Republic*, June 5, 2000.

52. Patricia Miller, "The Bush Administration Welcomes Conservative Catholics with Open Arms," *Conscience: The New Journal of Catholic Opinion* (Autumn 2001): www.catholicsforchoice.org/conscience/archives/cSummer2001_settingup shopatthegop.asp.

53. Thomas Edsall, "Bush Aims to Strengthen Catholic Base," *Washington Post*, April 16, 2001.

54. Bill Donohue, "Is Bush Catholic?" *Catalyst*, July-August 2001, www .catholicleague.org/is-bush-catholic/.

55. Daniel Burke, "Is George Bush Leading America's First Truly Catholic Presidency?" *Chron*, April 15, 2008, www.chron.com/life/houston-belief/article/NEWS-ANALYSIS-Is-George-Bush-leading-America-s-1758824.php.

56. See John Allen Jr., "Opus Dei Prestige on Display at Centenary Event," *National Catholic Reporter*, Jan. 18, 2002.

57. "The president, I half-kidded, is a closet Catholic"; see John DiIulio, *Godly Republic: A Centrist Blueprint for America's Faith-Based Future* (Berkeley: University of California Press, 2007), 117.

58. Quoted in Burke, "Is George Bush Leading America's First Truly Catholic Presidency?"

59. Ibid.

60. Miller, "Bush Administration Welcomes Conservative Catholics."

61. Alberto Gonzales (Attorney General), Mike Johanns (Agriculture), Carlos Miguel Gutierrez (Commerce), Mel Martinez (Housing and Urban Development), Anthony Principi and Jim Nicholson (Veterans Affairs), Tom Ridge (the first Secretary of Homeland Security), and John Walters (Office of National Drug Control Policy).

62. The law punishes the violence inflicted on an unborn child (Public Law 108-212 2004), yet it explicitly excludes abortion from the list of crimes.

63. Rooney, *The Global Vatican*, 153.

64. Ibid., 184.

65. Jim Nicholson, *The United States and the Holy See: The Long History* (Rome: 30 Giorni, 2002), 70.

66. "On the crest of war and justice, supporting victims should not allow us to forget the growing sentiment opposing armed solutions to conflicts between peoples" (*Avvenire*, Sept. 28, 2001).

67. See press release of November 5, 2001, and statement of Monsignor Diego Bona, president of Pax Christi in *Famiglia cristiana*, no. 46, Nov. 18, 2011.

68. See *ADISTA* (Agenzia Di Informazioni STAmpa), no. 78, Nov. 5, 2001.

69. In reality the decision had been made before the attacks in New York and Washington; see Manlio Graziano, "Perché, di preciso, gli americani sono andati in Iraq," *Limes*, no. 4 (June 2006). According to Bob Woodward, at 2:30 p.m. on September 11 Donald Rumsfeld already asked the Pentagon lawyers to find the connections between the terrorists and Saddam Hussein: "Hit S.H. @ same time—not only UBL [Usama Bin Laden]"; see Bob Woodward, *Plan of Attack* (New York: Simon and Schuster, 2004), 24–25.

70. Jean-Louis Tauran, speech delivered at the Immacolata Institute of Dermopathy, Feb. 24, 2003, *30 Giorni nella Chiesa e nel mondo*, March 2003.

71. *Angelus*, March 2, 2003.

72. See Franco, *Parallel Empires*, 105.

73. Donald B. Cozzens, *The Changing Face of the Priesthood: A Reflection on the Priest's Crisis of Soul* (Collegeville, MN: Liturgical Press, 2000), 125.

74. Franco, *Parallel Empires*, 157.

75. B. C., "Iraqi Christians and the West: A Rock and a Hard Place," *Economist*, July 14, 2014, www.economist.com/blogs/erasmus/2014/07/iraqi-christians-and-west.

76. Joseph Ratzinger to Cardinal McCarrick, "Worthiness to Receive Holy Communion: General Principles," memorandum, June 2004, www.ewtn.com/library/CURIA/cdfworthycom.HTM.

77. William P. Fay, "Catholics in Political Life," United States Conference of Catholic Bishops, June 21, 2004 (emphasis in the original), www.usccb.org/issues-and-action/faithful-citizenship/church-teaching/catholics-in-political-life.cfm.

78. Franco, *Parallel Empires*, 175–76. It is worth noting that in the Italian version Franco wrote "lesser evil over Evil," which is much more telling; see Massimo Franco, *Imperi paralleli: Vaticano e Stati Uniti—Due secoli di alleanza e conflitto, 1788–2005* (Milan: Mondadori, 2005), 194.

79. Karen Tumulty and Perry Bacon Jr., "A Test of Kerry's Faith," *Time*, April 5, 2004, http://content.time.com/time/magazine/article/0,9171,605436,00.html.

80. Al Gore won the popular vote; thus, even in that case Catholics voted with the majority.

81. See, e.g., Michael O'Brien, "Decision 2012 and the Myth of the 'Catholic Vote,'" *NBC Politics*, May 21, 2012. According to Domenico Montanaro, the main identity of the baptized voters is not religious: "White conservative Catholics vote Republican. White liberal Catholics vote Democratic. And Hispanics, who rank economic issues as their top priority, have voted overwhelmingly for Democrats"; see Domenico Montanaro, "The Myth of the Catholic Swing Vote," *PBS NewsHour*, March 27, 2014.

82. Patrick Basham, "How Many Votes Has the Pope? John Paul II, George W. Bush and the Changing Catholic Voter," Reason.com, April 15, 2005, reason.com/archives/2005/04/15/how-many-votes-has-the-pope. The statement "The Catholic vote is the most important swing vote" comes up in numerous articles on the topic.

83. Dan Gilgoff, *The Jesus Machine: How James Dobson, Focus on the Family, and Evangelical America Are Winning the Culture War* (New York: St. Martin's, 2007).

84. Ibid., 244.

85. Franco, *Imperi paralleli*, 189. I use again the Italian version of the quote since the word *outdated* has been omitted from the English translation.

86. Jodi Wilgoren and Bill Keller, "Kerry and Religion: Pressure Builds for Public Discussions," *New York Times*, Oct. 7, 2004.

87. Data from the Center for Responsive Politics. In the same campaign the Democratic Party raised $933 million, compared to $902 million raised by the Republicans.

88. Quoted in Pedro Nicolaci Da Costa, "Bernanke: 2008 Meltdown Was Worse Than Great Depression," *Wall Street Journal*, August 26, 2014.

89. Douglas Kmiec, "Reaganites for Obama? Sorry, McCain, Barack Obama Is a Natural for the Catholic Vote," *Slate*, Feb. 13, 2008.

90. Address at the Call to Renewal's Building a Covenant for a New America, Washington, DC, June 28, 2006.

91. Remarks by President Obama and His Holiness Pope Francis at Arrival Ceremony, Sept. 23, 2015, www.whitehouse.gov/the-press-office/2015/09/23/remarks-president-obama-and-his-holiness-pope-francis-arrival-ceremony.

92. In reality that obligation existed before; the first requests for exemption from these health contributions were submitted at the time of the Bush administration but were rejected by the Supreme Court; see Massimo Gaggi, *Dio, patria, ricchezza: Inchiesta sull'America* (Milan: Rizzoli, 2006), 33. At any rate, in July 2014 the Supreme Court accepted the appeal of some groups of religious inspiration, thus cancelling this objection.

93. Dario Fabbri, "The Roman Factor: I cattolici alla conquista di Washington," in *Limes*, no. 3 (April 2013): 109. The people in question are Joe Biden, Denis McDonough, Robert Gates, Mike Mullen, Tom Donilon, William Daley, Audrey Tomason, John Brennan, and James Clapper.

94. Before Antonin Scalia's untimely death in February of 2016, the Court seated six Catholic justices and three Jewish justices.

NOTES TO CHAPTER 7

1. Charles Morris, *American Catholic: The Saints and Sinners Who Built America's Most Powerful Church* (New York: Times Books, 1997), vii.

2. According to a survey conducted by the Catholic University in 2011, only 40 percent of American Catholics considered the teaching of the Church on abortion "very important," and 35 percent thought the teaching on same-sex marriage relevant; however, 30 percent said that the Roman authority must be accepted regardless and always. See William D'Antonio et al., *Catholics in America: Persistence and Change in the Catholic Landscape* (Washington, DC: Catholic University Survey, 2011).

3. Joseph Ratzinger, *Salt of the Earth: Christianity and the Catholic Church at the End of the Millennium: An Interview with Peter Seewald* (San Francisco: Ignatius Press, 1997), 16.

4. Here I have to make reference to another statistical basis—much less precise and especially less recent than CARA's, but which allows us to make a comparison with the situation in the rest of the world—proposed by David M. Cheney for the website catholic-hierarchy.org, updated in November 2005.

5. "The sacramental bond of belonging to the Body of Christ that is the Church, conferred by the baptismal character, is an ontological and permanent bond which is not lost by reason of any act or fact of defection" (*Actus formalis defectionis ab Ecclesia catholica*, March 13, 2006, sec. 7).

6. The last survey was carried out in 2008 with a sample basis of 54,461 people.

7. Mark M. Gray, "The 'Undercounted,'" *Nineteen Sixty-Four* (blog), March 18, 2014, http://nineteensixty-four.blogspot.com/2014/03/the-uncounted-11-million.html.

8. Sandro Magister, "Spretato, non sarai perdonato," *L'Espresso*, May 5, 2000.

9. Martin Arundel, " 'Thousands' of US Priests, Nuns Are Claimed Asking to Be Laicized," *Daily News* (US Virgin Islands), June 3, 1966. In the same article the spokesman of the archdiocese of New York denied these figures, claiming to see "no trend among American priests and sisters to be laicized."

10. Mark M. Gray, "Data in Context: New Ordinations and Seminarians," *Nineteen Sixty-Four* (blog), April 13, 2002, http://nineteensixty-four.blogspot.com /2012/04/data-in-context-new-ordinations-and.html.

11. Mary L. Gautier, Paul M. Perl, and Stephen J. Fichter, *Same Call, Different Men: The Evolution of the Priesthood since Vatican II* (Collegeville, MN: Liturgical Press, 2012), 2.

12. Gray, "Data in Context."

13. Ibid.

14. Melissa A. Cidade and Mary L. Gautier, "A Portrait of the Permanent Diaconate: A Study for the U.S. Conference of Catholic Bishops, 2009–2010" (Washington, DC: Center for Applied Research in the Apostolate, 2009), 12–13. Statistics from 2010 to 2014 show that the average percentage of "white, non-Hispanic" among the newly ordained was 68.8 percent; see Mary L. Gautier and Carolyne Saunders, *The Class of 2014: Survey of Ordinands to the Priesthood* (Washington, DC: Center for Applied Research in the Apostolate, 2014). Let us just recall that in 2011 the percentage of "white, non-Hispanic" Catholics among the American faithful was 63 percent, according to the *National Catholic Reporter*.

15. Joseph Ratzinger and Marcello Pera, *Without Roots: The West, Relativism, Christianity, Islam* (New York: Basic Books, 2006), 80.

16. In the original version colleges and universities are separate: as the distinction between the two is formal, I simplify things here by using only the term *university*.

17. Dario Fabbri, "The Roman Factor: I cattolici alla conquista di Washington," in *Limes*, no. 3 (April 2013): 110.

18. Ernesto Rossi, "Le speranze del Vaticano," *Il Ponte* 16, no. 6 (1960): 818–31.

19. Jordan's King Abdullah II, the former European Commission President Jose Barroso (1987); the former president of Costa Rica Laura Chinchilla Miranda; King Felipe VI of Spain; the president of Lithuania Dalia Grybauskaitė; the former president of the Philippines Gloria Macapagal-Arroyo; the Bosnian president Željko Komšić; and the Chinese foreign minister Wang Yi, to name a few.

20. Enzo Pace, *La nation italienne en crise: Perspectives européennes* (Paris: Bayard, 1998), 107.

21. Center for Applied Research in the Apostolate, CARA, 2015, http://cara .georgetown.edu/frequently-requested-church-statistics/ (2014 data).

22. Morris, *American Catholic*, 411, 430.

23. William D'Antonio, "New Survey Offers Portrait of U.S. Catholics," *National Catholic Reporter*, Oct. 24, 2011. On parish life between 1987 and 2011, "we see from the trends that Catholics remain attached to parish life. . . . Parishioners would like to have more say in the decisions that affect parish life"; see Mary L. Gautier, "How Parish Life Has Changed," *National Catholic Reporter*, Oct. 24, 2011.

24. Paul Kennedy, "Which Catholic Church?" *New York Times*, Feb. 26, 2013.

25. René Rémond, *Religion et société en Europe aux XIXe et XXe siècles: Essai sur la sécularisation* (Paris: Seuil, 1996), 274.

26. Mark M. Gray, "Pies, Damned Pies, and Statistics: Is the Catholic Population Growing?" *Nineteen Sixty-Four* (blog), Nov. 25, 2010, http://nineteensixty -four.blogspot.com/2010/11/pies-damned-pies-and-statistics-is.html.

27. In France it is prohibited to gather religious statistics, so the estimated percentage of people who attend church at least once a week varies between 4.5 and 15 percent of the entire population (i.e., between 2.8 and 9.5 million people), according to various hypotheses. The demonstrations against same-sex marriage had a total attendance of between 200,000 and 1.4 million people—just in Paris, according to various sources. To make a comparison, let us recall that about five thousand people marched in Paris during the traditional Labor Day rally on May 1, 2015.

28. Morris, *American Catholic*, 423.

29. By "rate of religiosity" I mean the percentage of people that answered affirmatively to the Gallup poll question, "Is religion important in your daily life?"

30. Jon Meacham, "The End of Christian America," in *Newsweek*, April 13, 2009.

31. John Micklethwait and Adrian Wooldridge, "God Still Isn't Dead," *Wall Street Journal*, April 9, 2009. Micklethwait and Wooldridge are the authors of a powerful book on the return of religion to the public arena; see *God Is Back: How the Global Revival of Faith Is Changing the World* (New York: Penguin, 2009).

32. Grace Davie, *Europe: The Exceptional Case: Parameters of Faith in the Modern World* (Maryknoll, NY: Orbis, 2002); Peter Berger, "Desecularization of the World," in *The Desecularization of the World: Resurgent Religion and World Politics*, ed. Peter Berger (Grand Rapids, MI: Wm. B. Eerdmans, 1999).

33. Alexis de Tocqueville, *Democracy in America*, Historical-Critical Edition of *De la démocratie en Amérique*, ed. Eduardo Nolla, translated from the French by James T. Schleifer (Indianapolis: Liberty Fund, 2010), http://oll.libertyfund.org/ titles/2286#lf1532-02_head_107.

34. Ibid.

35. Pope Francis, interview by Antonio Spadaro, *La civiltà cattolica*, Sept. 19, 2013, w2.vatican.va/content/francesco/en/speeches/2013/september/documents/ papa-francesco_20130921_intervista-spadaro.html.

36. Ibid.

37. Morris, *American Catholic*, 92.

38. Pope Leo XIII, *Rerum novarum*, sec. 49.

39. Tocqueville, *Democracy in America*, bk. 2, chap. 5, "Of the Use Which the Americans Make of Public Associations in Civil Life."

40. The International Catholic-Jewish Historical Commission, "The Vatican & the Holocaust: Preliminary Report on the Vatican During the Holocaust," Oct. 2000, www.jewishvirtuallibrary.org/jsource/Holocaust/vatrep.html. The text informs us that despite the detailed report of the nuncio in Berlin and the communi-

cation of the Apostolic Delegate to the United States, "there appears to have been no official reaction by the Vatican." A few months before *Kristallnacht*, the influential Jesuit journal *La civiltà cattolica* had written that "the Jews have brought on themselves every time, and still today, people's just aversion with their all too frequent abuses of power and with their hatred toward Christ himself, his religion, and his Catholic Church" (*La civiltà cattolica*, July 2, 1938, 62–71).

41. See Chapter 3.

42. Leonard Dinnerstein, *Anti-Semitism in America* (New York: Oxford University Press, 1994), 114.

43. Thomas Stransky, "The Genesis of Nostra Aetate," *America: The National Catholic Review*, Oct. 24, 2005, http://americamagazine.org/issue/547/article/genesis-nostra-aetate.

44. During the debate those who spoke in favor of a text even more open to Jews were, among others, Joseph Ritter, archbishop of St. Louis; Richard Cushing, archbishop of Boston; Albert Meyer (Chicago); Lawrence Shehan (Baltimore); Patrick O'Boyle (Washington, DC); and Stephen Leven, auxiliary bishop of San Antonio. See John Oesterreicher, *The New Encounter: Between Christians and Jews* (New York: Philosophical Library, 1986), 103–295. The *Decretum de Judæis*, completed in 1961, was actually later withdrawn from the discussion but was replaced by another document, *Nostra aetate*, on the relation of the Church to non-Christian religions, including Judaism.

45. Daniel Jonah Goldhagen, *A Moral Reckoning: The Role of the Catholic Church in the Holocaust and Its Unfilled Duty of Repair* (London: Abacus, 2003), 422.

46. John Tracy Ellis, "Les États-Unis depuis 1850," in *Nouvelle histoire de l'Église*, vol. 5, ed. Jean Daniélou, Ludovicus Jacobus Rogier, Roger Aubert, and David Knowles (Paris: Seuil, 1975), 332.

47. Ibid., 334.

48. Quoted in Agostino Bono, "Religious Freedom: Vatican II Modernizes Church-State Ties," *Catholic News Service*, Oct. 12, 2005.

49. Morris, *American Catholic*, 274.

50. Olivier Roy, *Holy Ignorance: When Religion and Culture Part Ways* (Oxford: Oxford University Press, 2013), 30.

51. The commission is chaired by Archbishop O'Malley of Boston, and directed de facto by his secretary, Robert W. Oliver, a priest from New York, former member of the Boston Archdiocesan Review Board, a body that deals with child protection, and a prosecutor for cases of sexual harassment at the Congregation for the Doctrine of the Faith.

52. Francis Rooney, *The Global Vatican: An Inside Look at the Catholic Church, World Politics, and the Extraordinary Relationship Between the United States and the Holy See* (Lanham, MD: Rowman and Littlefield, 2013), 156.

53. He did so more than once, however, during his visit to the United States in September 2015.

54. Lucio Caracciolo and Fabrizio Maronta, "Riportare la Chiesa nel mondo: Questa è la sfida di Francesco," interview with Andrea Riccardi, *Limes*, no. 3 (April 2013): 37–42, 41.

55. Marco Politi, *Francesco tra i lupi: Il segreto di una rivoluzione* (Rome: Laterza, 2014), 48–53.

56. Samuel Huntington, *The Clash of Civilizations and the Remaking of World Order* (New York: Simon and Schuster, 1996), 111.

57. Ibid., 240.

NOTES TO CONCLUSION

1. Francis Rooney, *The Global Vatican: An Inside Look at the Catholic Church, World Politics, and the Extraordinary Relationship Between the United States and the Holy See* (Lanham, MD: Rowman and Littlefield, 2013), 221.

2. Anne Goujon, Éric Caron Malenfant, and Vegard Skirbekk, "Towards a Catholic North America? Projections of Religious Denominations in Canada and the US up to 2060," Vienna Institute of Demography, April 21, 2011.

3. Quoted in Olivier Le Gendre, *Confession d'un cardinal* (Paris: JC Lattès, 2007), 14.

4. Quoted in Kenneth A. Briggs, "Church Groups Denounce Reagan Move," *New York Times*, Jan. 11, 1984.

5. Dario Fabbri, "The Roman Factor: I cattolici alla conquista di Washington," *Limes*, no. 3 (April 2013): 111.

6. Leahy, a Democrat, was replaced in office in January 2015 by Republican Orrin Hatch, a Mormon from Utah. Boehner announced his resignation as Speaker of the House in September 2015, the day of the pope's speech in Washington, and was replaced by Republican Paul Ryan, a Catholic.

7. Congregation for the Doctrine of the Faith, "Doctrinal Note on Some Questions Regarding the Participation of Catholics in Political Life," sec. 2, Nov. 24, 2002, www.vatican.va/roman_curia/congregations/cfaith/documents/rc_con_cfaith_doc_20021124_politica_en.html.

8. Peter Berger, "The Desecularization of the World: A Global Overview," in *The Desecularization of the World: Resurgent Religion and World Politics*, ed. Peter Berger (Grand Rapids, MI: Wm. B. Eerdmans, 1999), 7.

9. Charles Morris, *American Catholic: The Saints and Sinners Who Built America's Most Powerful Church* (New York: Times Books, 1997), 421.

Bibliography

Adams, Charles Francis, ed. *The Works of John Adams, Second President of the United States*. Vol. 7. Boston: Little, Brown, 1856.

Allen, John, Jr. "Opus Dei Prestige on Display at Centenary Event." *National Catholic Reporter*, Jan. 18, 2002.

Andreotti, Giulio. *Intervista su De Gasperi*. Rome: Laterza, 1977.

Arundel, Martin. "'Thousands' of US Priests, Nuns Are Claimed Asking to Be Laicized." *Daily News* (US Virgin Islands), June 3, 1966.

Association of Statisticians of American Religious Bodies. *Religion Census: Religious Congregations and Membership Study*. Lenexa, KS: ASARB, 2010.

Aubert, Roger. "Le demi-siècle qui a préparé Vatican II." In Daniélou et al., *Nouvelle histoire de l'Église*, 581–689.

———. "L'Église catholique de la crise de 1848 à la Première Guerre mondiale." In Daniélou et al., *Nouvelle histoire de l'Église*, 7–218.

Baker, David P. "Schooling All the Masses: Reconsidering the Origins of American Schooling in the Postbellum Era." *Sociology of Education* 72, no. 4 (1999): 197–215.

Balmer, Randall. *Thy Kingdom Come: How the Religious Right Distorts the Faith and Threatens America*. New York: Basic Books, 2006.

Barbier, Emmanuel. *Rome et l'action libérale populaire: Histoire et documents*. Poitiers: Blais and Roy Imprimeurs, 1906.

Barone, Michael. "Franklin D. Roosevelt: A Protestant Patrician in a Catholic Party." In *FDR, the Vatican, and the Roman Catholic Church in America, 1933–1945*, edited by David B. Woolner and Richard G. Kurial, 3–10. New York: Palgrave Macmillan, 2003.

Basham, Patrick. "How Many Votes Has the Pope? John Paul II, George W. Bush and the Changing Catholic Voter." Reason.com, April 15, 2005. http://reason.com/archives/2005/04/15/how-many-votes-has-the-pope.

B. C. "Iraqi Christians and the West: A Rock and a Hard Place." *Economist*, July 14 2014. www.economist.com/blogs/erasmus/2014/07/iraqi-christians-and-west.

Beale, Jonathan. "Pope May Find US on His Wavelength." *BBC News*, April 15, 2008. http://news.bbc.co.uk/2/hi/europe/7348087.stm.

Beecher, Lyman. *A Plea for the West*. New York: Truman and Smith, 1835.

Berger, Peter L. "The Desecularization of the World: A Global Overview." In *The Desecularization of the World: Resurgent Religion and World Politics*, edited by Peter Berger, 1–18. Grand Rapids, MI: Wm. B. Eerdmans, 1999.

Berlinerblau, Jacques. *Thumpin' It: The Use and Abuse of the Bible in Today's Presidential Politics*. Louisville, KY: Westminster John Knox Press, 2008.

Bernstein, Carl. "The Holy Alliance." *Time*, Feb. 24, 1992.

Blet, Pierre, Robert A. Graham, Angelo Martini, and Burkhart Schneider. *Actes et documents du Saint Siège relatifs à la Seconde Guerre mondiale*. Vol. 9, *Le Saint Siège et les victimes de la guerre janvier–décembre 1943*. Rome: Libreria editrice vaticana, 1975.

Bolce, Louis, and Gerald De Maio. "Our Secularist Democratic Party." *Public Interest* 149 (Fall 2002): 3–20.

Bono, Agostino. "Religious Freedom: Vatican II Modernizes Church-State Ties." *Catholic News Service*, Oct. 12, 2005.

Booth, Charles E. *Bridging the Breach: Evangelical Thought and Liberation in the African-American Preaching Tradition*. Chicago: Urban Ministries, 2000.

Boyer, Peter J. "Party Faithful: Can the Democrats Get a Foothold on the Religious Vote?" *New Yorker*, Sept. 8, 2008. www.newyorker.com/magazine/2008/09/08/party-faithful.

Briggs, Kenneth A. "Church Groups Denounce Reagan Move." *New York Times*, Jan. 11, 1984.

Brownson, Orestes A. "Are Catholics Pro-Slavery and Disloyal?" *Brownson's Quarterly Review* 25 (July 1863): 372–73.

Brugerette, Joseph. *Le prêtre français et la société contemporaine*. Tome 2, *Vers la séparation (1871–1901)*. Paris: J. de Gigord, 1935.

Bucley, Kevin. *Panama*. New York: Touchstone, 1991.

Burke, Daniel. "Is George Bush Leading America's First Truly Catholic Presidency?" *Chron*, April 15, 2008, www.chron.com/life/houston-belief/article/NEWS-ANALYSIS-Is-George-Bush-leading-America-s-1758824.php.

Burnham, Walter D. *Critical Elections and the Mainsprings of American Politics*. New York: Norton, 1970.

Byrnes, Timothy A. *Catholic Bishops in American Politics*. Princeton, NJ: Princeton University Press, 1991.

Callaghan, James. "The San Patricios." *American Heritage*, Nov. 1995. www.americanheritage.com/content/san-patricios?page=show.

Caracciolo, Alberto. *Roma capitale: Dal Risorgimento alla crisi dello stato liberale*. Rome: Editori Riuniti, 1956.

Caracciolo, Lucio, and Maronta Fabrizio. "Riportare la Chiesa nel mondo: Questa è la sfida di Francesco." Interview with Andrea Riccardi. *Limes*, no. 3 (April 2013): 37–42.

Cardinale, Gianni. "Il cardinale Hummes: 'Sette, aborto e laicismo i nodi del Continente ma il cattolicesimo è forte.'" *Avvenire*, May 6, 2007.

Carty, Thomas. "White House Outreach to Catholics." In *Catholics and Politics: The Dynamic Tension Between Faith and Power*, edited by Kristin E. Heyer, Mark J. Rozell, and Michael A. Genovese, 175–98. Washington, DC: Georgetown University Press, 2008.

Casanova, José. "Religion and Conflict in Latin America: Conversation with Otto Maduro." *Telos* 58 (Jan. 1983): 185–95.

Casaroli, Agostino. *Il martirio della pazienza: La Santa Sede e i paesi comunisti (1963–1989)*. Turin: Einaudi, 2000.

Castagna, Luca. *A Bridge Across the Ocean: The United States and the Holy See Between the Two World Wars*. Washington, DC: Catholic University of America Press, 2014.

———. *Un ponte oltre l'oceano: Assetti politici e strategie diplomatiche tra Stati Uniti e Santa Sede nella prima metà del Novecento (1914–1940)*. Bologna: Il Mulino, 2011.

Center for Applied Research in the Apostolate. "Frequently Requested Church Statistics." Washington, DC: CARA, 2014.

Chenaux, Philippe. *Une Europe vaticane? Entre le plan Marshall et les Traités de Rome*. Bruxelles: Éditions Ciaco, 1990.

Christopher, Robert C. *Crashing the Gates: The De-WASPing of America's Power Elite*. New York: Simon and Schuster, 1989.

Cidade, Melissa A., and Mary L. Gautier. "A Portrait of the Permanent Diaconate: A Study for the U.S. Conference of Catholic Bishops, 2009–2010." Washington, DC: CARA, 2009.

Collectanea Sacrae Congregationis de Propaganda Fide: Seu decreta, instructiones, rescripta pro apostolicis missionibus. Vol. 1. Rome: Typographia polyglotta, 1907.

Commissione per la pubblicazione dei documenti diplomatici. *I Documenti diplomatici italiani*. Vol. 11, Dec. 31, 1861–July 31, 1862. Rome: Libreria dello Stato, 1986.

Conley, Patrick, and Matthew Smith. *Catholicism in Rhode Island: The Formative Era*. Providence, RI: Diocese of Providence Press, 1976.

Connelly, James F. *The Visit of Archbishop Gaetano Bedini to the United States of America*. Rome: Libreria editrice dell'Università gregoriana, 1960.

Cooney, John. *The American Pope: The Life and Times of Francis Cardinal Spellman*. New York: Times Books, 1984.

Coudenhove-Kalergi, Richard Nikolaus von. *Pan-Europa*. Zurich: Paneuropa, 1923.

Cox, Charlie. "Democrats Paved the Way for Their Own Decline." *National Journal*, Dec. 1, 2014.

Cozzens, Donald B. *The Changing Face of the Priesthood: A Reflection on the Priest's Crisis of Soul*. Collegeville, MN: Liturgical Press, 2000.

Cremonesi, Lorenzo. "Quando i cattolici accusavano Israele di 'nazismo.'" *Corriere della Sera*, April 29, 2012.

Curley, Charles. "Delaware." *The Catholic Encyclopedia*. Vol. 4. New York: Robert Appleton, 1908.

Curran, Charles E. *Catholic Moral Theology in the United States: A History*. Washington, DC: Georgetown University Press, 2008.

Daniélou, Jean, Ludovicus Jacobus Rogier, Roger Aubert, and David Knowles, eds. *Nouvelle histoire de l'Église*. Vol. 5. Paris: Seuil, 1975.

D'Antonio, William. "New Survey Offers Portrait of U.S. Catholics." *National Catholic Reporter*, Oct. 24, 2011.

D'Antonio, William, et al. *Catholics in America: Persistence and Change in the Catholic Landscape*. Washington, DC: Catholic University Survey, 2011.

Davie, Grace. *Europe: The Exceptional Case: Parameters of Faith in the Modern World*. Maryknoll, NY: Orbis, 2002.

Davis, Kenneth C. "America's True History of Religious Tolerance." *Smithsonian Magazine*, Oct. 2010.

Day, Dorothy. "Where Are the Poor?" *Catholic Worker*, no. 1 (Jan. 1955): 6.

De Moidrey, Joseph. *La hiérarchie catholique en Chine, en Corée et au Japon (1307–1914)*. Chang-Hai (Shanghai): Imprimerie de l'Orphelinat de T'ou-Sè-Wè, 1914.

De Tocqueville, Alexis. *Democracy in America*. Historical-Critical Edition of *De la démocratie en Amérique*. Edited by Eduardo Nolla. Translated from the French by James T. Schleifer. Indianapolis: Liberty Fund, 2010. http://oll.libertyfund .org/titles/2286#lf1532-02_head_107

Dickerson, John S. "The Decline of Evangelical America." *New York Times*, Dec. 15, 2012. www.nytimes.com/2012/12/16/opinion/sunday/the-decline-of -evangelical-america.html?_r=0.

Diggins, Patrick. *Mussolini and Fascism: The View from America*. Princeton, NJ: Princeton University Press, 1972.

DiIulio, John. *Godly Republic: A Centrist Blueprint for America's Faith-Based Future*. Berkeley: University of California Press, 2007.

Dillingham, William P., et al. *Senate Documents, 61st Congress, 3rd Session: Statistical Review of Immigration, 1820–1910*. Washington, DC: Government Printing Office, 1911.

Dinnerstein, Leonard. *Anti-Semitism in America*. New York: Oxford University Press, 1994.

Di Nolfo, Ennio. *Vaticano e Stati Uniti, 1939–1952: Dalle carte di Myron C. Taylor*. Milan: Franco Angeli, 1978.

Dolan, Jay P. *The Immigrant Church: New York's Irish and German Catholics, 1815–1865*. Baltimore: Johns Hopkins University Press, 1975.

Dolan, Jay P. *The American Catholic Experience: A History from Colonial Times to the Present*. New York: Doubleday, 1985.

Donaldson, Gary A. *The First Modern Campaign: Kennedy, Nixon, and the Election of 1960*. Lanham, MD: Rowman and Littlefield, 2007.

Donohue, Bill. "Is Bush Catholic?" *Catalyst*, July-August 2001. www.catholic league.org/is-bush-catholic/.

Duncan, Jason K. *Citizens or Papists? The Politics of Anti-Catholicism in New York: 1685–1821*. New York: Fordham University Press, 2005.

Dunstan, Leslie. *Protestantism*. New York: George Braziller, 1961.

Edsall, Thomas. "Bush Aims to Strengthen Catholic Base." *Washington Post*, April 16, 2001.

Ellis, John Tracy. *American Catholicism*. Chicago: University of Chicago Press, 1956.

———. "American Catholics and the Intellectual Life." *Thought* 30 (Autumn 1955): 351–88.

———. *Catholics in Colonial America*. Baltimore: Helicon, 1965.

———. "Les États-Unis depuis 1850." In Daniélou et al., *Nouvelle histoire de l'Église*, 276–350.

Esbeck, Carl H. "Dissent and Disestablishment: The Church-State Settlement in the Early American Republic." *BYU Law Review*, no. 4 (2004): 1385–1592.

Eskridge, Larry. "Evangelicals and Politics." Wheaton College, Institute for the Study of American Evangelicals, 1996–2012. www.wheaton.edu/ISAE/Defining-Evangelicalism/Politics.

Fabbri, Dario. "The Roman Factor: I cattolici alla conquista di Washington." *Limes*, no. 3 (April 2013): 109–16.

Fallo, Elena. *Antisemitismo in America*. Boves: Araba Fenice, 2008.

Fazzini, Gerolamo. "Oltre i confini." *Avvenire*, June 1, 2007.

Feldstein, Mark. "JFK's Own Dirty Trick." *Washington Post*, Jan. 14, 2011.

Flint, Andrew R., and Joy Porter. "Jimmy Carter: The Re-emergence of Faith-Based Politics and the Abortion Rights Issue." *Presidential Studies Quarterly* 35, no. 1 (2005): 28–51.

Flynn, George Q. *American Catholics and the Roosevelt Presidency, 1932–1936*. Lexington: University Press of Kentucky, 1968.

Foer, Franklin. "Spin Doctrine." *New Republic*, June 5, 2000.

Fogarty, Gerald P. *The Vatican and the American Hierarchy from 1870 to 1965*. Collegeville, MN: Liturgical Press, 1985.

Forster, Greg. "Evangelicals and Politics: The Religious Right (Born 1979, Died 2000)." *Public Discourse*, May 2, 2012, www.thepublicdiscourse.com/2012/05/5216/.

Franco, Massimo. "Dietro il sacrificio estremo di un intellettuale le ombre di un 'rapport segreto' choc." *Corriere della Sera*, Feb. 12, 2013.

———. *Imperi paralleli: Vaticano e Stati Uniti—Due secoli di alleanza e conflitto, 1788–2005*. Milano: Mondadori, 2005.

———. *Parallel Empires: The Vatican and the United States—Two Centuries of Alliance and Conflict*. New York: Doubleday, 2008.

Freston, Paul. "Christianity and Conflict in Latin America." A panel held at the National Defense University's School for National Security, Washington, DC, April 6, 2006.

Fukuyama, Francis. *The End of History and the Last Man*. New York: Avon, 1992.

Gaggi, Massimo. *Dio, patria, ricchezza: Inchiesta sull'America*. Milan: Rizzoli, 2006.

Gallagher, Charles R. *Vatican Secret Diplomacy: Joseph P. Hurley and Pope Pius XII*. New Haven, CT: Yale University Press, 2008.

Garzia, Italo. "La diplomazia vaticana e il problema dell'assetto postbellico." In *Pio XII*, edited by Andrea Riccardi, 211–64. Rome-Bari: Laterza, 1984.

Gates, Robert. *From the Shadows: The Ultimate Insider's Story of Five Presidents and How They Won the Cold War*. New York: Simon and Schuster, 2006.

Gautier, Mary L. "How Parish Life Has Changed." *National Catholic Reporter*, Oct. 24, 2011.

Gautier, Mary L., Paul M. Perl, and Stephen J. Fichter. *Same Call, Different Men: The Evolution of the Priesthood since Vatican II*. Collegeville, MN: Liturgical Press, 2012.

Gautier, Mary L., and Carolyne Saunders. *The Class of 2014: Survey of Ordinands to the Priesthood*. Washington, DC: CARA, 2014.

Gibson, Campbell J., and Emily Lennon. "Mother Tongue of the Foreign-Born Population: 1910 to 1940, 1960, and 1970." In *Historical Census Statistics on the Foreign-Born Population of the United States: 1850–1990*. Washington, DC: United States Census Bureau, March 9, 1999.

Gilgoff, Dan. *The Jesus Machine: How James Dobson, Focus on the Family, and Evangelical America Are Winning the Culture War*. New York: St. Martin's, 2007.

Ginsborg, Paul. *Storia d'Italia dal dopoguerra ad oggi: Società e politica, 1943–1988*. Torino: Einaudi, 1988.

Gleason, Everett, and Frederick Aandahl, eds. *Foreign Relations of the United States, 1950*. Vol. 3, *Western Europe*. Washington, DC: US Department of State, 1950.

Goldberg, Michelle. *Kingdom Coming: The Rise of Christian Nationalism*. New York: Norton, 2000.

Goldhagen, Jonah. *A Moral Reckoning: The Role of the Catholic Church in the Holocaust and Its Unfilled Duty of Repair*. London: Abacus, 2003.

Goujon, Anne, Éric Caron Malenfant, and Vegard Skirbekk. "Towards a Catholic North America? Projections of Religious Denominations in Canada and the US up to 2060." Vienna Institute of Demography, April 21, 2011.

Gray, Mark M. "Data in Context: New Ordinations and Seminarians." *Nineteen Sixty-Four* (blog). April 13, 2002. http://nineteensixty-four.blogspot.com/2012/04/data-in-context-new-ordinations-and.html.

———. "Pies, Damned Pies, and Statistics: Is the Catholic Population Growing?" *Nineteen Sixty-Four* (blog). Nov. 25, 2010. http://nineteensixty-four.blogspot.com/2010/11/pies-damned-pies-and-statistics-is.html.

———. "The 'Undercounted.'" *Nineteen Sixty-Four* (blog). March 18, 2014. http://nineteensixty-four.blogspot.com/2014/03/the-uncounted-11-million.html.

Graziano, Manlio. *Essential Geopolitics: A Handbook—Manuel essentiel de géopolitique*. Amazon e-book, 2011.

———. "Europa magistra mundi: La grande strategia della Chiesa di Roma." *Limes*, no. 5 (Oct. 2009): 91–106.

———. *Guerra santa e santa alleanza: Religioni e disordine internazionale nel XXI secolo*. Bologna: Il Mulino, 2014.

———. *Il secolo cattolico: La strategia geopolitica della Chiesa*. Rome: Laterza, 2012.

———. "La Chiesa e l'Europa, cinquant'anni di vantaggio." *Limes*, no. 1 (Feb. 2008): 269–83.

————. "Perché, di preciso, gli americani sono andati in Iraq." *Limes*, no. 4 (June 2006): 279–89.

Greely, Andrew. *The Catholic Myth: The Behavior and Beliefs of American Catholics*. New York: Touchstone, 1990.

Green, John C. "Seeking a Place: Evangelical Protestants and Public Engagement in the Twentieth Century." In *Toward an Evangelical Public Policy: Political Strategies for the Health of the Nation*, edited by Ronald J. Sider and Diane Knippers, 15–32. Grand Rapids, MI: Baker Books, 2005.

Guilday, Peter. *The Life and Times of John Carroll, Archbishop of Baltimore, 1735–1815*. New York: Encyclopedia Press, 1922.

Hachey, Thomas E., ed. *Anglo-Vatican Relations, 1914–1939: Confidential Annual Reports of the British Ministers to the Holy See*. Boston: G. K. Hall, 1972.

Hamilton, Jeanne. "The Nunnery as Menace: The Burning of the Charlestown Convent, 1834." *U.S. Catholic Historian* 14 (Winter 1996): 35–65.

Hanson, Eric O. *The Catholic Church in the World Politics*. Princeton, NJ: Princeton University Press, 1987.

Harding, Susan F. *The Book of Jerry Falwell: Fundamentalist Language and Politics*. Princeton, NJ: Princeton University Press, 2000.

Haynes, Jeffrey. *An Introduction to International Relations and Religion*. Harlow, UK: Pearson Education, 2007.

Hebblethwaite, Peter. "Pope Pius XII: Chaplain of the Atlantic Alliance?" In *Italy in the Cold War: Politics, Culture and Society*, edited by Christopher Duggan and Christopher Wagstaff, 67–75. Washington, DC: Berg, 1995.

Heinz, Helen A. " 'We Are All as One Fish in the Sea . . . ' Catholicism in Protestant Pennsylvania: 1730–1790." PhD diss., Temple University, 2008. ProQuest.

Hennesey, James J. *American Catholics: A History of the Roman Catholic Community in the United States*. New York: Oxford University Press, 1981.

Herr, Daniel C., and Joel Wells. *Through Other Eyes: Some Impressions of American Catholicism by Foreign Visitors from 1777 to the Present*. Westminster, MD: Newman Press, 1965.

Hinckley, Ted C. "American Anti-Catholicism During the Mexican War." *Pacific Historical Review* 31, no. 2 (1962): 121–37.

Hogan, Michael. *The Irish Soldiers of Mexico*. Trafford, UK: Intercambio Press, 1997.

Hominal, François. "L'évangélisation de la Chine et la querelle des rites." Ricci Institute of Paris, Seminar in Nantes, Dec. 1, 2014.

Huntington, Samuel. *The Clash of Civilizations and the Remaking of World Order*. New York: Simon and Schuster, 1996.

International Catholic-Jewish Historical Commission. "The Vatican and the Holocaust: Preliminary Report on the Vatican During the Holocaust." Jewish Virtual Library, Oct. 2000. www.jewishvirtuallibrary.org/jsource/Holocaust/vatrep.html.

Jemolo, Carlo Arturo. *Chiesa e stato in Italia negli ultimi cento anni*. Torino: Einaudi, 1948.

Kennedy, Paul. *The Rise and Fall of the Great Powers: Economic Change and Military Conflict from 1500 to 2000*. New York: Random House, 1987.

———. "Which Catholic Church?" *New York Times*, Feb. 26, 2013.

Kent, Peter C., and John F. Pollard. "A Diplomacy Unlike Any Other: Papal Diplomacy in the Nineteenth and Twentieth Centuries." In *Papal Diplomacy in the Modern Age*, edited by Peter C. Kent and John F. Pollard, 11–21. Westport, CT: Praeger, 1994.

Kertzer, David I. *Prisoner of the Vatican: The Popes, the Kings, and Garibaldi's Rebels in the Struggle to Rule Modern Italy*. Boston: Houghton Mifflin, 2006.

Kirkpatrick, David D. "The Evangelical Crackup." *New York Times*, Oct. 28, 2007.

Kissinger, Henry. *Diplomacy*. New York: Simon and Schuster, 1995.

Kmiec, Douglas. "Reaganites for Obama? Sorry, McCain. Barack Obama Is a Natural for the Catholic Vote." *Slate*, Feb. 13, 2008.

Kruse, Kevin M. *One Nation Under God: How Corporate America Invented Christian America*. New York: Basic Books, 2015.

Lally, Francis J. *The Catholic Church in a Changing America*. Boston: Little, Brown, 1962.

Lambert, Frank. *The Founding Fathers and the Place of Religion in America*. Princeton, NJ: Princeton University Press, 2003.

Le Gendre, Olivier. *Confession d'un cardinal*. Paris: JC Lattès, 2007.

Levison, Andrew. *The White Working Class Today: Who They Are, How They Think and How Progressives Can Regain Their Support*. Lexington, KY: Democratic Strategist Press, 2013.

Luxmoore, Jonathan, and Jolanta Babiuch. *The Vatican and the Red Flag: The Struggle for the Soul of Eastern Europe*. London: Geoffrey Chapman, 1999.

Magister, Sandro. "Con Hummes arriva in curia un Brasile campione del mondo." *L'Espresso*, Nov. 3, 2006.

———. *La politica vaticana e l'Italia, 1943–1978*. Rome: Editori Riuniti, 1979.

———. "Spretato, non sarai perdonato." *L'Espresso*, May 5, 2000.

Man, Albon P., Jr. "The Church and the New York Draft Riots of 1863." *Records of the American Catholic Historical Society of Philadelphia* 62, no. 1 (1951): 33–50.

Martin, Philip, and Peter Duignan. *Making and Remaking America: Immigration into the United States*. Stanford: Hoover Institution on War, Revolution, and Peace, Stanford University, 2003.

Martina, Giacomo. *Pio IX: 1851–1866*. Rome: Editrice Pontificia Università Gregoriana, 1985.

Masket, Seth. "Minority Rule: How Labor Unions and Civil Rights Activists Beat the Big Guys." *Pacific Standard*, Jan. 9, 2014.

McAvoy, Thomas T. *A History of the Catholic Church in the United States*. Notre Dame, IN: University of Notre Dame Press, 1969.

McDonough, Peter. *The Catholic Labyrinth: Power, Apathy, and a Passion for Reform in the American Church*. New York: Oxford University Press, 2013.

McEniry, Blanche Marie. *American Catholics in the War with Mexico*. Washington, DC: Catholic University of America Press, 1937.

McGreevy, John T. *Catholicism and American Freedom: A History*. New York: Norton, 2003.

———. "Catholics in America: Antipathy and Assimilation." In *American Catholics, American Culture: Tradition and Resistance*. Vol. 2 of *American Catholics in the Public Square*, edited by Margaret O'Brien Steinfels, 3–26. Lanham, MD: Rowman and Littlefield, 2004.

McGuire, Edward. "State of New York." *The Catholic Encyclopedia*. Vol. 11. New York: Robert Appleton, 1911. www.newadvent.org/cathen/11029a.htm.

McPherson, James M. *Battle Cry of Freedom: The Civil War Era*. New York: Oxford University Press, 1988.

Meacham, Jon. "The End of Christian America." *Newsweek*, April 13, 2009.

Mendes de Almeida, Luciano. "Brasile: Le sette ci interrogano." *Nuovo progetto*, April 2009, www.sermig.org/it/dom-luciano-mendes-de-almeida/141-nuovoprogetto/speciali/foresta-che-cresce/1215-brasile-le-sette-ci-interrogano.

Menozzi, Daniele. *Chiesa e diritti umani: Legge naturale e modernità politica dalla Rivoluzione francese ai nostri giorni*. Bologna: Il Mulino, 2012.

Merkley, Paul Charles. *Christian Attitudes Towards the State of Israel*. Montreal: McGill-Queen's University Press, 2001.

Merritt, Jonathan. "Election 2012 Marks the End of Evangelical Dominance in Politics." *Atlantic*, Nov. 13, 2012.

———. "The Religious Right Turns 33: What Have We Learned?" *Atlantic*, Jan. 8, 2012.

Michael, Robert. *A Concise History of American Antisemitism*. Lanham, MD: Rowman and Littlefield, 2005.

Micklethwait, John, and Adrian Wooldridge. *God Is Back: How the Global Revival of Faith Is Changing the World*. New York: Penguin, 2009.

———. "God Still Isn't Dead." *Wall Street Journal*, April 9, 2009.

Mieli, Paolo. "Chiesa e diritti umani: Una lunga diffidenza." *Corriere della Sera*, April 17, 2012.

Miller, Patricia. "The Bush Administration Welcomes Conservative Catholics with Open Arms." *Conscience: The New Journal of Catholic Opinion* (Autumn 2001): www.catholicsforchoice.org/conscience/archives/cSummer2001_settingupshopatthegop.asp.

Miller, Robert R. *Shamrock and Sword: The Saint Patrick's Battalion in the US-Mexican War*. Norman: University of Oklahoma Press, 1989.

Miller-Davenport, Sarah. " 'Their Blood Shall Not Be Shed in Vain': American Evangelical Missionaries and the Search for God and Country in Post–World War II Asia." *Journal of American History* 99, no. 4 (2013): 1109–32.

Montanaro, Domenico. "The Myth of the Catholic Swing Vote." *PBS NewsHour*, March 27, 2014.

Monti, Carlo. *La conciliazione ufficiosa: Diario del Barone Carlo Monti incaricato d'affari del governo italiano presso la Santa Sede: 1914–1922*. Rome: Libreria editrice vaticana, 1997.

Monzell, Thomas I. "The Catholic Church and the Americanization of the Polish Immigrant." *Polish American Studies* 26, no. 1 (1969): 1–15.

Moore, David W. "Little Prejudice Against a Woman, Jewish, Black or Catholic Presidential Candidate." Gallup Institute, June 10, 2003. www.gallup.com/poll/8611/little-prejudice-against-woman-jewish-black-catholic-presidenti.aspx.

Morgan, Thomas Brynmor. *The Listening Post: Eighteen Years on Vatican Hill*. New York: G. P. Putnam, 1944.

Morris, Charles. *American Catholic: The Saints and Sinners Who Built America's Most Powerful Church*. New York: Times Books, 1997.

Moskin, J. Robert. *American Statecraft: The Story of the U.S. Foreign Service*. New York: St. Martin's, 2013.

National Council of Churches. *Yearbook of American and Canadian Churches*. Edited by Eileen W. Lindner. Nashville, TN: Abingdon Press, 2006.

Nemenzo, Francisco. "A Nation in Ferment: Analysis of the February Revolution." In *The Aquino Alternative*, edited by Murugaiah Rajaretnam, 28–53. Singapore: Institute of Southeast Asian Studies, 1986.

Neuhaus, John Richard. "Mechanic of the New Right—With No Apologies." *Commonweal*, Oct. 9, 1981, 555–57.

———. *The Naked Public Square: Religion and Democracy in America*. 2nd ed. Grand Rapids, MI: William B. Eerdmans, 1986.

Newport, Frank. "In U.S., Four in 10 Report Attending Church in Last Week." Gallup Institute, Dec. 24, 2013. www.gallup.com/poll/166613/four-report-attending-church-last-week.aspx

Nicholson, Jim. *The United States and the Holy See: The Long History*. Rome: 30 Giorni, 2002.

Nicolaci Da Costa, Pedro. "Bernanke: 2008 Meltdown Was Worse Than Great Depression." *Wall Street Journal*, August 26, 2014.

Nixon, Richard M. *Memoirs*. New York: Touchstone, 1978.

Noll, Mark A. "Jesus and Jefferson." *New Republic*, June 9, 2011. https://newrepublic.com/article/88644/review-daniel-williams-darren-dochuk-christian-right.

O'Brien, Michael. "Decision 2012 and the Myth of the 'Catholic Vote.'" *NBC Politics*, May 21, 2012.

O'Connor, Charles, and William Lucey. "Massachusetts, Catholic Church In." *New Catholic Encyclopedia*, 2003. www.highbeam.com/doc/1G2-3407707255.html.

O'Donnell, James H. "Diocese of Hartford." In *History of the Catholic Church in the New England States*, edited by William Byrne and William A. Leahy, 148–63. Boston: Hurd and Everts, 1899.

Oesterreicher, John. *The New Encounter: Between Christians and Jews*. New York: Philosophical Library, 1986.

Pace, Enzo. *La nation italienne en crise: Perspectives européennes*. Paris: Bayard, 1998.

Pacelli, Eugenio, ed. "Circa la situazione della Santa Sede in Italia." Minutes of the Internal Meeting of the Congregation, March 29, 1917. In "Le città di Dio," *Limes*, no. 3 (1993): 113–27.

Palumberi, Franco. "Bipartitismo e strategia a Sud." *Lotta comunista*, no. 457, Sept. 2008.

Panzer, Joel S. *The Popes and Slavery*. New York: Alba House, 1996.

Perry, Lewis. *Intellectual Life in America: A History*. Chicago: University of Chicago Press, 1989.

Phillips, Kevin. *American Theocracy: The Peril and Politics of Radical Religion, Oil, and Borrowed Money in the 21st Century*. New York: Penguin, 2006.

———. *The Emerging Republican Majority*. New Rochelle, NY: Arlington House, 1969.

Pike, Fredrick B. "Le catholicisme en Amérique Latine." In Daniélou et al., *Nouvelle histoire de l'Église*, 353–418.

Pinheiro, John C. *Missionaries of Republicanism: A Religious History of the Mexican-American War*. New York: Oxford University Press, 2014.

Pizzorni, Reginaldo. *Diritto, etica e religione: Il fondamento metafisico del diritto secondo Tommaso d'Aquino*. Bologna: Edizioni Studio Domenicano, 2006.

Politi, Marco. *Francesco tra i lupi: Il segreto di una rivoluzione*. Rome: Laterza, 2014.

Pollard, John F. *Money and the Rise of the Modern Papacy*. Cambridge: Cambridge University Press, 2005.

Pope, Liston. "Religion and Class Structure." *Annals of the American Academy of Political and Social Science* 256 (March 1948): 84–91.

Ratzinger, Joseph. *Europe: Today and Tomorrow*. San Francisco: Ignatius Press, 2007.

———. *Il sale della terra: Cristianesimo e Chiesa cattolica nel XXI secolo*. Cinisello Balsamo: Ed. S. Paolo, 1997.

———. *Salt of the Earth: The Church at the End of the Millennium: An Interview with Peter Seewald*. Translated by Adrian Walker. San Francisco: Ignatius Press, 1997.

Ratzinger, Joseph, and Marcello Pera. *Without Roots: The West, Relativism, Christianity, Islam*. New York: Basic Books, 2006.

Reagan, Ronald. "The King James Bible." *Newsweek*, Dec. 27, 1982.

Reardon, Patrick J. "JFK and the Cafeteria Bishops: 50 Years After Kennedy Asserted Independence from the Pope, the Tide Has Turned." *National Catholic Reporter*, August 10, 2010.

Rémond, René. *Religion et société en Europe: Essai sur la sécularisation des sociétés européennes aux XIXᵉ et XXᵉ siècles, 1789–2000*. Paris: Seuil, 1998.

Romano, Sergio. *I falsi protocolli: Il "complotto ebraico" dalla Russia di Nicola II a oggi*. Milan: Corbaccio, 1992.

Rooney, Francis. *The Global Vatican: An Inside Look at the Catholic Church, World Politics, and the Extraordinary Relationship Between the United States and the Holy See*. Lanham, MD: Rowman and Littlefield, 2013.

Rossi, Ernesto. "Le speranze del Vaticano." *Il Ponte* 16, no. 6 (1960): 818–31.

Rossi, Joseph S. *Uncharted Territory: The American Catholic Church at the United Nations, 1946–1972.* Washington, DC: Catholic University of America Press, 2006.

Roy, Olivier. *Holy Ignorance: When Religion and Culture Part Ways.* Oxford: Oxford University Press, 2013.

Russell, William T. *Maryland, the Land of Sanctuary: A History of Religious Toleration in Maryland from the First Settlement Until the American Revolution.* Baltimore: J. H. Furst, 1907.

Saad, Lydia. "Churchgoing Among U.S. Catholics Slides to Tie Protestants." Gallup Institute, April 9, 2009. www.gallup.com/poll/117382/church-going-among-catholics-slides-tie-protestants.aspx.

Samuelson, Robert J. "The Shutdown Heralds a New Economic Norm." *Washington Post,* Oct. 14, 2013.

Scalfari, Eugenio. "Il Papa a Scalfari: 'Così cambierò la Chiesa.'" *La Repubblica,* Oct. 1, 2013.

Schmitt, Carl. *Roman Catholicism and Political Form.* Westport, CT: Greenwood Press, 1996. Originally published as *Römischer Katholizismus und politische Form* (Hellerau, Dresden: Jakob Hegner, 1923).

Shelley, Thomas J. *The History of the Archdiocese of New York: New York Catholicism in the Twentieth Century.* Vol. 2. Strasbourg: Éditions du Signe, 1998.

Sheriff, Carol. *The Artificial River: The Erie Canal and the Paradox of Progress, 1817–1862.* New York: Hill and Wang, 1996.

Sine, Tom. "A Wakeup Call for Evangelicals." *Patheos,* August 13, 2010. www.patheos.com/Resources/Additional-Resources/A-Wakeup-Call-for-Evangelicals.

Snyder, Thomas D., ed. *120 Years of American Education: A Statistical Portrait.* Washington, DC: National Center for Education Statistics, 1993.

Soderini, Edoardo. *Il pontificato di Leone XIII.* Milano: Mondadori, 1932.

Sorge, Friedrich Adolph. *Il movimento operaio negli Stati Uniti d'America: Corrispondenze dal Nord America.* Milan: Edizioni Pantarei, 2002.

Spalding, Thomas W. *The Premier See: A History of the Archdiocese of Baltimore, 1789–1994.* Baltimore: Johns Hopkins University Press, 1989.

Spykman, Nicholas J. "Geography and Foreign Policy." *American Political Science Review* 32, no. 1 (1938): 28–50.

Stahr, Walter. *John Jay: Founding Father.* New York: Hambledon and London, 2005.

Stehlin, Stewart A. "The Emergence of a New Vatican Diplomacy During the Great War and Its Aftermath, 1914–1929." In *Papal Diplomacy in the Modern Age,* edited by Peter C. Kent and John F. Pollard, 75–86. Westport, CT: Praeger, 1994.

Stransky, Thomas. "The Genesis of Nostra Aetate." *America: The National Catholic Review,* Oct. 24, 2005. http://americamagazine.org/issue/547/article/genesis-nostra-aetate.

Strode, Hudson, ed. *Jefferson Davis: Private Letters, 1823–1899.* New York: Harcourt, Brace and World, 1966.

Tager, Jack. *Boston Riots: Three Centuries of Social Violence*. Boston: Northeastern University Press, 2000.

Tardini, Domenico. *Pio XII*. Città del Vaticano: Tipografia poliglotta vaticana, 1960.

Teixeira, Ruy, and Joel Rogers. *America's Forgotten Majority: Why the White Working Class Still Matters*. New York: Basic Books, 2000.

Terp, Navy Vet. "The Emerging Republican Majority—44 Years Later." *Daily Kos*, August 19, 2013.

Tierney, Dominic. *FDR and the Spanish Civil War: Neutrality and Commitment in the Struggle That Divided America*. Durham, NC: Duke University Press, 2007.

Tooley, Mark. "Eisenhower's Religion." *American Spectator*, Feb. 14, 2011.

Traniello, Francesco. "Pio XII." In *Enciclopedia dei Papi*. Rome: Istituto dell'enciclopedia Treccani, 2000.

Tumulty, Karen, and Perry Bacon Jr. "A Test of Kerry's Faith." *Time*, April 5, 2004.

United States Conference of Catholic Bishops. *The Challenge of Peace: God's Promise and Our Response*. May 3, 1983. www.usccb.org/upload/challenge-peace-gods-promise-our-response-1983.pdf.

United States National Intelligence Council. *Global Trends 2025: A Transformed World*. Washington, DC: US Government Printing Office, 2008.

Vinovskis, Maris A. "Abortion and the Presidential Election of 1976: A Multivariate Analysis of Voting Behavior." *Michigan Law Review* 77, no. 7 (1979): 1750–71.

Wallis, Jim. *God's Politics: Why the Right Gets It Wrong and the Left Doesn't Get It*. New York: HarperCollins, 2005.

Walsh, Edward. "Bishops Like Ford's Stand on Abortion." *Washington Post*, Sept. 11, 1976.

Wear, Michael. "The Changing Face of Christian Politics." *Atlantic*, Feb. 17, 2014.

Webman, Esther. "Adoption of the Protocols in the Arab Discourse on the Arab-Israeli Conflict, Zionism, and the Jews." In *The Global Impact of the Protocols of the Elders of Zion: A Century-Old Myth*, edited by Esther Webman, 175–89. London: Routledge, 2011.

West, Albert. "Rhode Island." *The Catholic Encyclopedia*. Vol. 13. New York: Robert Appleton, 1912. www.newadvent.org/cathen/13020a.htm.

Whelan, Frank. "French-Indian War Fueled Anti-Catholic Fears." *Morning Call*, April 28, 1985.

White, Mel. *Religion Gone Bad: The Hidden Dangers of the Christian Right*. New York: Penguin, 2006.

White, Theodor H. *The Making of the President 1960*. New York: Atheneum House, 1961.

———. *The Making of the President 1968*. New York: Atheneum House, 1969.

———. *The Making of the President 1972*. New York: Atheneum House, 1973.

Wilgoren, Jodi, and Bill Keller. "Kerry and Religion: Pressure Builds for Public Discussions." *New York Times*, Oct. 7, 2004.

Willey, David. *God's Politician: Pope John Paul II, the Catholic Church, and the New World Order*. New York: St. Martin's, 1992.

Wilson, John K. "Religion Under the State Constitutions, 1776–1800." *Journal of Church and State* 32, no. 4 (1990): 753–73.

Wilson, Kathryn, and Jennifer Coval. "City of Unbrotherly Love: Violence in Nineteenth-Century Philadelphia." In *Exploring Diversity in Pennsylvania History*. Philadelphia: Historical Society of Pennsylvania, n.d. http://hsp.org/sites/default/files/legacy_files/migrated/thephiladelphiariotsof1844.pdf.

Wojtyła, Karol. *Mémoire et identité: Conversations au passage entre deux millénaires*. Paris: Flammarion, 2005.

Woodward, Bob. *Plan of Attack*. New York: Simon and Schuster, 2004.

Woolley, John T., and Gerhard Peters. *The American Presidency Project*. www.presidency.ucsb.edu/ws/?pid=9920.

Yurica, Katherine. "Excerpts from the New Messiahs." Yurica Report. www.yuricareport.com/Art Essays/The New Messiahs Excerpts.htm.

Zanini, Paolo. *Aria di Crociata: I cattolici italiani di fronte alla nascita dello Stato di Israele (1945–51)*. Milan: Unicopli, 2012.

Index

Abdullah II, King, 208n19

Abington School District v. Schempp,
   193n23

abortion, 17, 115, 117, 198n23,
   205n62; opposed by Catholic
   Church, 107–9, 119, 136, 141–42,
   207n2; popular referenda regarding,
   198n20; *Roe v. Wade,* 92, 104, 106,
   107–8, 110, 124

Adams, John, 50, 51

Afghanistan: Soviet invasion, 125, 134–
   35; US-led invasion, 139, 140

Africa, 7, 21, 167, 168, 191n43

Aguiar Retes, Carlos, 121

Alabama, 101, 196n53

Albright, Madeleine, 204n49

Alito, Samuel, 138

America, 133

American Carpatho-Ruthenian
   Orthodox Church, 182n50

American Catholics: appointed to
   Supreme Court, 4–5, 8, 9, 13,
   25, 126, 138, 146; attendance at
   religious services, 92, 108, 149,
   151, 158–59; attitudes regarding
   Church teaching, 149, 207n2;
   attitudes regarding Israel, 74;
   attitudes regarding slavery, 57–59;
   "cafeteria Catholicism" among,
   149; cardinals, 2, 24, 43, 65,
   69, 74, 76, 98, 140, 162, 166,
   167, 168, 169, 181n41, 188n9;
   Conference of Catholic Bishops, 9,
   108, 133, 202n24; vs. evangelicals,
   17, 19, 106, 112, 116, 119–21;
   as immigrants, 15–16, 27, 28,
   34–35, 36, 180n23; integration
   into American life, 28, 41–46, 48,
   91; vs. Jewish Americans, 14–15,
   93, 97, 114; legal quarantine of,
   27, 32–36; vs. Mormons, 14; and
   New Deal, 84–85, 88–92, 93–94,
   96; number of, 8, 13, 14, 15–16,
   21, 28, 32, 36–41, 42, 45, 84, 97,
   149–51, 156, 157, 171, 177n12,
   179n12, 207n5; number of monks,
   156; number of nuns, 149, 152,
   156, 208n9; number of permanent
   deacons, 20–21, 149, 153, 154,
   156; number of priests, 149, 150,
   151–53, 156, 181n43, 208nn9,14;
   number of seminarians, 149, 152–
   53, 154; ostracism in American
   colonies, 27–31; parish activities,
   21, 156–58, 208n23; prelates/
   episcopate, 1, 2, 3–4, 7, 9, 13, 21,
   24, 32, 42, 43, 48, 51–52, 54, 55,
   56, 57, 58–60, 63, 64, 65, 69, 71,
   73, 74, 88, 90, 91, 97, 99, 104,
   107–8, 128, 133, 137, 140, 141,
   147, 162, 163, 164, 166, 181n41,
   202n24, 210n44; presence by states,
   157; presence in Congress, 4, 8, 9,
   13, 111; religious marriages among,
   149; role and influence in American
   political life, 1, 2, 3–5, 8–10,
   12–14, 15–16, 18, 25, 44–46, 48,
   81–82, 84–85, 88–91, 96–99, 104,
   106–8, 111, 123–24, 126, 128,
   137, 138, 145–46, 155, 159, 171–
   72, 173, 188n9, 204n49, 205n61;
   role and influence in Catholic
   Church, 1, 3–4, 21–24, 42, 43, 48,
   49–52, 63–66, 69, 73, 76, 77, 133,
   146, 147–48, 159, 161–65, 168,
   170, 171–72; and social services,
   3, 18, 144–45, 149, 154–56;
   socioeconomic status, 45–46, 89,

227